Peachtree COMPLETE® AC

RELEASE 8.0

to accompany

ACCOUNTING PRINCIPLES

Peachtree COMPLETE® ACCOUNTING RELEASE 8.0

to accompany

ACCOUNTING PRINCIPLES

6th Edition

MEL COE JR. M.B.A.
DeVry Institute of Technology
Atlanta, Georgia

JERRY J. WEYGANDT Ph.D., C.P.A.
Arthur Andersen Alumni Professor of Accounting
University of Wisconsin - Madison
Madison, Wisconsin

DONALD E. KIESO Ph.D., C.P.A.
KPMG Peat Marwick Emeritus Professor of Accountancy
Northern Illinois University
DeKalb, Illinois

PAUL D. KIMMEL Ph.D., C.P.A.
Associate Professor of Accounting
University of Wisconsin - Milwaukee
Milwaukee, Wisconsin

JOHN WILEY & SONS, INC.

For LeA, Alyce, my DeVry Institute students
And Kay

EXECUTIVE EDITOR	Brent Gordon
ASSISTANT EDITOR	Ed Brislin
MARKETING MANAGER	Clancy Marshall
PRODUCTION EDITOR	Lenore Belton
COPY EDITOR	Pam Landau
COVER PHOTO	©James Bareham/Stone

ACKNOWLEDGEMENTS

Thanks to:

Al Ruggiero, Suffolk County Community College
Linda Schain, Hofstra University
Rex Schildhouse, University of Phoenix - San Diego
Charles Wolgamott, Ferris State University

ISBN 0-471-41956-7

Printed in the United States of America

10 9 8 7 6 5 4 3 2 1

Printed and bound by Bradford & Bigelow, Inc.

PREFACE

The *Peachtree Complete Accounting Workbook* will walk you through the accounting process detailed in the first 18 chapters of *Accounting Principles, Sixth Edition*, by Jerry Weygandt, Donald Kieso, and Paul Kimmel. Upon completion of this Peachtree workbook you will have an excellent understanding of both basic accounting principles and of the ways in which Peachtree will enhance your accounting success.

The exercises at the end of each chapter are based on corresponding problems found in the text. These problems are identified in the text with the Peachtree® logo. The text problems and their corresponding Peachtree® problems are listed on the following page. To successfully use this workbook you must also work through the Demonstration Problems near the end of each chapter. Please note that because not all concepts in the textbook are covered by the workbook, the workbook exercises are not a substitute for all the problems found in Accounting Principles, Sixth Edition.

Each company discussed in this workbook has a corresponding file in the data sets folder on the Peachtree Complete® Accounting CD-ROM. Because the same few companies are used throughout the workbook, you are encouraged to make a separate disk, as needed, for each company and use the same data disk as you progress through the chapters. This helps you see the "big picture" in the Peachtree accounting process.

The CD that comes with this workbook has an autorun feature that will by design load a Peachtree menu on start-up. Once Peachtree is installed, you must then unzip the data sets following the nine steps below. If you already have Peachtree Complete Accounting, version 8.0 on your network or computer, you will want to only load the data sets and not the application.

Step 1: Insert the CD-ROM that came with the workbook into your CD drive (usually the "d:" drive). A menu to install the Peachtree application will be displayed.

Step 2: Click on the last option "EXIT INSTALLATION". Leave the CD in the drive.

Step 3: Select Start/Run in the space provided.

Step 4: Enter "d:\datasets\datasets.exe" (Where "d:" is your CD drive.)

Step 5: Click "OK". A self-extracting Zip program will open in a small window.

Step 6: Click "Unzip to folder".

Step 7: Enter "c:\peachw"

Step 8: Click "Unzip". Your files will then "extract" into your Peachtree application folder making them available for your use within the Peachtree system.

Step 9: When the files are finished "unzipping", click on "OK" and then click on "CLOSE".

If you need to install a network version of Peachtree and you are a professor, you can now obtain a license for a free network version of Peachtree by visiting the following URL:

http://www.peachtree.com/training/html/educational_partnerships.cfm

Should you have any comments or questions regarding this workbook, you may contact me directly via e-mail: mcoe@faculty.atl.devry.edu

Good Luck and Have Fun!

Mel

Correlation Guide

Accounting Principles Chapter Number	Corresponding *Peachtree Workbook* Chapter Number	Chapter Title	*Accounting Principles* Problem Number	Corresponding Peachtree Workbook Problem Number
1	1	Accounting In Action	None	None
2	2	Recording Process	P2-1a P2-5a	P2-1a P2-5a
3	3	Adjusting the Accounts	P3-2a P3-5a	P3-2a P3-5a
4	4	Completion of The Accounting Cycle	P4-2a P4-5a	P4-2a P4-5a
5	5	Accounting for the Merchandising Operation	P5-2a P5-4a	P5-2a P5-4a
6	6	Inventories	None	None
7	7	Accounting Information Systems	P7-1a P7-3a P7-5a	P7-1a P7-3a P7-5a
		Mini Practice Set		
8	8	Internal Control and Cash	P8-2a P8-5a	P8-2a P8-5a
9	9	Accounting for Receivables	P9-5a	P9-5a
10	10	Plant Assets	None	None
11	11	Current Liabilities and Payroll	P11-1a P11-4a	P11-1a P11-4a
12	12	Accounting Principles	None	None
13	13	Partnerships	P13-1a P13-5a	P13-1a P13-5a
14	14	Corporations: Organizations	P14-1a P14-4a	P14-1a P14-4a
15	15	Corporations: Income Reporting, Retained Earnings	P15-1a P15-2a	P15-1a P15-2a
16	16	Long Term Liabilities	None	None
17	17	Investments	P17-2a	P17-2a
18	18	Statement of Cash Flows	None	None

CONTENTS

CHAPTER 1

Accounting in Action

OBJECTIVES

- Be able to understand the basic accounting equation and relate it to entries made in Peachtree Accounting
- Be able to launch the Peachtree accounting application
- Be able to open a previously set up business
- Be able to enter transactions into Peachtree's general journal system
- Be able to understand how to generate and read the four basic financial statements in Peachtree Accounting
- Be able to check for errors in entries made into the general journal
- Be able to edit a general journal entry

BASIC ACCOUNTING

Before we start entering data into the Peachtree software, there are several simple basic principles of accounting you must learn first. Specifically, you must be aware that there are two groupings in which fiscal events are classified: what a business owns and what a business owes. Assets are what a company owns. They are the resources owned by a business. The means under which the business operates are assets. The second group, liabilities and owner's equity, are the rights or claims against these resources. The claims by creditors are called liabilities. Claims by the owners are called owner's equity. We use these groupings whether we're using a computerized or a manual accounting system.

The relationship between the assets and the liabilities and owner's equity is referred to as the basic accounting equation. The total assets of a firm must be equal to the sum of liabilities and owner's equity. The accounting equation applies to all economic and business entities regardless of size, nature of the business, or how the organization is formed and operated.

Let's look in more detail at the categories that comprise the basic accounting equation.

- **Assets**

  Assets are all of the resources owned by a business. They are used in carrying out activities such as production, consumption of goods, and exchange.
- **Liabilities**

  Liabilities are the company's existing debts and obligations. They are the claims against the assets by creditors. For example, businesses usually borrow money from banks and purchase merchandise on credit. These transactions result in the business *owing* money and are recorded in the books as liabilities.
- **Owner's Equity.**

  The ownership claim on total assets is known as owner's equity. It is equal to total assets minus total liabilities. Here's why: The assets of a business are supplied or claimed by either creditors or owner. To find out what belongs to owners, we subtract the creditors' claims, the liabilities, from the assets. The remainder is the owner's claim on the assets, the owner's equity. Because the claims of creditors must be paid before ownership claims, the owner's equity is sometimes referred to as residual equity. In a proprietorship, the owner's investments and revenues increase owner's equity.

  Investments by the Owner

  Investments by the owner are the assets that the owner puts into the business. These investments increase owner's equity. The investments may be cash or material items.

  Drawings

  An owner may take cash or other assets from the business, a withdrawal, for personal use. Drawings decrease owner's equity.

  Revenues

  Revenues are the gross increase in owner's equity resulting from business activities that have been entered into for the purpose of earning income. Generally, revenues result from the sale of merchandise (a retail establishment) or the performance of services (a service related company). A business may also earn money by other means including the rental of property or the lending of money to another company.

  Expenses

  Expenses decrease owner's equity. A business incurs expenses that result from the actual operation of the business. The cost of assets purchased and consumed or services that are used in the process of earning revenue are considered expenses. Expenses are the actual or expected cash outflows (payments) of doing business.

THE TRANSACTION PROCESS

A transaction is often referred to as an external or internal economic event of an enterprise. Transactions are recorded. An external transaction involves economic events between the company and some outside enterprise. For example, the purchase of equipment from a supplier or the payment of rent to a landlord are external transactions. Sales and revenue are also external transactions.

An internal transaction is an economic event that occurs entirely within a company; for example, when office supplies are used up.

A company may also carry on activities that do not in themselves represent business transactions. Hiring employees, answering the phone, and taking a sales order are examples. Some of those activities will eventually lead to a business transaction. We will soon have to pay wages to workers we hired and merchandise must be delivered to customers

Before we enter any transaction, we must install (if needed) and launch Peachtree, then open the company in which you wish to work. Only then can any data can be entered.

REQUIRED COMPUTER EQUIPMENT

Please see the note in the Preface if you have Peachtree Complete, Release 8.0 already installed on your system.

To install Peachtree Complete Accounting, Release 8.0 (Educational) from the CD-ROM included with this workbook, Peachtree Software, Inc. recommends you have the following hardware and software available on your system:

- IBM PC compatible with a Pentium processor, 150 MHz or higher
- 32 MB (megabytes) of RAM (Random Access Memory; 64 MB or higher is highly recommended
- Microsoft Windows 95, Windows 98, Windows 2000, or Windows NT 4 (with Service Pack 3 or higher already installed)
- Hard Disk with the following free space requirements:

The Educational version of Peachtree Complete Accounting	48 MB
The uncompressed (unzipped) Data Files that go along with the workbook	52 MB

Note: The recommended Peachtree Accounting memory requirements are in addition to the memory required by your system software and memory used when working with company data.

- MPC compatible CD-ROM drive
- SVGA monitor that can display at least 256 colors and a minimum resolution of 640x480; 64K colors and 800x600 resolution (or higher) are highly recommended

Use small fonts in your Windows Control Panel Display settings; DO NOT USE LARGE FONTS – Peachtree will not display properly.

- Printers supported by Microsoft Windows 95, Windows 98, Windows 2000 or Windows NT 4
- Mouse or compatible pointing device
- If multiple users will access company data, Peachtree Complete Accounting can operate on any peer-to-peer network that supports Microsoft Winodws 95, Windows 98, Windows 2000 or Windows NT 4 (with Service Pack 3 or higher applied). Peachtree can also operate on client/server networks such as Windows NT Server and Novell NetWare 4.x (or higher). For more information on networking Peachtree Complete and obtaining a site license contact Peachtree Software, Inc.

LAUNCHING PEACHTREE ACCOUNTING SOFTWARE

Step 1: Follow the instructions given to you by your instructor or lab administrator in opening the Peachtree software package.
Step 2: Once Peachtree is open, you will see the Peachtree splash screen.
Step 3: This screen will change to Peachtree's main menu screen as shown in Figure 1.1.

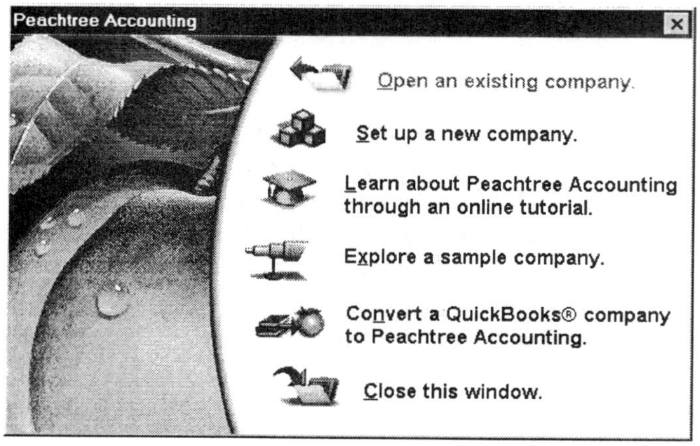

Figure 1. 1 Opening Peachtree menu screen.

Step 4: Click on the first icon. Open an existing company, to get the screen shown in Figure 1.2. Depending on your system, your screen may or may not have the exact same companies listed.
Step 5: Click on "Softbyte Computer Software" which should appear if the Data Sets were correctly loaded from the CD-ROM. (Reload the Data Sets if "Softbyte Computer Software does not appear.)
Step 6: Check to make sure "Softbyte Computer Software" appears in the Title bar above the main window of Peachtree. The full screen is illustrated in Figure 1.3.

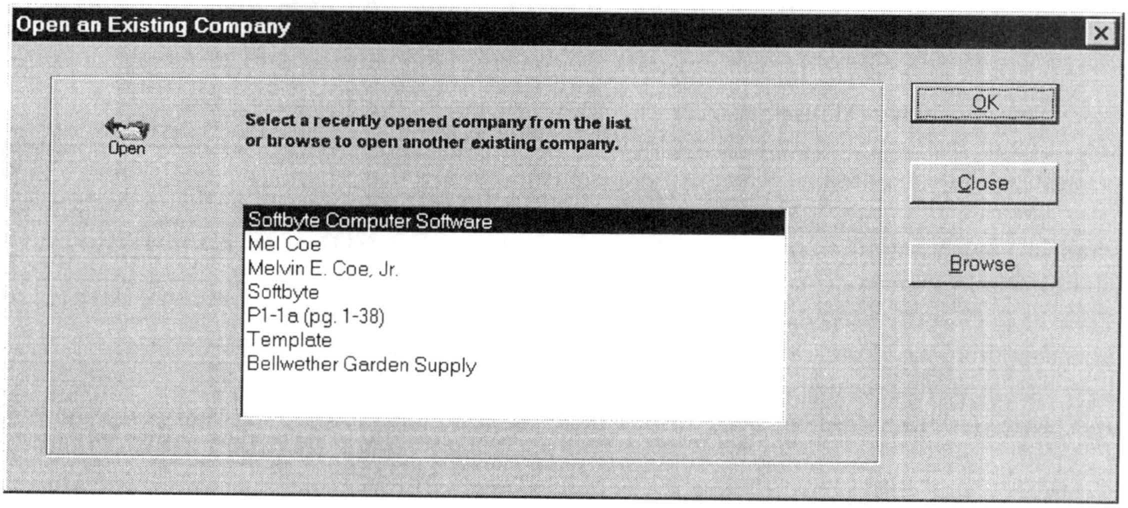

Figure 1. 2 Open company menu screen.

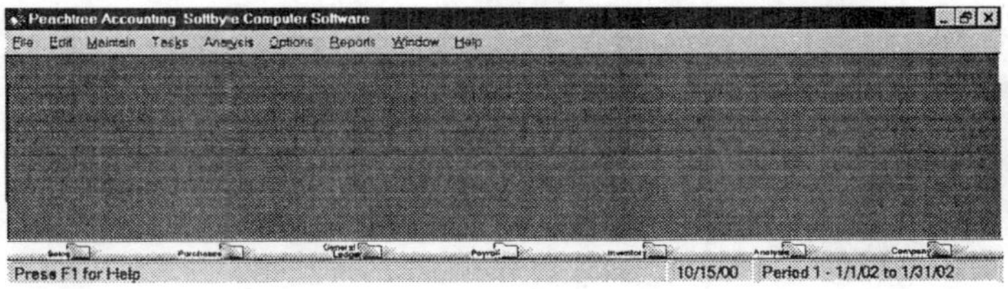

Figure 1. 3 Main Window of Peachtree Accounting.

Even though your text does not cover General Journal entries in the first chapter, you can get a little ahead by working in Peachtree and start to understand how the accounting process works.

With that in mind, now you may enter transactions into Peachtree Accounting by following the step by step instructions that follow. You will be working with a make believe company called Softbyte Computer Services which can be found on your student data disk and in the first chapter of your text. You will build on this file for the next several chapters. So, be sure to <u>*back up your data*</u> on a regular basis. Good luck and have fun.

ENTERING GENERAL JOURNAL TRANSACTIONS

Transaction (1) Investment by Owner. Ray Neal decides to open a computer programming service. On January 1, 2002 he invests $15,000 cash in the business, which he names Softbyte. This transaction results in an equal increase in assets and owner's equity. The asset cash increases by $15,000 and the owner's equity, R. Neal, capital increases by the same amount.

Using Peachtree Accounting, let's step through this initial entry.

Step 1: Using the menu bar from the main Peachtree window, click on Tasks.
Step 2: On the pull down menu, as shown in Figure 1.4, click on General Journal Entries.

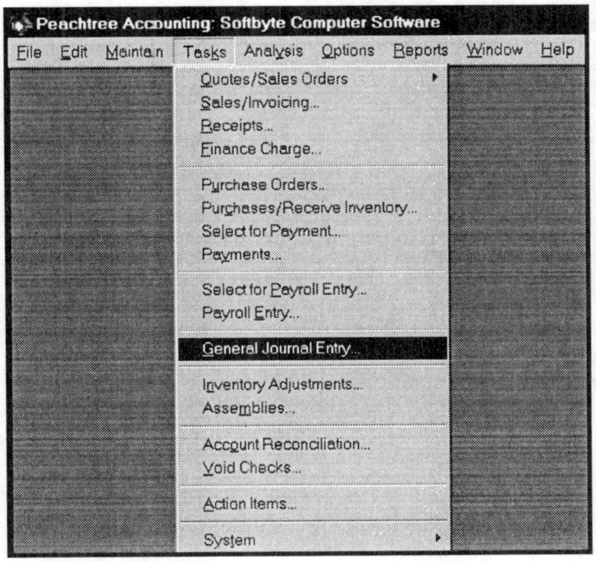

Figure 1. 4 Pull down menu from "Maintain" on menu bar.

Step 3: Make sure that your window looks like that shown in Figure 1.5.

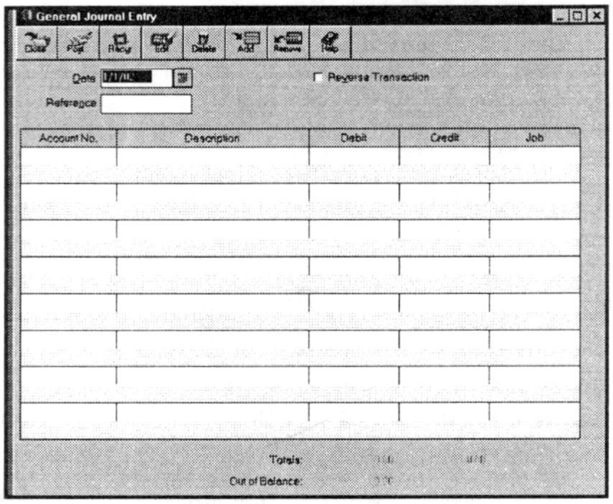

Figure 1. 5 Blank screen for General Journal entry.

Step 4: As a reference, type in "Transaction 1" in the blank Reference Box, just under the date which is preset for January 1, 2002.

Step 5: Click on the magnifying glass that appears next to the Account No. column to get a pull down menu that lists the available accounts for Softbyte, the Chart of Accounts, as shown in Figure 1.6.

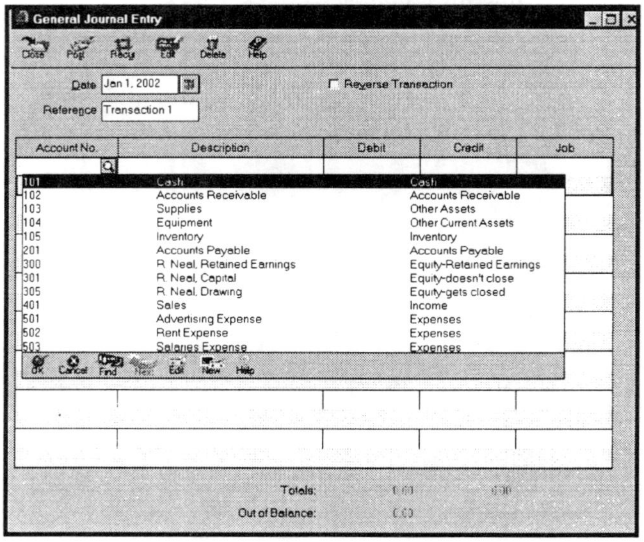

Figure 1. 6 Chart of Accounts

Step 6: Double click on Account Number 101 (Cash). In the description column type in "Initial Investment." And, in the Debit column, type in "1-5-0-0-0-decimal point-0-0."

> Be careful in Peachtree Accounting how you enter numbers requiring decimal points. The "system" will *automatically* insert a decimal point two places to the right of the entered number. For example, if you entered "1-5-0-0," Peachtree would recognize it as $15.00 not $1,500.00, a capital mistake. Make sure your screen looks like Figure 1.7.

Account No.	Description	Debit	Credit	Job
101	Initial Investment	15000.00		
Cash		*Account Increased/Decreased*		

Figure 1. 7 First entry line for the first transaction.

Step 7: Press the enter key (or tab key) three times to get your insertion point to the next line, as shown in Figure 1.8.

Account No.	Description	Debit	Credit	Job
101	Initial Investment	15,000.00		
Cash		Account will be increased		
	Initial Investment			
	Account Description	*Account Increased/Decreased*		

Figure 1. 8 Beginning the second entry line for Transaction 1.

Using the illustrated examples above, enter the amount for owner's equity by:

Step 8: Clicking on the magnifying glass in the Account No. column.
Step 9: Double clicking the account number 301
Step 10: In the Credit column, entering the amount, $15,000.00 – the dollar sign is not necessary, but the decimal point should be entered manually. Your entry should look like Figure 1.9.

Account No.	Description	Debit	Credit	Job
101	Initial Investment	15,000.00		
Cash		Account will be increased		
301	Initial Investment		15,000.00	
R. Neal, Capital		Account will be increased		

Figure 1. 9 Entry for owner's investment of cash in the business.

BEFORE YOU CONTINUE

Look at the window in Figure 1.10. Notice the amounts at the bottom of the window, in the gray area outside the entry area. They indicate whether or not your entry is in balance. In Figure 1.10, $15,000 appears under the Debit column and under the Credit column. The figure next to "Out of Balance" is zero. Therefore, your entry is in balance.

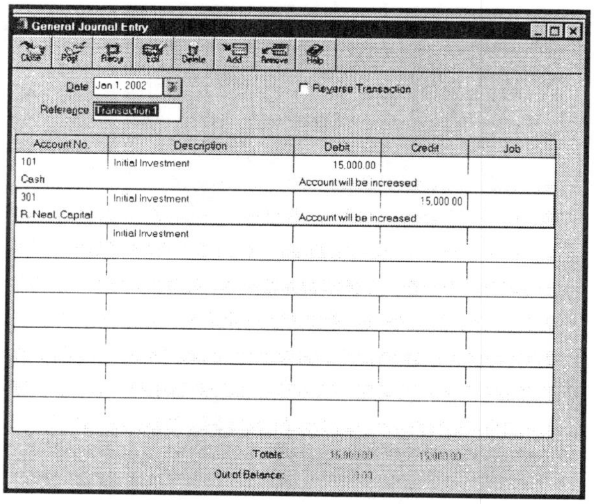

Figure 1. 10 In balance journal entries.

If we had mistakenly entered both amounts in the Debit column as shown in Figure 1.11 (or even both amounts in the credit column), we would be "Out of Balance."

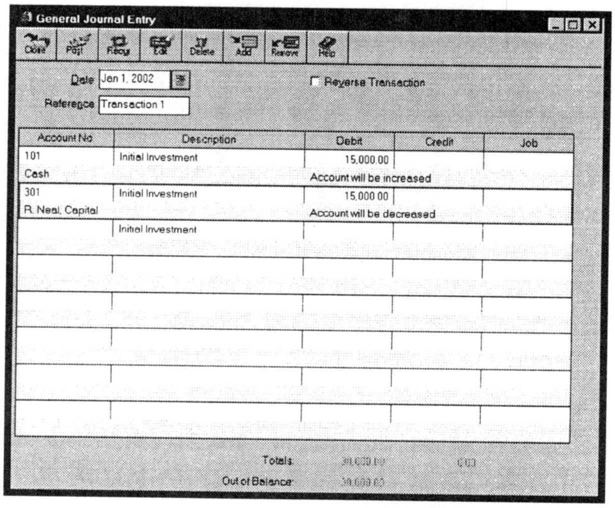

Figure 1. 11 Entry error as shown by out of balance tally.

Always double-check your entries before continuing. Just because the system indicates you are "In Balance" does not necessarily mean your transaction is correct. It just means what you have entered is "In Balance." However, as shown in Figure 1.12, the system will not let you continue if you are "Out of Balance" and will return an error message.

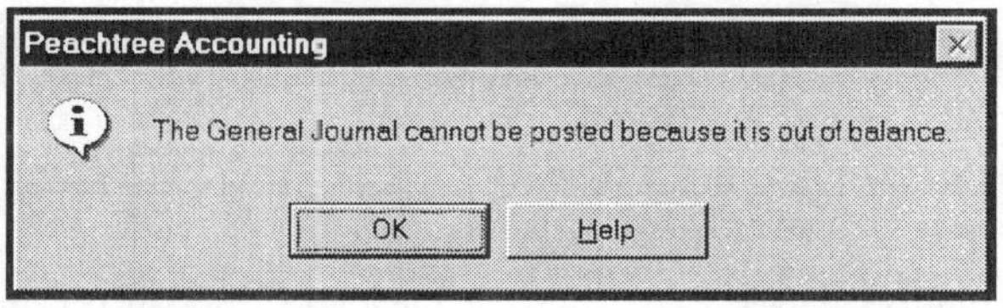

Figure 1. 12 The system will not let you continue if you are "Out of Balance" on your entry.

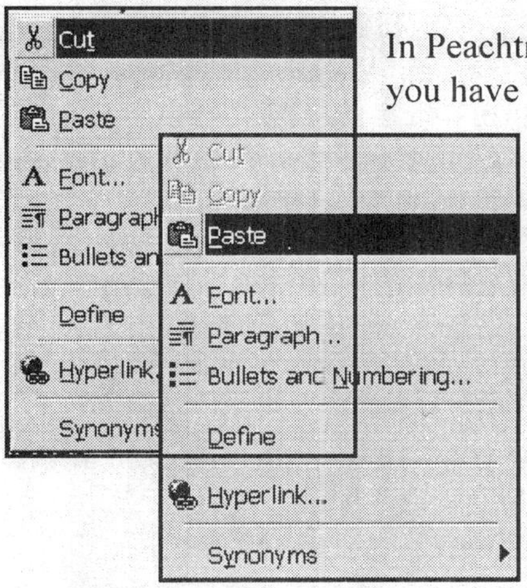

In Peachtree Accounting, as in any Microsoft Windows product, you have "cut," "copy" and "paste" capabilities. You may click on the right button of your mouse to get the "Edit" pull down menu. Highlight the field you want to move by double clicking on the field. Click on "Cut". Move the insertion point to the correct field where you want the data, right click to get the pull down edit menu then click on "Paste".

POSTING THE TRANSACTION

Step 1: To post the transaction (enter it into the system) click on the "Post" icon (see Figure 1.13) in the tool bar section toward the top of the window.

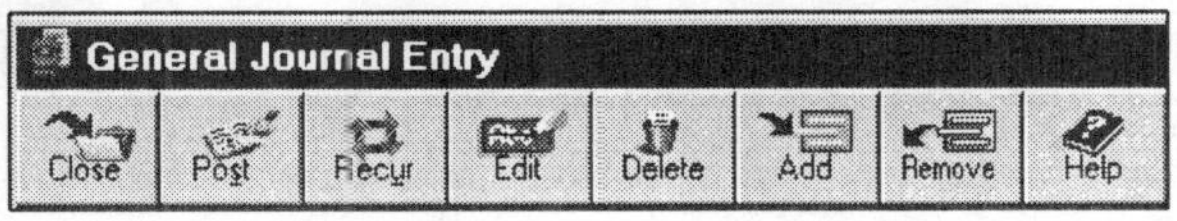

Figure 1. 13 Click on the "Post" icon to enter your transaction.

Step 2: The General Journal window clears all that has been previously entered and is now ready for the second transaction. Notice that the General Journal window's Transaction Number has now automatically advanced to "Transaction 2".

You are now ready for the next transaction.

Transaction (2). Purchase of Equipment for Cash. Softbyte purchases computer equipment for $7,000 cash. This transaction will result in an equal increase and decrease in total assets. Cash is decreased by $7,000 whereas the asset Equipment is increased by $7,000.

Using the process you learned in Transaction 1 make this General Journal entry.

Step 1: Type in "Transaction 2" in the reference box, if it is different. Leave the date as it is, January 1, 2002.
Step 2: Click on the magnifying glass to get the pull down menu of the Chart of Accounts. Highlight "Equipment" and double click (you may also press the <ENTER> key).
Step 3: Press the <TAB> key to move your insertion point over to the Description column and type in "Paid cash for equipment."
Step 4: Press the <TAB> key to move your insertion point to the next column, the Debit column and enter, in error the amount $8,000.00. This amount is in error because in the second part of this exercise you will learn how to edit a General Journal entry, after it has been posted. Remember you do not have to enter the "$," but you should enter the decimal point.
Step 5: Press the <ENTER> key three times so that your insertion point is in the Account No. column of the next line. Click on the magnifying glass to get the pull down menu of the Chart of Accounts. Highlight "Cash" and double click (you may also press the <ENTER> key).
Step 6: Press the <TAB> key to move your insertion point over to the Description column and type in "Paid cash for equipment." (The system may have already generated this for you.)
Step 7: Press the <TAB> key twice to move your insertion point to the credit column and enter the amount, *purposely in error* $8,000.00. We enter this amount in error for our books to balance. This will be edited in the next part of this exercise. Again, remember you do not have to enter the "$," but you should enter the decimal point.
Step 8: Make sure your screen looks like Figure 1.14 before continuing. If there are no errors (besides the intentional ones you typed in) go ahead and post your transaction. Notice that even though we know there is an error, the system will let you post because technically your books are in balance.

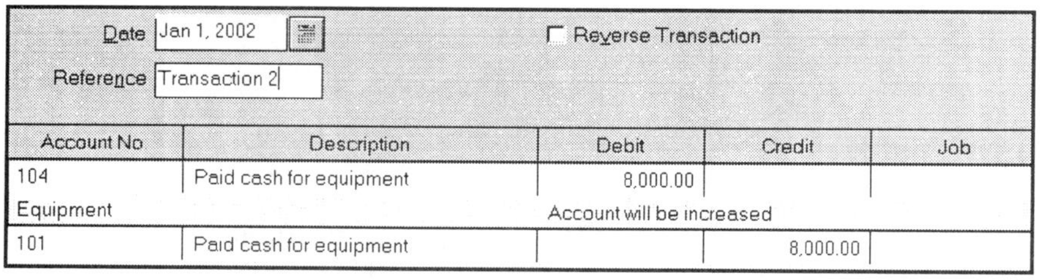

Figure 1. 14 General Journal entry shown in error.

EDITING A GENERAL JOURNAL ENTRY

Editing a General Journal entry is just as simple as making the original entry.

Step 1: Make sure you have a blank General Journal screen. If not, create one by clicking on Tasks, then General Journal Entries.
Step 2: On the Toolbar menu, illustrated in Figure 1.15, click on the EDIT tool.

Figure 1. 15 General Journal tool bar.

Step 3: You will be presented with a Select General Journal Entry menu listing all of the General Journal entries you have entered in this accounting period. Do not worry about accounting periods at this time. Figure 1.16 shows only two entries. The first transaction, for $15,000 is the first entry you made and the second one, for $8,000 is the one with the error, which you are going to correct. Click on the second entry.

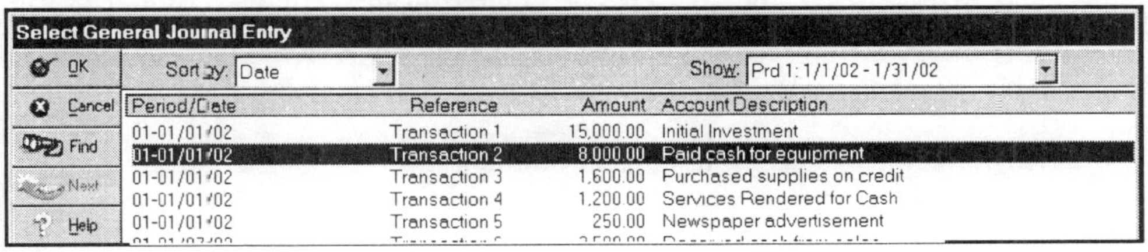

Figure 1. 16 Select General Journal entry menu.

Step 4: You will be returned to the General Journal entry screen like the one you had when you made the earlier entry. Your screen should look like Figure 1.17.

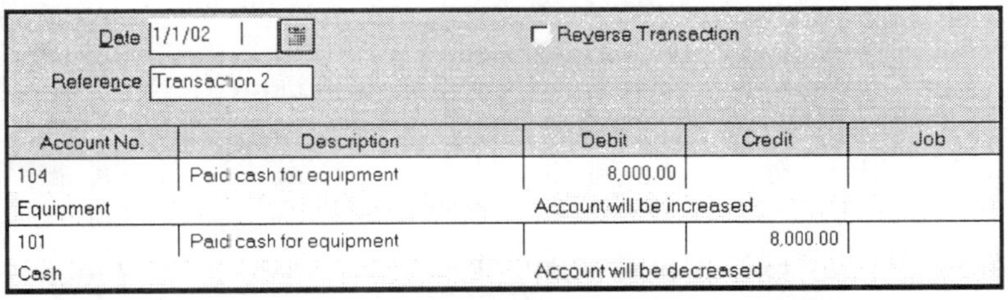

Figure 1. 17 General Journal entry screen showing second transaction in error.

Step 5: Any field on the screen can be changed and reposted. However, we are only interested in changing the amounts, $8,000 to $7,000. Place the insertion point in the first amount field, highlight the $8,000, and change it to $7,000.

Step 6: Do the same with the second amount. Your screen should match the one shown in Figure 1.18.

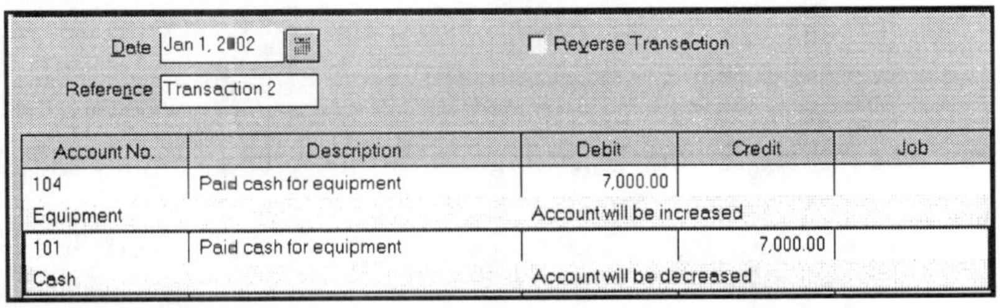

Figure 1. 18 Corrected General Journal Entry for Transaction 2.

SOME ADDITIONAL POINTS

Notice that written below the amount you entered in the "Debit" column in Figure 1.18, the system has told you that the account is going to be *increased* by the amount you entered. A "Debit" entry will always increase an Asset account.

Also, notice that written below the amount you entered in the "Credit" column in Figure 1.18, the system has told you that the account is going to be *decreased* by the amount you entered. A "Credit" entry will always decrease an Asset account.

Step 1: Click on POST on the General Journal Entry toolbar.

Transaction (3). Purchase of Supplies on Credit. Softbyte purchases computer paper and other supplies expected to last several months for $1,600.00 from Acme Supply Company. Acme will allow Softbyte to pay this bill next month. This transaction is referred to as a purchase on account or a credit purchase. Assets will be increased (a debit entry will increase an asset account) because the expected future benefits of using the paper and supplies. Liabilities will also be increased (a credit entry will increase an liability account) by the amount due to Acme Company. With an equal debit and credit entry, your accounting equation will remain in balance.

Using the process you learned in Transaction 1 make this General Journal entry on your own.

Step 1: Type in "Transaction 3" in the reference box, if it is different. Leave the date as it is, January 1, 2002.
Step 2: Click on the magnifying glass to get the pull down menu of the Chart of Accounts. Highlight "Supplies" and double click (you may also press the <ENTER> key).
Step 3: Press the <TAB> key to move your insertion point over to the Description column and type in "Purchased supplies on account."
Step 4: Press the <TAB> key to move your insertion point to the next column, the Debit column and enter $1,600.
Step 5: Press the <ENTER> key three times so that your insertion point is in the Account No. column of the next line. Click on the magnifying glass to get the pull-down menu of the Chart of Accounts. Highlight "Accounts Payable" and double click (you may also press the <ENTER> key).
Step 6: Press the <TAB> key to move your insertion point over to the Description column "Purchased supplies on account" should have automatically been generated for you; if not go ahead and enter it.
Step 7: Press the <TAB> key twice to move your insertion point to the credit column and enter the amount $1,600.
Step 8: Make sure your screen looks like Figure 1.22 and correct any errors before continuing.

Before you post your entry, double-check what you have entered. Make sure your entries match Figure 1.19.

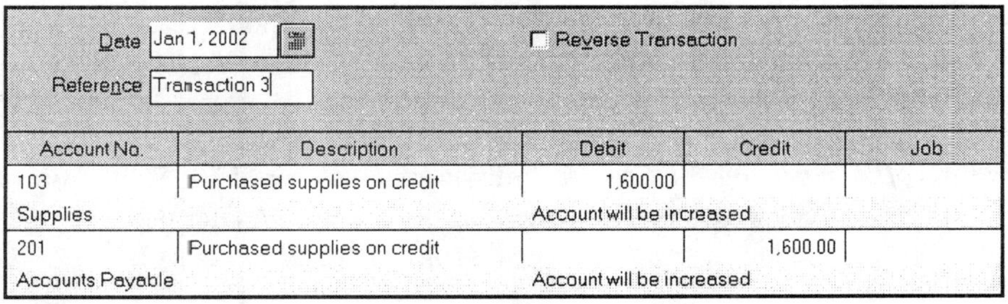

Date: Jan 1, 2002 — Reverse Transaction
Reference: Transaction 3

Account No.	Description	Debit	Credit	Job
103 Supplies	Purchased supplies on credit	1,600.00		
	Account will be increased			
201 Accounts Payable	Purchased supplies on credit		1,600.00	
	Account will be increased			

Figure 1.19 Journal entry for a credit (on account) purchase.

Before you "Post" Transaction 3, notice that both accounts, Supplies and Accounts Payable, are going to be increased by this operation. We have added $1,600 worth of supplies to our company (an asset) and we have also incurred $1,600 worth of liabilities (money we owe).

Looking at the "big picture," total assets are now $16,600. This total is matched by a $1,600 creditor's claim (the supplies just purchased on account)) and a $15,000 ownership claim (the initial cash the owner put into the business).

Step 1: Click on the "Post" icon on the toolbar to post your transaction into the General Journal.

Transaction (4). Services Rendered for Cash. Softbyte receives $1,200 cash from customers for programming services it has provided. This transaction represents the company's principal revenue producing activity. Remember that revenue will increase owner's equity. However, revenue does have its own separate account under "Equity" .

Make the General Journal entry:

Step 1: The account no. 101, Cash, should be increased by $1,200 (a debit entry).
Step 2: The account no. 401, Revenue, should be increased by $1,200 (a credit entry).

Remember that an asset is increased by a debit entry and that revenue (in reality an increase to equity) is increased by a credit entry. As a rule of thumb, it is rare that any income (revenue) account will be debited, so, it is relatively safe to say that <u>all revenue</u> (income) accounts will only be credited.

Step 3: Before posting, make sure your entry matches the one below in Figure 1.20.

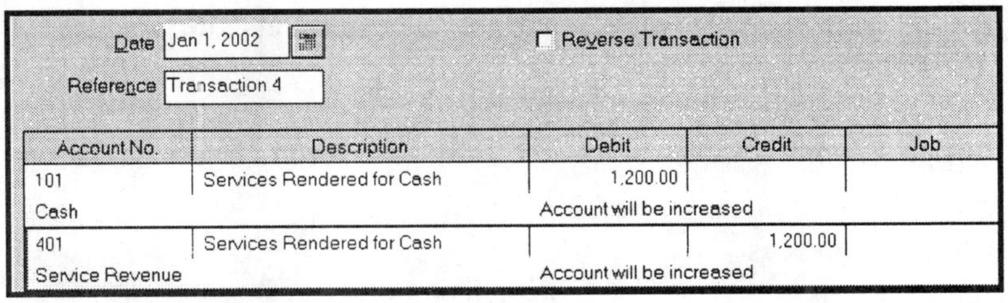

Date: Jan 1, 2002 — Reverse Transaction
Reference: Transaction 4

Account No.	Description	Debit	Credit	Job
101 Cash	Services Rendered for Cash	1,200.00		
	Account will be increased			
401 Service Revenue	Services Rendered for Cash		1,200.00	
	Account will be increased			

Figure 1. 20 General Journal entry for Service Revenue.

Step 4: If there are no errors, "Post" the entry.

The two sides of the equation remain in balance at $17,800. The source of the increase in owner's equity is indicated as Service Revenue, which will be included in determining Softbyte's net income.

Transaction (5). Purchase of Advertising on Credit. Softbyte receives a bill for $250 from the *Daily News* for advertising. Softbyte decides to postpone payment of the bill until a later date. This transaction results in an increase in liabilities and an increase in expenses (or a decrease in equity).

Step 1: The expense Account No. 501, Advertising Expense, is increased (debited) by $250.
Step 2: The Accounts Payable Account No. 201, is also increased (credited) by $250.

As a rule of thumb, it is rare that <u>any</u> expense account would be credited. So it is relatively safe to say that all expense accounts will only be debited. The entry is shown in Figure 1.21 below.

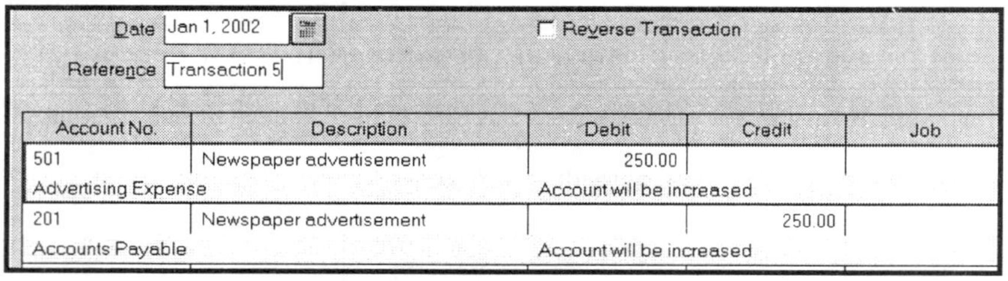

Date Jan 1, 2002 ☐ Reverse Transaction
Reference Transaction 5

Account No.	Description	Debit	Credit	Job
501 Advertising Expense	Newspaper advertisement	250.00 Account will be increased		
201 Accounts Payable	Newspaper advertisement	Account will be increased	250.00	

Figure 1. 21 Advertising Expense to be paid later.

Step 3: If your entries are correct, go ahead and post the General Journal entry.

The two sides of the equation still balance at $17,800. Owner's Equity will be decreased when the expense (Advertising Expense) is incurred and is noted. Expenses do not have to be paid in cash at the time they are incurred. When payment is made at a later date, the liability Accounts Payable will be decreased and the asset Cash will be decreased. You will see how that works in Transaction 8. The cost of advertising is considered an expense, as opposed to an asset. That is because the benefits of the ads have been used up. This expense is included in determining net income.

Transaction (6). Services Rendered for Cash and Credit. Softbyte provides $3,500 of programming services for customers. On January 7, 2002, Cash, $1,500 is received from customers and the balance of $2,200 is billed on account. This transaction results in an equal increase in assets and owner's equity.
Three specific accounts are affected:

- Cash is increased by $1,500
- Accounts Receivable is increased by $2,000
- The revenue account is increased by $3,500.

Cash and Accounts Receivable, both assets, will be increased (debited). Cash increases by $1,500 whereas Accounts Receivable increase by $2,000. The third entry will increase the revenue account by $3,500.

Step 1: Change the date from January 1 to January 7. You may enter the date directly in the date box or by clicking on the calendar icon, you will be able to click the appropriate date for entry directly from a pull-down calendar as shown in Figure 1.22.

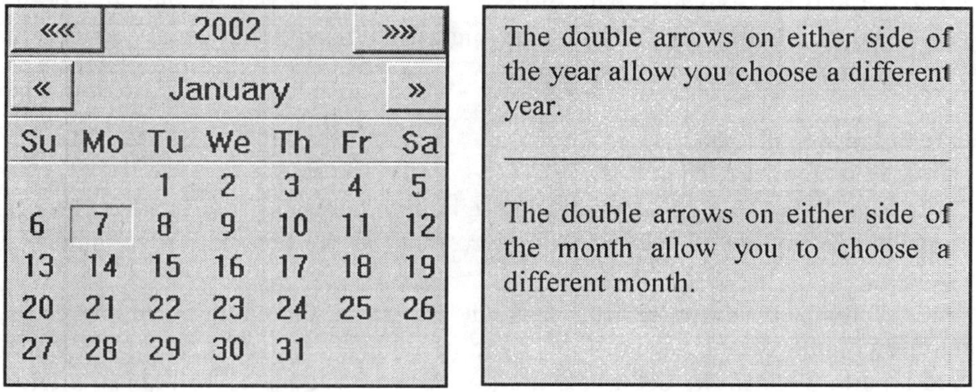

Figure 1. 22 Pull down calendar.

Step 2: Change the Transaction number under the date to "Transaction 6".

Step 3: Using the magnifying glass, find the account number (#101) for Cash and press <ENTER>. In the Description column type in "Cash from sales" and enter the amount, $1,500 in the Debit column.

Step 4: Using the magnifying glass, find the account number (#102) for Accounts Receivable and press <ENTER>. In the Description column type in "Sales On Account" and enter the amount, $2,000, in the Debit column.

Step 5: And again, using the magnifying glass, find the account number (#401) for Service Revenue and press <ENTER>. In the Description column type in "Sales." Tab over to the Credit column and enter the amount, $1,500.

Step 6: Notice that all three entries will increase the appropriate accounts and that glancing at the bottom of the window, you should be in balance at $3,500.

Step 7: Your entry should match Figure 1.23. Make any necessary changes before posting your entry.

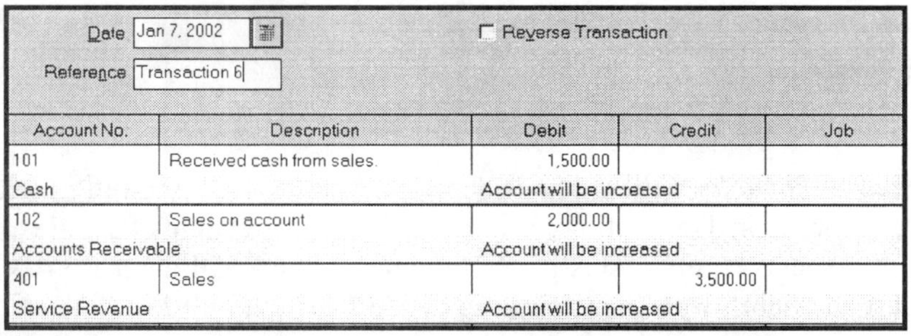

Figure 1. 23 General Journal Entry showing date change and account entries.

Why did we increase Service Revenue (Owner's Equity) by $3,500 when only $1,500 has been collected? Answer: Because the inflow of assets resulting from the earning of revenues does not have to be in the form of cash. Remember that owner's equity is increased when revenues are earned, in Softbyte's case, when the service is provided. When collections on account are received later, Cash will then be increased and Accounts Receivable will be decreased. That will happen in Transaction 9.

Transaction (7). Payment of Expenses. Expenses paid in cash on January 15 include the Store Rent $600; Salaries of employees $900; and Utilities $200. These payments will result in an equal decrease in assets (cash) and owner's equity (the individual expense items).

Step 1: Change the date to January 15, 2002.
Step 2: Change the transaction number to "Transaction 7".
Step 3: Identify the Store Rent Expense account, #501, highlight it and press <ENTER> (or click) to place it the account number column. Type in "Paid store rent" in the description column and $600 in the debit column.
Step 4: On the next line, identify the salaries expense account number, #503 making sure it appears in the account number column on the second line. Type in "Paid Employee's salaries" on the description line and type in $900 in the debit column. (We'll worry about payroll tax in a later chapter.)
Step 5: On the third line, identify and place account #504, the utilities expense account number in the appropriate column. In the description column, type in "Paid utilities". And, in the debit column, type in $200.
Step 6: Cash will be decreased by the total amount of the above expenses, $1,700. By now you should know that the account number for Cash is 101. You may type that in directly or search for it using the magnifying glass. Type in "Paid monthly expenses" in the description column. The total credit amount (we're decreasing an asset) is $1,700.
Step 7: Check to see that your entries are in balance before posting. Your entry should match the one in Figure 1.24.

Date: Jan 15, 2002 ☐ Reverse Transaction
Reference: Transaction 7

Account No.	Description	Debit	Credit	Job
502	Paid rent on store	600.00		
Rent Expense		Account will be increased		
503	Paid salaries of employees	900.00		
Salaries Expense		Account will be increased		
504	Paid utilities expense	200.00		
Utilities Expense		Account will be increased		
101	Paid utilities expense		1,700.00	
Cash		Account will be decreased		

Figure 1. 24 Paid cash for monthly expenses.

Transaction (8). Payment of Accounts Payable. Softbyte pays its *Daily News* advertising bill of $250 in cash. The bill had been previously recorded in Transaction (5) as an increase in Accounts Payable and an increase in expenses (a decrease in owner's equity). This payment "on account" will decrease the asset cash (a credit) and will also decrease the liability accounts payable (a debit) – both by $250.

Step 1: Keep the date, January 15, 2002 as is, but change the transaction number to "Transaction 8".
Step 2: Entering the debit amount first, the account number is 201 for Accounts Payable.
Step 3: Type in "Paid Daily News for ads on account" in the description column. And, type in $250 in the debit column to complete the first line.

Step 4: Account number 101 is the number for the cash account which goes in the first column of the second line.

Step 5: "Paid *Daily News* for ads on account." This should have been automatically generated by the system. If so, press the <TAB> key twice to move to the credit column and enter $250.

Step 6: Check to make sure your entry is in balance and matches Figure 1.25.

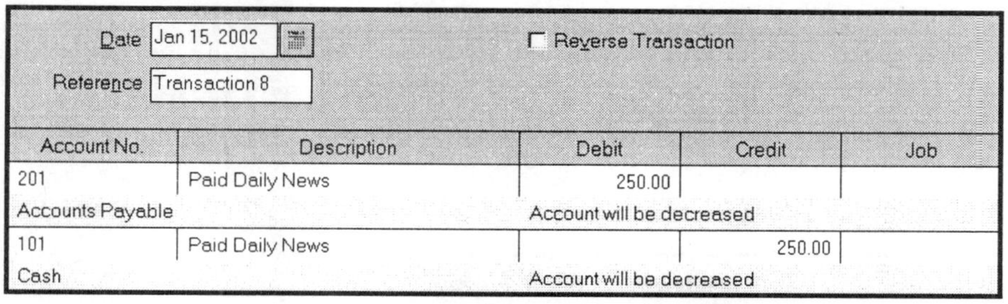

Figure 1. 25 Paid Daily News account due.

Remember that the payment of liability related to an expense that has previously been recorded will not affect owner's equity. The expense was recorded in Transaction 5.

Transaction (9). Receipt of Cash on Account. The sum of $600 in cash is received from those customers who have previously been billed for services in Transaction 6. This transaction does not change any of the totals in assets, but it will change the composition of those accounts. Cash is increased by $600 and Accounts Receivable is decreased by $600.

Step 1: If you went directly to Transaction 9 from Transaction 8, you will notice that the reference has automatically changed to "Transaction 9." If that change did not occur, enter "Transaction 9" in the reference box. Leave the date at January 15.

Step 2: Enter account number 101 for the Cash account. And, in the Description column type in "Received Cash from customers." In the Debit column, enter $600.

Step 3: On the second line, enter account number 102 for the Accounts receivable account. "Received Cash from customers" should have been automatically entered by the system. However, you need to enter $600 in the Credit column so that your entry will balance.

Step 4: Check your entry with the one in Figure 1.26 before posting. Make any necessary changes.

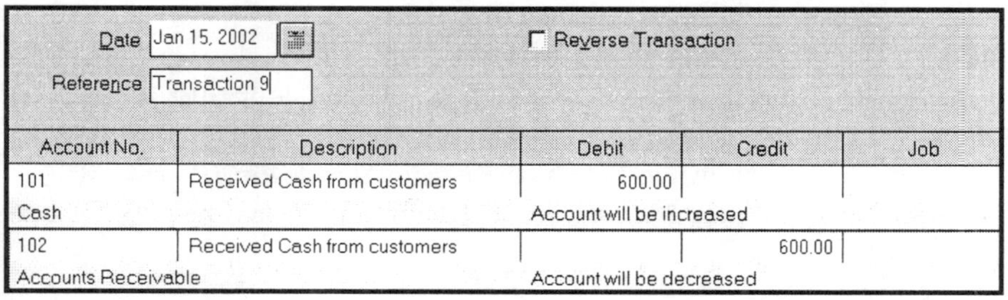

Figure 1. 26 Received cash from customers on account.

Transaction (10). Withdrawal of Cash By Owner. On January 31, Ray Neal withdraws $1,300 in cash from the business for his personal use. This transaction results in an equal decrease in assets (Cash) and Owner's Equity (Drawing).

Step 1: Change the date to January 31. Also, make sure that Transaction 10 is in the reference window.

Step 2: Account number 302 is the Drawing account that will be debited. Enter 302 as the account number. In the Description column, type in "Ray Neal, Drawing" and in the Debit column (a decrease to capital), enter $1,300.

Step 3: Because Neal wants cash for his withdrawal, the asset cash must be decreased (a credit). Enter account number 101 for the Cash account. "Ray Neal, Drawing" will most likely have been defaulted in the Description column; if not, make the appropriate entry. And, in the Credit column, enter $1,300.

Step 4: Check your entry with Figure 1.27 and make any corrections before posting your entry.

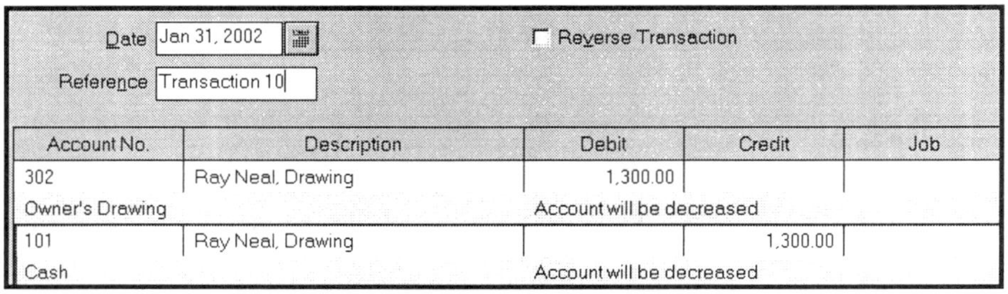

Figure 1. 27 Owner withdraws cash from the business for personal use.

Be aware that the effect of a cash withdrawal by the owner is the opposite of the effect of an investment by the owner. Owner's Drawings are not like expenses. Just like the investment made by the owner, they (withdrawals) are not included in the determination of net income.

FINANCIAL STATEMENTS

After transactions have been identified, analyzed, and entered into the computer, four financial statements can be prepared from your data. In fact, when you made your first entry each of the statements was updated, and kept up to date as you went along.

Those statements are:

- An income statement
  - Presents the revenues and expenses and resulting net income or net loss for a specific period of time.
- An owner's equity statement (also known as the change in capital or equity)
  - The statement of owner's equity summarizes the changes in owner's equity for a specific period of time.
- A balance sheet
  - A company's report of the assets, liabilities, and owner's equity at a specific date.
- A statement of cash flow
  - A summary of information about the cash inflows (receipts) and outflows (payments) for a specific period of time.

Each Peachtree financial statement provides management, owners, and other interested parties with relevant financial data. The statements are interrelated. For example, Net income of $2,750 shown on the income statement is added to the beginning balance of owner's capital (equity) in the owner's equity statement. Owner's capital of $16,450 at the end of the reporting period shown in the owner's equity statement is reported on the balance sheet. Cash of $8,050 on the balance sheet is reported on the statement of cash flows.

Every set of financial statements is accompanied by explanatory notes and supporting schedules that are an integral part of the statements.

The reports used throughout this workbook are provided already preset for each of your assignments. The assignments in Peachtree accounting appear in the 6th edition of *Accounting Principles* by Weygandt, Kieso, and Kimmel and are noted by the Peachtree logo - a peach in the margin.

The customizing of the appearance and information appearing on the reports is outside the scope of this text.

In addition to the four statements mentioned previously, several other reports also deserve attention. They are included, under the General Ledger heading:

- The Chart of Accounts
- The General Journal
- The General Ledger

GENERATING THE INCOME STATEMENT

Step 1: On the main menu bar, Figure 1.28, click on "Reports" to get the pull down menu shown in Figure 1.29.

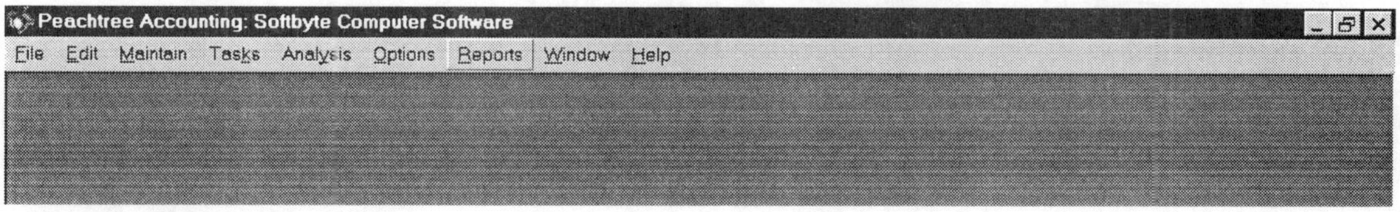

Figure 1. 28 Main Menu Bar.

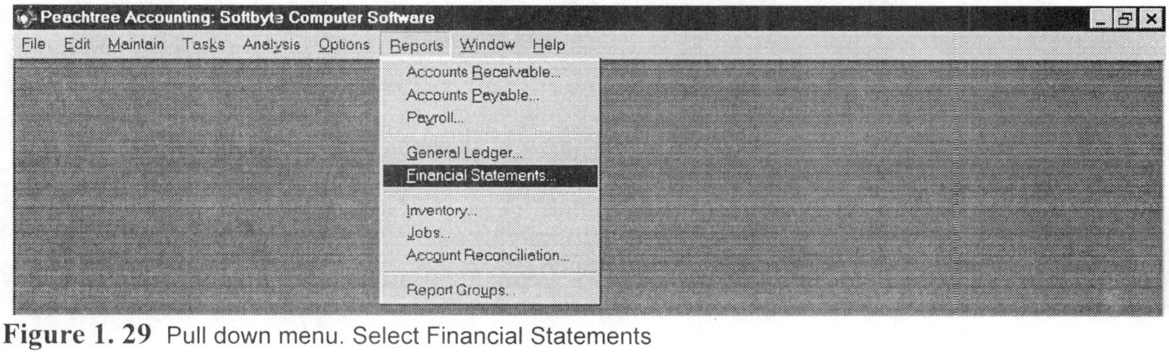

Figure 1. 29 Pull down menu. Select Financial Statements

Step 2: Click on Financial Statements to get the "Select A Report" menu of shown in Figure 1.30.

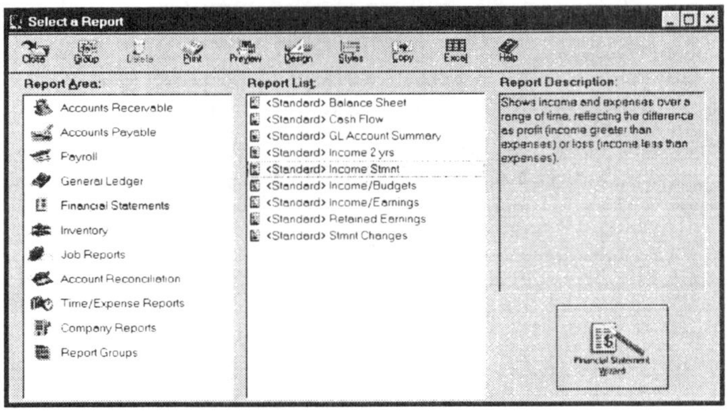

Figure 1. 30 Select A Report menu.

Step 3: Double click on <Predefined> Income Statement toward the middle of the list.

Step 4: The Dialog Box, shown in Figure 1.31, gives several option choices including the choice of financial periods, the margins for the printer, whether or not we want to show accounts that have a zero balance, whether or not we want page numbers, and so on. If you wish to print the Income Statement, make sure the printer at the bottom of the dialog box matches the printer you are using on your computer system.

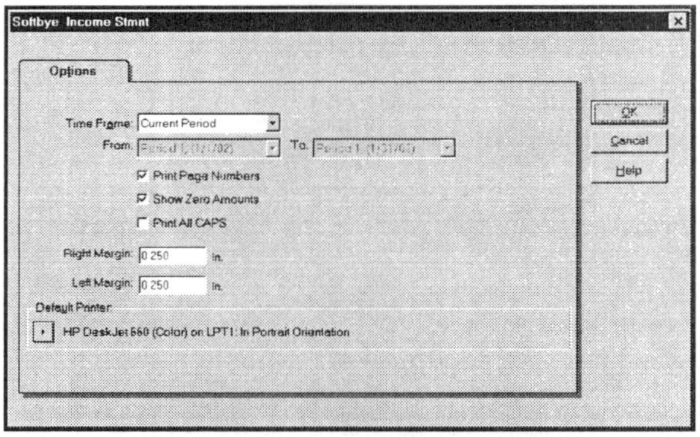

Figure 1. 31 Dialog box to prepare Income Statement for display

Step 5: Click OK to show the income statement, Figure 1.32, on your computer screen.

The <Predefined> Income Statement is a complete income statement already set up by the Peachtree system during the original company set up.

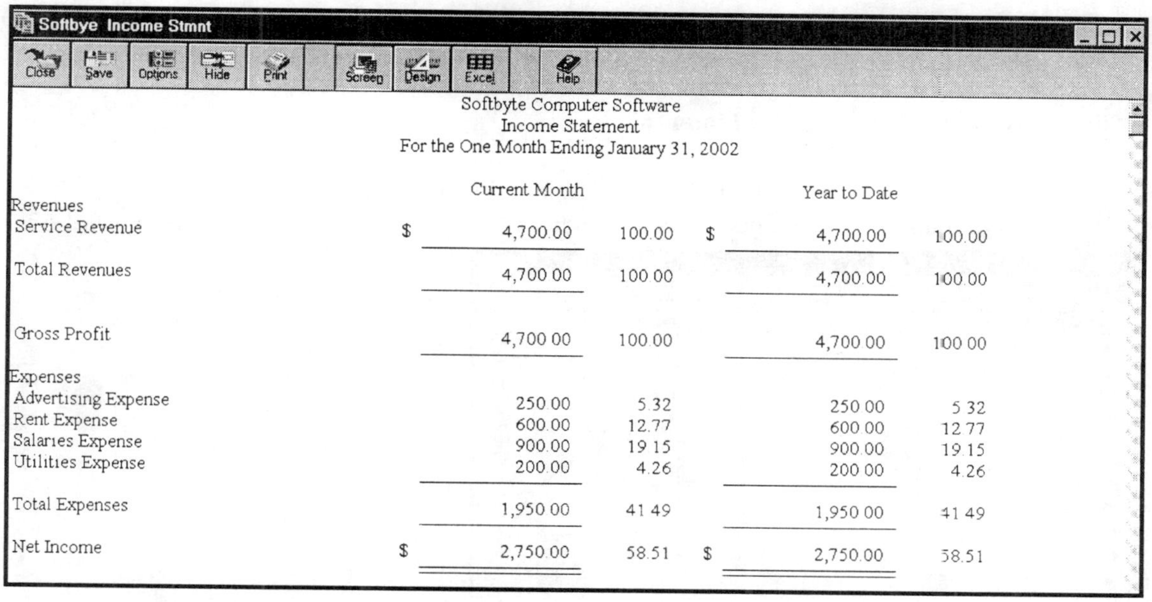

Softbyte Computer Software
Income Statement
For the One Month Ending January 31, 2002

	Current Month		Year to Date	
Revenues				
Service Revenue	$ 4,700.00	100.00	$ 4,700.00	100.00
Total Revenues	4,700.00	100.00	4,700.00	100.00
Gross Profit	4,700.00	100.00	4,700.00	100.00
Expenses				
Advertising Expense	250.00	5.32	250.00	5.32
Rent Expense	600.00	12.77	600.00	12.77
Salaries Expense	900.00	19.15	900.00	19.15
Utilities Expense	200.00	4.26	200.00	4.26
Total Expenses	1,950.00	41.49	1,950.00	41.49
Net Income	$ 2,750.00	58.51	$ 2,750.00	58.51

Figure 1. 32 Full Screen display of the Income Statement for Softbyte.

The revenues and expenses are reported for a specific period of time, the month ending on January 31, 2002. The statement was generated from all of the data you entered since the beginning of the chapter. Make sure your data matches what is shown in Figure 1.32. Go back and edit changes if your figures do not match.

On the income statement the revenues are listed first, followed by expenses. Finally net income (or net loss) is determined. Although practice sometimes varies in the "real world," the expenses in our example have been generated based on account number. In some cases, expenses appear in order of financial magnitude.

Investment and withdrawal transactions between the owner and the business are not included in the measurement of net income. Remember, R. Neal's withdrawal of cash from Softbyte was not regarded as a *business* transaction.

GENERATING THE STATEMENT OF OWNER'S EQUITY

In Peachtree Accounting, changes in Owner's Equity are presented in the Retained Earnings report and Statement of Changes in Financial Position. This data, again, was obtained from the entries you made in the earlier transactions.

When learning accounting principles, Retained Earnings, is usually covered as a part of corporate accounting and not while learning about sole proprietorships. We will look at Retained Earnings more in depth in our section on corporate accounting. However, the Peachtree Complete accounting system, when setting up the original company, requires the creation of a Retained Earnings account in the set up procedure.

By definition, retained earnings are the net income retained in a corporation. Net income is recorded and added to Retained Earnings by a closing entry in which Income Summary is debited and Retained Earnings is credited just as you credited the capital account. Closing entries will also be covered later. R. Neal's Capital account would contain all of the paid-in contributions by the sole proprietor (R. Neal).

To generate the Retained Earnings Statement:

Step 1: On the main menu bar, click on "Reports" to get the pull down menu.
Step 2: Click on Financial Statements to get the "Select A Report" menu of shown in Figure 1.33.

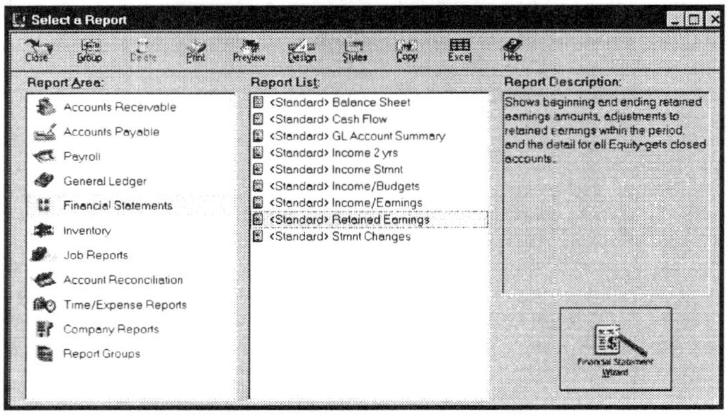

Figure 1. 33 Select A Report Menu

Step 3: Double click on <Predefined> Retained Earnings toward the bottom of the list.
Step 4: Again, the Dialog Box, as shown in Figure 1.34, gives us several choices including the choice of financial periods, the margins for the printer, whether or not we want to show accounts that have a zero balance, whether or not we want page numbers, etc. If you wish to print the Retained Earnings Statement, make sure the printer at the bottom of the dialog box matches the printer you are using on your computer system.

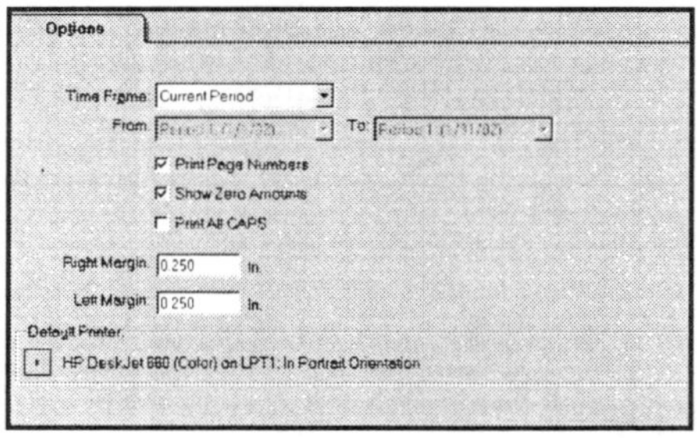

Figure 1. 34 Dialog box to prepare Income Statement for display

Step 5: Click OK to show the Retained Earnings statement, Figure 1.35, on your computer screen.

Softbyte Computer Software
Statement of Retained Earnings
For the One Month Ending January 31, 2002

Beginning Retained Earnings	$	0.00
Adjustments To Date		15,000.00
Net Income		2,750.00
Subtotal		17,750.00
Owner's Drawing		<1,300.00>
Ending Retained Earnings	$	16,450.00

Figure 1. 35 The Retained Earnings statement.

The beginning Retained Earnings is shown on the first line of the statement. The balance is zero since this is a start up company with no previous earned income. Next month, the amount should equal (for the beginning balance) the ending balance, $16,45 as of January 31, 2002.

The next line shows the amount of money invested, paid-in by Neal not earned through revenue, this accounting period. Recall that Neal invested $15,000 in his business. The net income, obtained from the Income Statement produced earlier shows a net income of $2,700. This figure was acquired by subtracting all of this period's expenses from all of the period's revenue. The results: Net Income, which will eventually be "rolled into" Retained Earnings.

The amount Neal took out or withdrew from the company is shown next as a subtraction from equity. And, the final figure is the ending Owner's Equity balance, $16,450 that will be the beginning balance for the next accounting period.

The statement of changes in financial condition is obtained in a similar manner and not covered here.

THE BALANCE SHEET

The balance sheet also is prepared from all of the data you previously entered. The assets will appear at the top of the balance sheet, followed by liabilities, then owner's equity. Recall from the beginning of the chapter that assets must equal the total of the liabilities plus (in addition to) the owner's equity. Peachtree Accounting will make sure this balances for you. The system will let you know if it does not balance.

The balance sheet is obtained in the same way the Income Statement and Retained Earnings Statement were obtained.

Step 1: On the main menu bar click on Reports to get the pull-down menu. .

Step 2: Click on Financial Statements to get the "Select A Report" menu.

Step 3: Double click on Softbyte Balance Sheet toward the bottom of the list, just above the Softbyte Income Statement used earlier.

Step 4: Again, the Dialog Box gives us several choices including the choice of financial periods, the margins for the printer, whether or not we want to show accounts that have a zero balance, whether or not we want page numbers, and so on. If you wish to print the Retained Earnings Statement, make sure the printer at the bottom of the Dialog Box matches the printer you are using on your computer system.

Step 5: Click OK to show the Softbyte Balance sheet, Figure 1.36, on your computer screen. It is shown below in full screen.

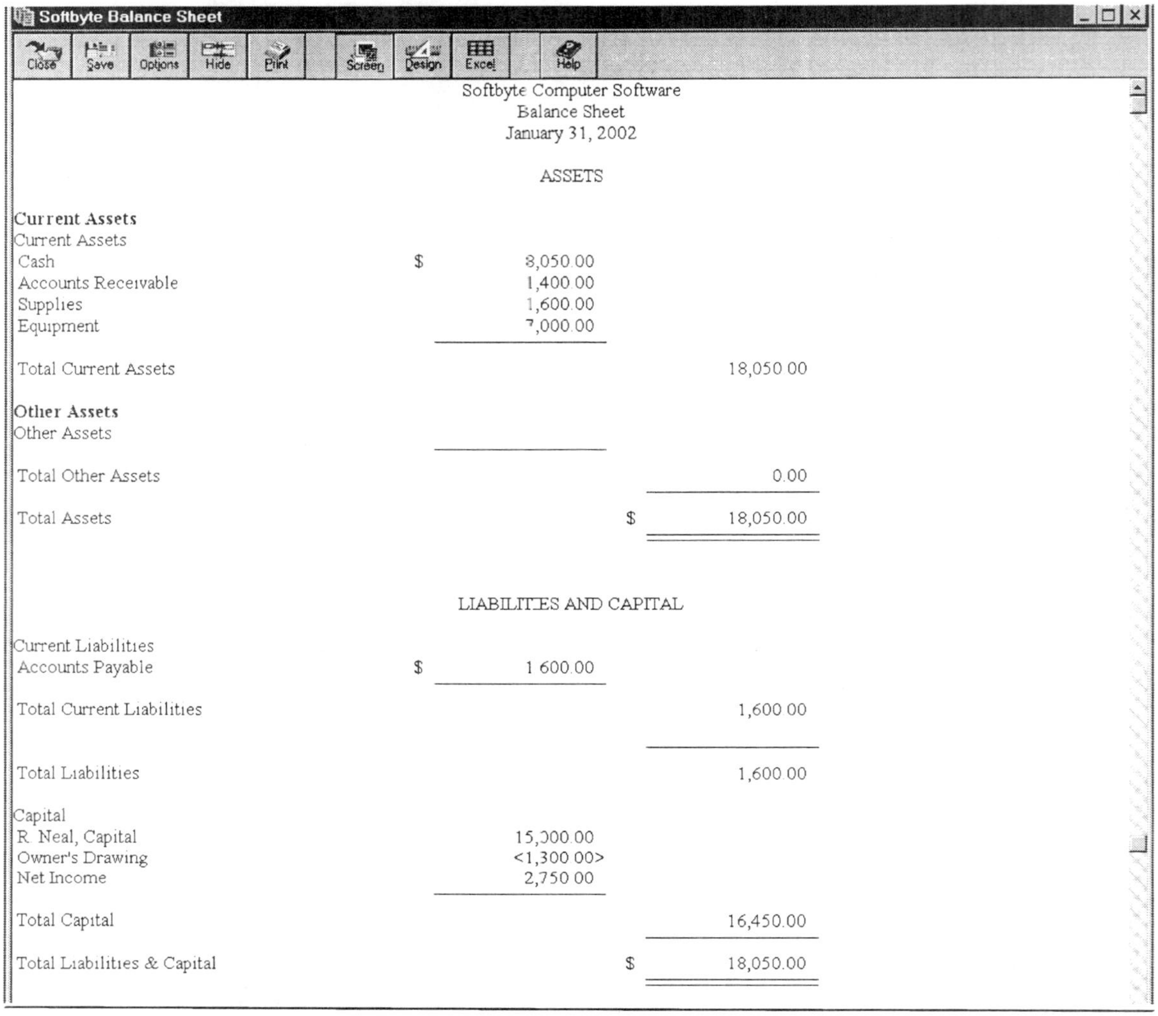

Softbyte Computer Software
Balance Sheet
January 31, 2002

ASSETS

Current Assets		
Current Assets		
Cash	$ 8,050.00	
Accounts Receivable	1,400.00	
Supplies	1,600.00	
Equipment	7,000.00	
Total Current Assets		18,050.00
Other Assets		
Other Assets		
Total Other Assets		0.00
Total Assets		$ 18,050.00

LIABILITIES AND CAPITAL

Current Liabilities		
Accounts Payable	$ 1 600.00	
Total Current Liabilities		1,600.00
Total Liabilities		1,600.00
Capital		
R. Neal, Capital	15,000.00	
Owner's Drawing	<1,300.00>	
Net Income	2,750.00	
Total Capital		16,450.00
Total Liabilities & Capital		$ 18,050.00

Figure 1. 36 Full screen balance sheet for Softbyte.

GENERATING THE STATEMENT OF CASH FLOW

The statement of cash flows reports:

1. The cash effects of a company's operations during a period
2. Its investing transactions
3. Its financing transactions
4. The net increase or decrease in cash during the period
5. The cash amount at the end of the period

Reporting the sources, uses, and net increase or decrease in cash is useful because investors, creditors, and others want to know what is happening to a company's most liquid resource. Thus the statement of cash flows, provides answers to the following simple but important questions:

- Where did the cash come from during the period?
- What was the cash used for during the period?
- What was the change in the cash balance during the period?

The statement of cash flows for Softbyte is shown in Figure 1.36. Cash increased by $8,050 during the period (January). Net Cash flow provided from operating activities increased cash $1,350. Cash flow from investing transactions decreased cash $7,000 and cash flow from financing transactions increased cash $13,700. Do not be concerned at this point with how these amounts were determined, but, be aware that they are based on your earlier entries.

Step 1: On the main menu bar click on "Reports" to get the pull down menu. Click on Financial Statements to get the "Select A Report" menu.
Step 2: Double click on <Predefined> Cash Flow.
Step 3: Again, the Dialog Box gives us several choices including the choice of financial periods, the margins for the printer, whether or not we want to show accounts that have a zero balance, whether or not we want page numbers, etc. If you wish to print the Retained Earnings Statement, make sure the printer at the bottom of the dialog box matches the printer you are using on your computer system.
Step 4: Click OK to show the Cash Flows statement for Softbyte, Figure 1.37, on your computer screen. It is shown full screen below.

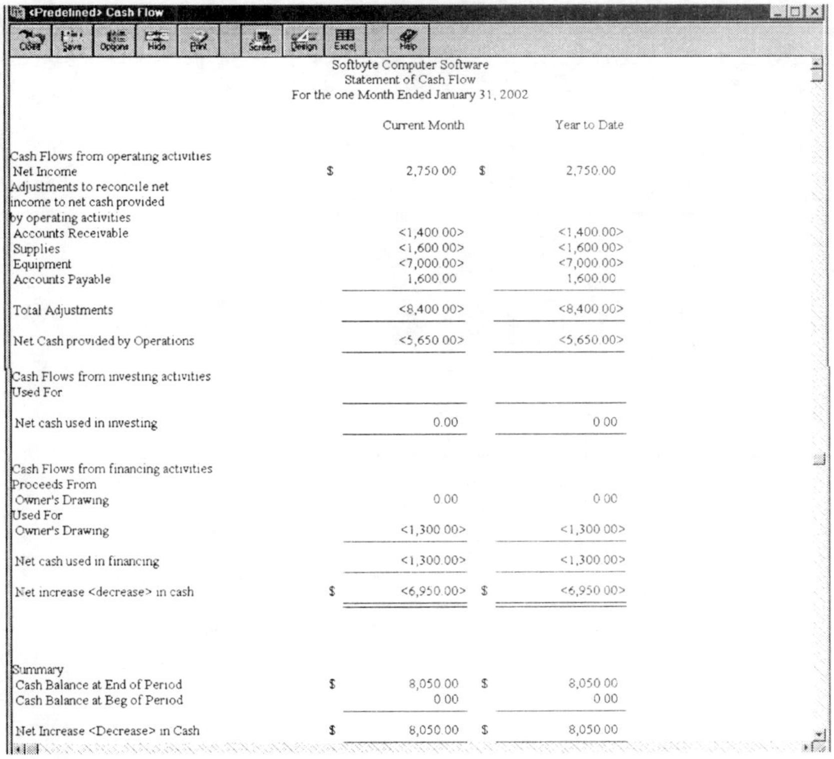

Softbyte Computer Software
Statement of Cash Flow
For the one Month Ended January 31, 2002

		Current Month		Year to Date
Cash Flows from operating activities				
Net Income	$	2,750.00	$	2,750.00
Adjustments to reconcile net income to net cash provided by operating activities				
Accounts Receivable		<1,400.00>		<1,400.00>
Supplies		<1,600.00>		<1,600.00>
Equipment		<7,000.00>		<7,000.00>
Accounts Payable		1,600.00		1,600.00
Total Adjustments		<8,400.00>		<8,400.00>
Net Cash provided by Operations		<5,650.00>		<5,650.00>
Cash Flows from investing activities				
Used For				
Net cash used in investing		0.00		0.00
Cash Flows from financing activities				
Proceeds From				
Owner's Drawing		0.00		0.00
Used For				
Owner's Drawing		<1,300.00>		<1,300.00>
Net cash used in financing		<1,300.00>		<1,300.00>
Net increase <decrease> in cash	$	<6,950.00>	$	<6,950.00>
Summary				
Cash Balance at End of Period	$	8,050.00	$	8,050.00
Cash Balance at Beg of Period		0.00		0.00
Net Increase <Decrease> in Cash	$	8,050.00	$	8,050.00

Figure 1. 37 Statement of Cash Flows

Demonstration Problem

Mary Malone opens her own law office on July 1, 2002. During the first month of operations, the following transactions occurred:

1. July 1, 2002, Mary invested $10,000 in cash to open her law practice.
2. July 15, 2002, paid $800 for July rent on her office space.
3. Purchased office equipment on July 18, 2002, on account, $3,000
4. July 20, 2002, Rendered legal services to clients for cash, $1,500
5. Borrowed $700 cash, on July 22, 2002 from a bank on a note payable.
6. Billed legal services on July 23, 2002 to a client (on account) for $2,000.
7. On July 31, 2002, she paid additional monthly expenses: salaries $500; utilities $300 and telephone $100.

Instructions

a. Open the company "Mary Malone" found on your Peachtree Accounting data disk.
b. Enter and post the above transactions in Peachtree Accounting.
c. Print out Mary Malone's <Predefined> Income Statement, Retained Earnings Statement, <Predefined> Balance Sheet and Statement of Cash Flows

Solution To Demonstration Problem

General Journal Entries

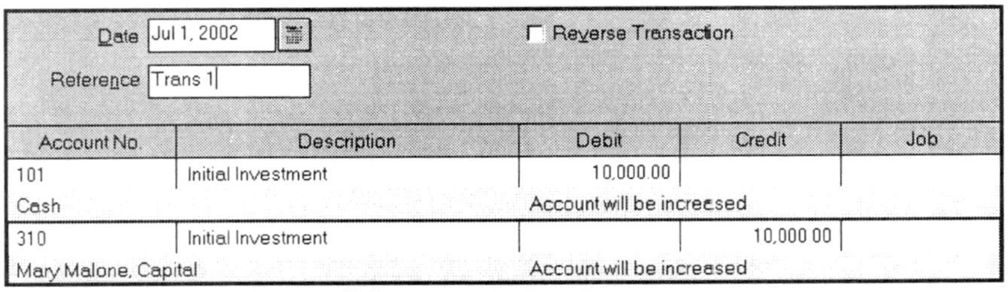

Date: Jul 1, 2002 — Reverse Transaction
Reference: Trans 1

Account No.	Description	Debit	Credit	Job
101 Cash	Initial Investment	10,000.00 Account will be increased		
310 Mary Malone, Capital	Initial Investment	Account will be increased	10,000.00	

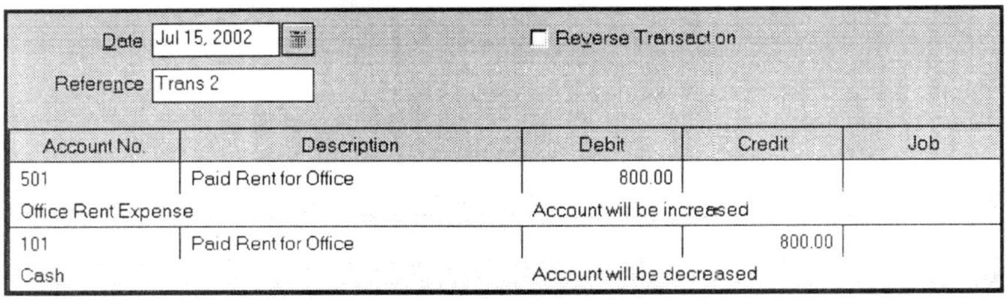

Date: Jul 15, 2002 — Reverse Transaction
Reference: Trans 2

Account No.	Description	Debit	Credit	Job
501 Office Rent Expense	Paid Rent for Office	800.00 Account will be increased		
101 Cash	Paid Rent for Office	Account will be decreased	800.00	

Date 7/18/02 ☐ Reverse Transaction

Reference Trans 3

Account No.	Description	Debit	Credit	Job
110	Purchased Office Equipment	3,000.00		
Office Equipment		Account will be increased		
201	Purchased Office Equipment		3,000.00	
Accounts Payable		Account will be increased		

Date Jul 20, 2002 ☐ Reverse Transaction

Reference Trans 4

Account No.	Description	Debit	Credit	Job
101	Legal Services for Cash	1,500.00		
Cash		Account will be increased		
401	Legal Services for Cash		1,500.00	
Legal Service Fees		Account will be increased		

Date Jul 20, 2002 ☐ Reverse Transaction

Reference Trans 5

Account No.	Description	Debit	Credit	Job
101	Borrowed money from bank	700.00		
Cash		Account will be increased		
210	Borrowed money from bank		700.00	
Notes Payable		Account will be increased		

Income Statement

Mary Malone, attorney at law
Income Statement
For the One Month Ending July 31, 2002

		Current Month			Year to Date	
Revenues						
Legal Service Fees	$	3,500.00	100.00	$	3,500.00	100.00
Total Revenues		3,500.00	100.00		3,500.00	100.00
Cost of Sales						
Total Cost of Sales		0.00	0.00		0.00	0.00
Gross Profit		3,500.00	100.00		3,500.00	100.00
Expenses						
Office Rent Expense		800.00	22.86		800.00	22.86
Salaries Expense		500.00	14.29		500.00	14.29
Utilities Expense		300.00	8.57		300.00	8.57
Telephone Expense		100.00	2.86		100.00	2.86
Total Expenses		1,700.00	48.57		1,700.00	48.57
Net Income	$	1,800.00	51.43	$	1,800.00	51.43

Retained Earnings Statement

Mary Malone, attorney at law
Statement of Retained Earnings
For the One Month Ending July 31, 2002

Beginning Retained Earnings	$	0.00
Adjustments To Date		0.00
Net Income		1,800.00
Subtotal		1,800.00
Ending Retained Earnings	$	1,800.00

Balance Sheet

Mary Malone, attorney at law
Balance Sheet
July 31, 2002

ASSETS

Current Assets				
Cash	$	10,500.00		
Accounts Receivable		2,000.00		
Total Current Assets				12,500.00
Property and Equipment				
Office Equipment		3,000.00		
Total Property and Equipment				3,000.00
Other Assets				
Total Other Assets				0.00
Total Assets			$	15,500.00

LIABILITIES AND CAPITAL

Current Liabilities				
Accounts Payable	$	3,000.00		
Notes Payable		700.00		
Total Current Liabilities				3,700.00
Long-Term Liabilities				
Total Long-Term Liabilities				0.00
Total Liabilities				3,700.00
Capital				
Mary Malone, Capital		10,000.00		
Net Income		1,800.00		
Total Capital				11,800.00
Total Liabilities & Capital			$	15,500.00

Statement of Cash Flow

Mary Malone, attorney at law
Statement of Cash Flow
For the one Month Ended July 31, 2002

	Current Month	Year to Date
Cash Flows from operating activities		
Net Income	$ 1,800.00	$ 1,800.00
Adjustments to reconcile net income to net cash provided by operating activities		
Accounts Receivable	<2,000.00>	<2,000.00>
Accounts Payable	3,000.00	3,000.00
Notes Payable	700.00	700.00
Total Adjustments	1,700.00	1,700.00
Net Cash provided by Operations	3,500.00	3,500.00
Cash Flows from investing activities		
Used For		
Office Equipment	<3,000.00>	<3,000.00>
Net cash used in investing	<3,000.00>	<3,000.00>
Cash Flows from financing activities		
Proceeds From		
Mary Malone, Capital	10,000.00	10,000.00
Used For		
Mary Malone, Capital	0.00	0.00
Net cash used in financing	10,000.00	10,000.00
Net increase <decrease> in cash	$ 10,500.00	$ 10,500.00

	Current Month	Year to Date
Summary		
Cash Balance at End of Period	$ 10,500.00	$ 10,500.00
Cash Balance at Beg of Period	0.00	0.00
Net Increase <Decrease> in Cash	$ 10,500.00	$ 10,500.00

CHAPTER 2

Continuing the Recording Process

OBJECTIVES

- Explain what an account is, how it is created in Peachtree.
- Define debits and credits and explain how they are used to record business transactions.
- Generate the Trial Balance provided in Peachtree Accounting.
- Explain the General Journal and General Ledger in Peachtree Accounting

THE ACCOUNT

An account is an individual *accounting* record of the increases and decreases in a specific asset, liability, or owner's equity item. For example, Softbyte has separate *accounts* for Cash, Accounts Receivable, Accounts Payable, Service Revenue, Salaries Expense, and so on.

In its simplest form, an account has three parts:

1. The title
2. The left side or debit side
3. A right side or credit side

The accounting term *debit* refers to the left side of a column and *credit* refers to the right. Therefore, entering an amount on the left side is called debiting the account; the right side is called crediting the account. That is an accounting rule which is comparable the custom of driving on the right hand side of the road in the United States or stopping for a stoplight. The common abbreviations are Dr. for debit and Cr. for credit.

To "balance" your account, add up the debit amounts entered, then add up the credit amounts entered. Subtract the smaller total from the larger total. The difference is called the balance. Peachtree will balance your accounts for you.

In the first chapter, as you made General Journal entries for each of the Softbye transactions, you learned how a transaction affects the basic accounting equation. Each transaction must affect *two or more* accounts, and for each transaction debits must equal credits. That keeps the accounting equation in balance. This is the basis for the double entry accounting system, which is the heart of Peachtree Accounting.

THE GENERAL JOURNAL

In manual accounting, transactions are recorded in sequential order, as they happen, in a journal, before being transferred to the actual accounts. This journal is referred to as the Book of Original Entry. For each transaction the journal shows the debit and credit effects on the individual accounts. Companies use various kinds of journals but every company uses the most basic form of journal - a General Journal.

Peachtree's automated version of the General Journal was used when you made your entries for Softbyte Computer Software in Chapter 1. As you recall, the general journal has spaces for dates, account titles and explanations/references (descriptions) and money columns.

In Peachtree Accounting, you use the General Journal to enter those types of transactions that are not readily categorized in the Tasks menu. Typical General Journal entries include chart of account beginning balances, depreciation, and account transfers. Unlike other screens in Peachtree, you provide all the accounting distributions in the General Journal. At other times, Peachtree automatically distributes certain amounts, based on guidelines you set in Maintain menus.

Let's look at Softbyte's General Journal:

Open Softbyte Computer Software file on your data disk. This will be the same file you used during the exercises in Chapter 1.

Step 1: On the Menu bar click on Reports.
Step 2: On the pull down menu, click on General Ledger.
Step 3: Select General Journal from the Report Select menu.

The General Journal is shown in Figure 2.1. It shows the initial entry for Cash and Capital from the first transaction in the previous chapter. Notice the debit entry (increasing) cash and the credit entry (increasing) capital, each for $15,000. The other entries made on January 1 also appear in this General Journal entry.

Softbyte Computer Software
General Journal
For the Period From Jan 1, 2003 to Jan 31, 2003
Filter Criteria includes: Report order is by Date. Report is printed with Accounts having Zero Amounts and with Truncated Transaction Descriptions and in Detail Format.

Date	Account ID	Reference	Trans Description	Debit Amt	Credit Amt
1/1/03	101			15,000.00	
	301				15,000.00
	104			7,000.00	
	101				7,000.00
	103			1,600.00	
	201				1,600.00
	101			1,200.00	
	401				1,200.00
	501			250.00	
	201				250.00
	101			1,500.00	
	102			2,000.00	
	401				3,500.00
		Total		28,550.00	28,550.00

Figure 2. 1 General Journal entries for Softbyte

It is not shown in Figure 2.1, however during the operation of the Peachtree application, when you click on the General Journal report (as with each of the other reports) your cursor turns into a small magnifying glass with a "Z" in the middle. If you click on a specific transaction on the report with the magnifying glass Peachtree will go directly to the form or journal where that transaction was entered. In the case of the General Journal report, you will be taken directly to that specific General Journal entry.

One more point, when "Post" is clicked on the menu bar, after making General Journal entries, the entry made in the General Journal was then automatically posted to the appropriate journals and ledgers, one in particular: *The General Ledger.*

THE GENERAL LEDGER

The entire group of accounts maintained by a company is called the General Ledger. The ledger as it is commonly referred to, keeps in one place all of the information about any changes in individual account balances. Each transaction is entered in the ledger, which was the "posting" process performed in the previous chapter.

Every company has some type of general ledger that contains all of the assets, liabilities, and owner's equity accounts, their related transactions and balances.

The ledger provides management with the balances in various accounts. For example, the Cash account shows the amount of cash that is available to meet current obligations. Amounts due from customers can be found by examining Accounts Receivable and amounts owed to creditors can found by looking at Accounts Payable.

Let's look at the General Ledger for Softbyte.

Open Softbyte Computer Software file on your data disk. This will be the same file you used in Chapter 1.

Step 1: On the Menu bar click on Reports.
Step 2: On the pull down menu, click on General Ledger.
Step 3: Select General Ledger from the Report Selection menu as shown in Figure 2.2.

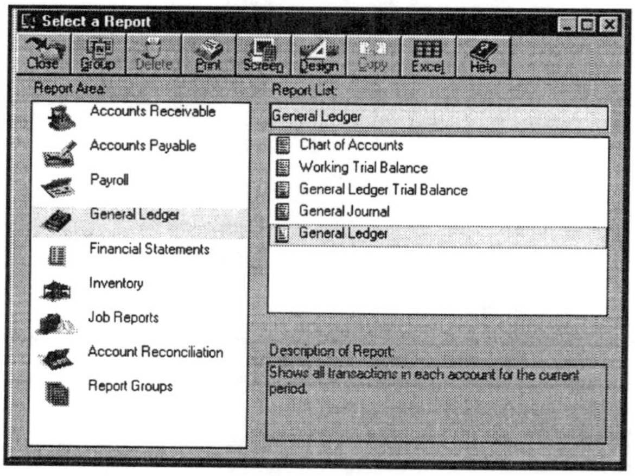

Figure 2. 2 Report Selection Menu

Peachtree then presents a complete (and rather lengthy for only 10 transactions) General Ledger report, a portion of which is shown Figure 2.3. The entire report would list each active account, the ones without a zero balance, and the associated transactions. However, you have an option to list the accounts with zero balances if you wish, which would make for an even longer report.

Softbyte Computer Software
General Ledger
For the Period From Jan 1, 2002 to Jan 31, 2002
Filter Criteria includes: Report order is by ID. Report is printed in Detail Format.

Account ID Account Description	Date Reference	Jrnl	Trans Description	Debit Amt	Credit Amt	Balance
101 Cash	1/1/02		Beginning Balance			
	1/1/02 Transaction	GENJ	Initial Investment	15,000.00		
	1/1/02 Transaction	GENJ	Paid cash for equipment		7,000.00	
	1/1/02 Transaction	GENJ	Services Rendered for Cash	1,200.00		
	1/7/02 Transaction	GENJ	Received cash from sales.	1,500.00		
	1/15/02 Transaction	GENJ	Paid utilities expense		1,700.00	
	1/15/02 Transaction	GENJ	Paid Daily News		250.00	
	1/15/02 Transaction	GENJ	Received Cash from customers	600.00		
	1/31/02 Transaction	GENJ	Ray Neal, Drawing		1,300.00	
			Current Period Change	18,300.00	10,250.00	8,050.00
	1/31/02		**Ending Balance**			**8,050.00**
102 Accounts Receivable	1/1/02		Beginning Balance			
	1/7/02 Transaction	GENJ	Sales on account	2,000.00		
	1/15/02 Transaction	GENJ	Received Cash from customers		600.00	
			Current Period Change	2,000.00	600.00	1,400.00
	1/31/02		**Ending Balance**			**1,400.00**

Figure 2. 3 Portion of General Ledger Report

ASSETS AND LIABILITIES

In the Softbyte exercise in Chapter 1, you were shown that increases in cash (an asset) were entered on the left side (debit side) of the journal amount column and decreases in cash were entered on the right side (credit side) of the journal amount column. We also know that both sides of the basic accounting equation (Assets = Liabilities + Owner's Equity) must be equal. It makes sense that increases and decreases in liabilities will be recorded opposite from each other, therefore, increases in liabilities must be entered on the right (credit side), and decreases in liabilities must be entered on the left (debit side).

Knowing the normal balance in an account may help you trace errors. For example, a credit balance in an asset account such as Land or a debit balance in a liability account such as Wages Payable would indicate an error. Occasionally, however, an abnormal balance may be correct. For example, the Cash account could have a credit balance when a company has overdrawn its bank balance.

OWNER'S EQUITY

Owner's equity is increased either by additional investments by the owner or by revenue earned in the business. Investments by the owner are credited to the owner's capital account. For example, when cash is invested in the business, cash is debited (increased) and owner's capital is credited (also increased). It is decreased by owner's drawings. An owner may withdraw cash or other assets from the business for personal use. Withdrawals could be debited directly to owner's capital to indicate a decrease in owner's equity. However, it is preferable to establish a separate account, the Owner's Drawing account. Expenses also decrease the owner's equity.

REVENUES AND EXPENSES

When revenues are earned, owner's equity is increased. That means simply that the effect of debits and credits on revenue accounts is the same as their effect on owner's capital. Revenue accounts are increased by credits (sales) and decreased by debits (expenses).

THE CHART OF ACCOUNTS

The number and type of accounts used are likely to differ for each enterprise depending on the amount of detail required by management. Although Softbyte is able to manage and report its activities with just a few accounts, a large corporation such as Robinson-Humphrey, a stock brokerage firm in Atlanta, requires thousands of accounts to keep track of its activities.

Companies have a chart of accounts, a master listing of the accounts and the account numbers, which identify their location in the ledger. The numbering system used to identify the accounts usually starts with the balance sheet accounts and ends with the expenses on the income statement.

Examine the Chart of Accounts for Softbyte.

Step 1: On the Menu bar, click on Reports.
Step 2: On the pull down menu, click on General Ledger.
Step 3: Then, select General Ledger from the Select Report menu as shown in Figure 2.4.

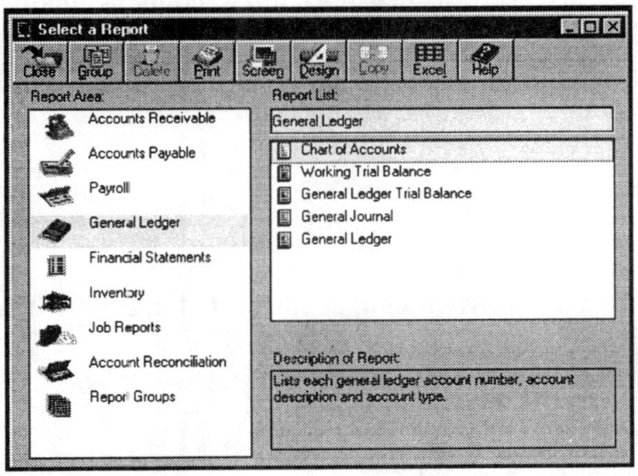

Figure 2. 4 Select Report menu for Chart of Accounts

The complete Chart of Accounts for Softbyte is shown in Figure 2.5. You may print the Chart of Accounts by clicking on the Print icon.

Softbyte Computer Software
Chart of Accounts
As of Jan 31, 2002

Filter Criteria includes: Report order is by ID. Report is printed with Accounts having Zero Amounts and in Detail Format.

Account ID	Account Description	Activ	Account Type
101	Cash	Yes	Cash
102	Accounts Receivable	Yes	Accounts Receivable
103	Supplies	Yes	Other Current Assets
104	Equipment	Yes	Other Current Assets
201	Accounts Payable	Yes	Accounts Payable
301	R. Neal, Capital	Yes	Equity-Retained Earnings
302	Owner's Drawing	Yes	Equity-gets closed
401	Service Revenue	Yes	Income
501	Advertising Expense	Yes	Expenses
502	Rent Expense	Yes	Expenses
503	Salaries Expense	Yes	Expenses
504	Utilities Expense	Yes	Expenses

Figure 2. 5 Chart of Accounts report for Softbyte.

HOW ACCOUNTS ARE ASSIGNED NUMBERS

The numbering system used to identify accounts can be quite sophisticated or as in Softbyte's case, fairly simple. For example, one major company uses an 18 digit account numbering system. The first three digits identify the division or plant; the second set of three digit numbers contain the plant location, and so on. Softbyte uses a three-digit classification.

Softbyte Computer Software
Account Number Classification

100 – 199	Assets
200 – 299	Liabilities
300 – 399	Equity/Capital
400 – 499	Revenue
500 – 599	Expenses

When setting up a new business, you will discover that Peachtree contains many sample companies and their related charts of accounts. You will be given a choice of setting up your own chart of accounts (which we'll do later in this chapter) or you may select one of the sample company's Chart of Account.

To see the sample companies and their Charts of Accounts:

Step 1: On the menu bar, click on Help.
Step 2: Select Contents and Index on the pull down menu, as illustrated in Figure 2.6.

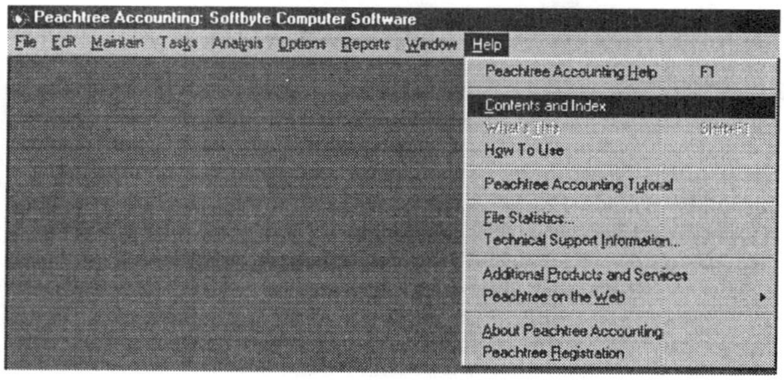

Figure 2. 6 Pull down window for help

Step 3: In Box 1, under the index tab, as shown in Figure 2.7, type in "chart of accounts," then click on set up (overview) and click on the "Display" button.

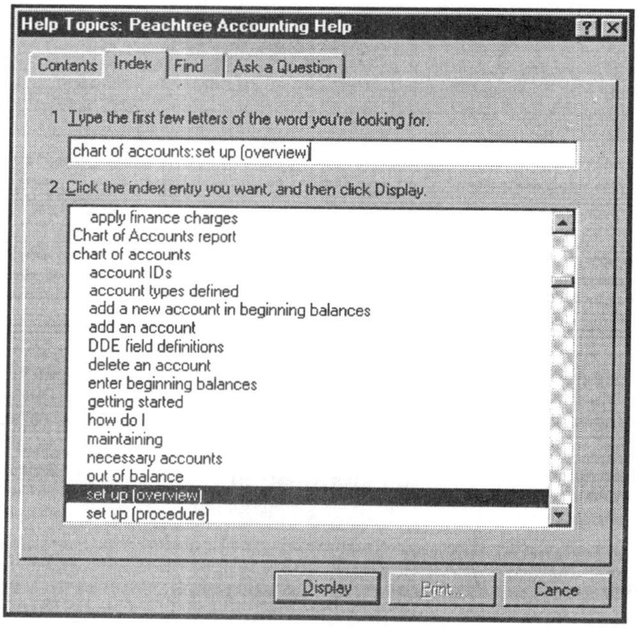

Figure 2. 7 Choices for Chart of Accounts assistance.

Step 4 Click on "Peachtree sample charts of accounts" on the help screen shown in Figure 2.8.

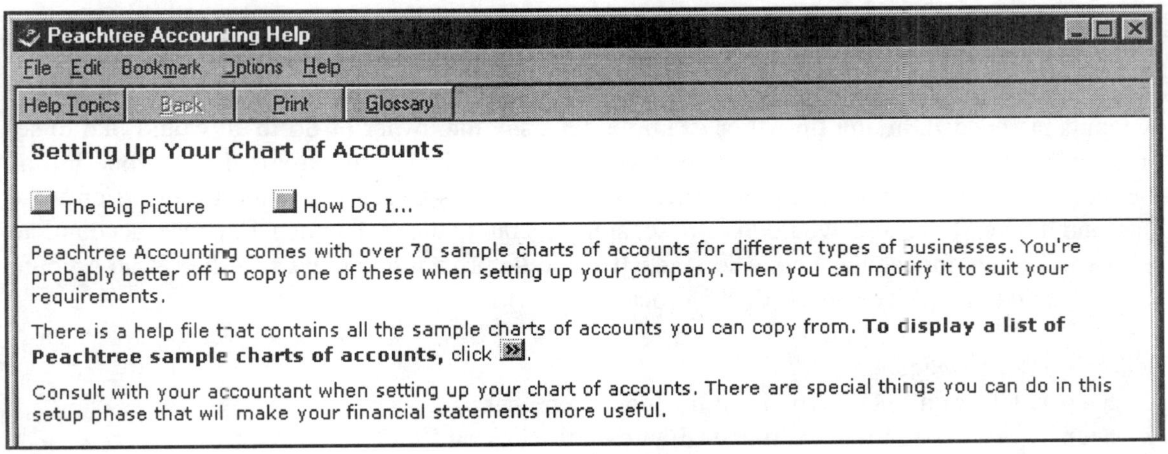

Figure 2. 8 Peachtree "Help" window for Chart of Accounts

Alphabetical listings of types of companies follow. Click on any one to see the sample listing of that type company's chart of accounts. A partial listing is shown in Figure 2.9.

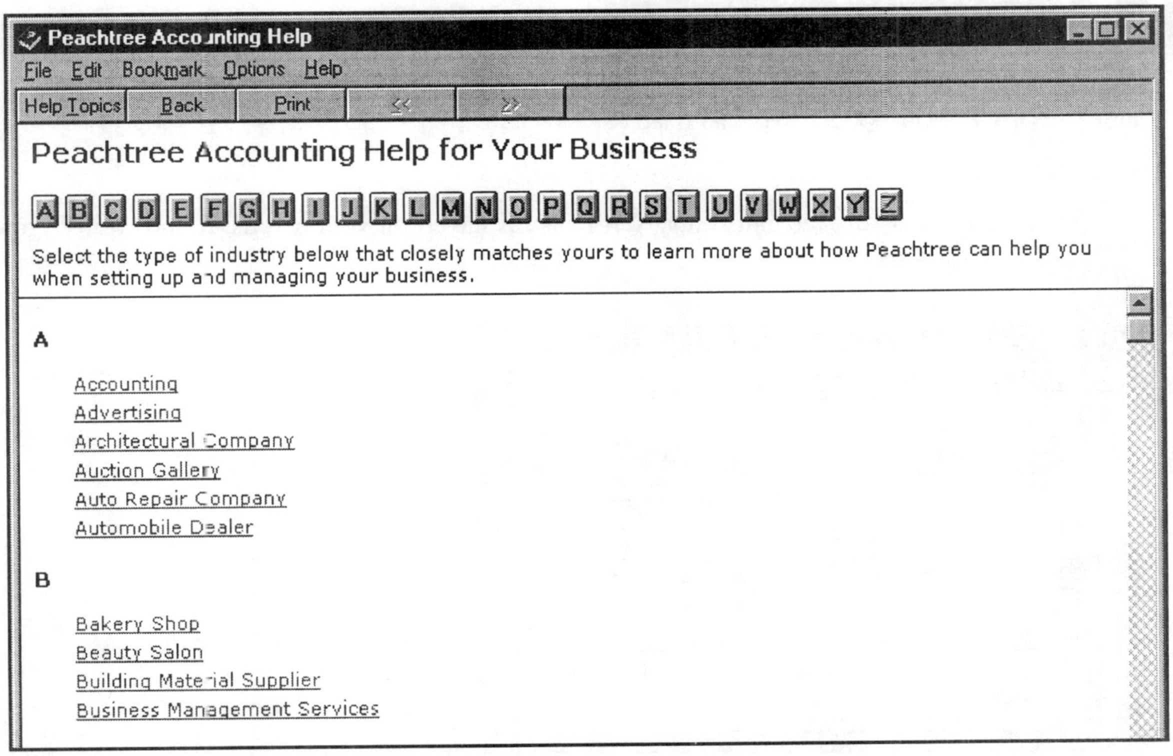

Figure 2. 9 Partial listing of sample Charts of Accounts

SETTING UP A NEW ACCOUNT

If you choose to use a company that has accounts already set up, you still may create new accounts, as needed, at any time. For example, let's say the owner of Softbyte would like to set up an account for the expense of Telephone Service. Originally he classified the phone bill as part of the Utilities Expenses. But now he wants the Utilities Expense account to reflect only the Gas and Power bills and would like a separate account, the Telephone Expense account, to reflect payments for regular phone service. (It could be broken down even further as an account for long-distance service and another for local service.)

Setting up the new account:

Step 1: Click on "Maintain" from the main menu bar.

Step 2: From the pull down menu (Figure 2.10) click on Chart of Accounts.

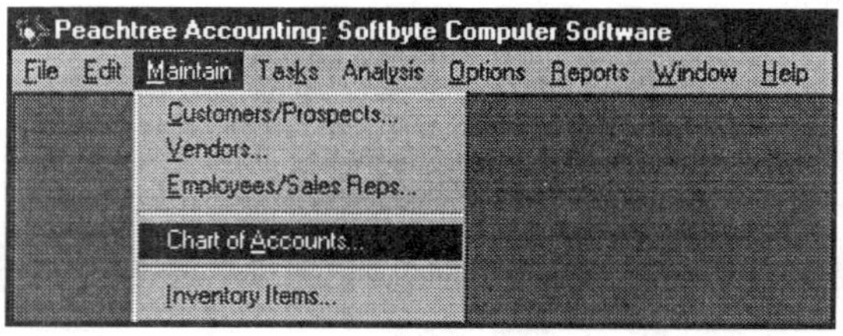

Figure 2. 10 Pull Down Menu - click on Chart of Accounts

Step 3: The Chart of Accounts entry screen is displayed on your screen as shown in Figure 2.11.

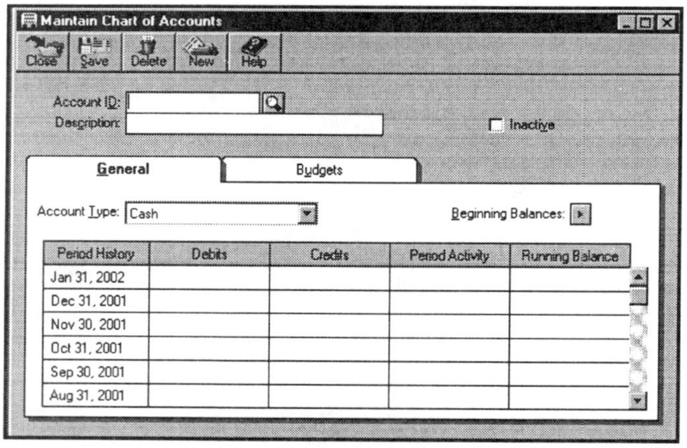

Figure 2. 11 Account entry form.

Step 4: In the Account No. window, enter "505" as the new Account Number. Recall that all of Softbyte's Expense accounts will be in the 500 range.

Step 5: The name of the account or description is "Telephone Expense."

Step 6: The account must have a type that is assigned by Peachtree. (Account Types are discussed in the next section.) Next to Account Type found under the "General" tab, click on the pull down menu and scroll down until "Expenses" is shown in the window. (See Figure 2.12.)

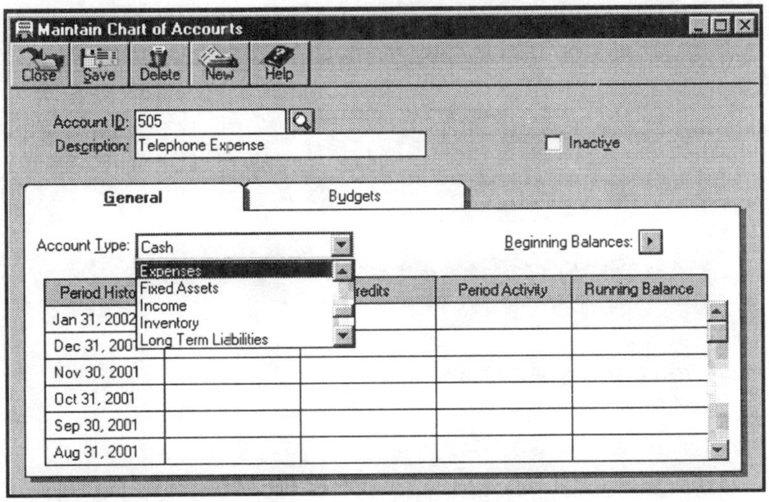

Figure 2. 12 New account entry, creating Account Type.

Step 7: Double click on "Expenses" to classify the account as an expense account within the Peachtree system. We will not enter a beginning balance nor any budget items at this time.

Step 8: Click Save on the toolbar to save the new account.

Step 9: To make sure your new account has been entered and saved properly, run a Chart of Accounts report (Figure 2.13.)

Softbyte Computer Software
Chart of Accounts
As of Jan 31, 2002
Filter Criteria includes: Report order is by ID. Report is printed with Accounts having Zero Amounts and in Detail Format.

Account ID	Account Description	Activ	Account Type
101	Cash	Yes	Cash
102	Accounts Receivable	Yes	Accounts Receivable
103	Supplies	Yes	Other Current Assets
104	Equipment	Yes	Other Current Assets
201	Accounts Payable	Yes	Accounts Payable
301	R. Neal, Capital	Yes	Equity-Retained Earnings
302	Owner's Drawing	Yes	Equity-gets closed
401	Service Revenue	Yes	Income
501	Advertising Expense	Yes	Expenses
502	Rent Expense	Yes	Expenses
503	Salaries Expense	Yes	Expenses
504	Utilities Expense	Yes	Expenses
505	Telephone Expense	Yes	Expenses

Figure 2. 13 New Chart of Accounts Report reflecting the Telephone Expense Account

ACCOUNT TYPES

When creating new accounts in Peachtree, account types will define how the account will be grouped in reports and financial statements. (Figure 2.14) They also control what happens during fiscal year-end.

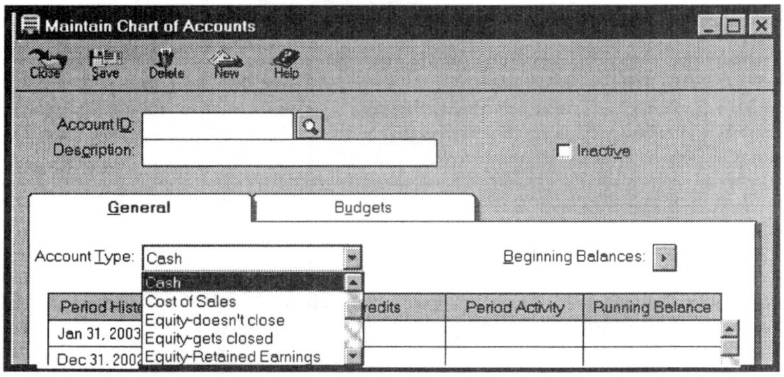

Figure 2. 14 Partial menu of account types in creating new accounts

Accounts Payable

Account balances owed to vendors for goods, supplies, and services purchased on an open account that are generally due in 30 or 60 days, and do not bear interest. Select this account type if you are setting up open vendor accounts or credit card (purchase) accounts.

Accounts Receivable

Account balances owed by customers for items or services sold to them when cash is not received at the time of sale. Typically, accounts receivable balances are recorded on sales invoices that include terms of payment.

Accumulated Depreciation

This is a contra asset account to depreciable (fixed) assets such as buildings, machinery, and equipment. Depreciation is an expense and is the difference between an asset's cost and its estimated salvage value. Recording depreciation is a way to indicate that assets have declined in service potential. *Accumulated depreciation* represents total depreciation taken to date on the assets.

Cash

This represents deposits in banks available for current operations, plus cash on hand consisting of currency, undeposited checks, drafts, and money orders. Select this account type if you are setting up bank checking accounts, petty cash accounts, money market accounts, and certificates of deposit (CDs).

Cost of Sales

This represents the known cost to your business for items or services when sold to customers. Cost of sales is also known as cost of goods sold for inventory items and computed based on inventory costing method FIFO, LIFO or Average. Select this account type if you are setting up cost-of-goods-sold accounts to be used when selling inventory items.

Equity - Doesn't Close

This represents the paid in equity or capital that is carried forward from year to year. It is also used for common stock.

Equity - Gets Closed

This represents equity that is closed or zeroed out at the end of the fiscal year, with their amounts moved to the capital or retained earnings account.

Equity - Retained Earnings

This represents the *earned* capital or equity of the enterprise. Its balance is the cumulative, lifetime earnings of the company that have not been distributed to owners. Peachtree Complete Accounting, Release 8.0 requires you to have a Retained Earnings accounting. It can be retitled Capital or Equity.

Expenses

These represent the costs incurred to produce revenues. The assets surrendered or consumed when serving customers are the company's expenses. If income exceeds expenses, *net income* results. If expenses exceed income, the business is said to be operating at a *net loss*.

Fixed Assets

These represent property, plant, or equipment assets that are acquired for use in a business rather than for resale. They are called *fixed* assets because they are to be used for long periods of time.
Select this account type if you are setting up any of the following fixed assets:

- **Land** - property, storage space, or parking lots.
- **Buildings** - structures in which the business is carried out.
- **Machinery** - heavy equipment used to carry out business operations.

For example, you may want to set up any of the following: store equipment or fixtures, factory equipment of fixtures, office equipment or fixtures (including computers and furniture), and delivery equipment (including autos, trucks, and vans used primarily in making deliveries to customers).

Income

Income (also known as revenue) is the inflow of assets resulting from the sale of products and services to customers. If income exceeds expenses, *net income* results. If expenses exceed income, the business is said to be operating at a *net loss*. Select this account type if you are setting up sales revenue accounts. It is common practice to create different income accounts for each category of revenue that you want to track (for example, retail income, service income, interest income, and so on).

Inventory

This represents the value of goods on hand and available for sale at any given time. Inventory is considered to be an asset that is purchased, manufactured (or assembled), and sold to customers for revenue. Select this account type if you are setting up assets that are intended for resale. It is common practice to create different accounts for each category of inventory that you want to track. For example, retail inventory, raw materials inventory, work in progress inventory, finished goods inventory, and so on can be tracked through the inventory account.

Long Term Liabilities

This represents debts that are not due for a relatively long period of time, usually more than one year. Portions of long-term loans due and notes payable with maturity dates at least one year or more beyond the current balance sheet date are considered to be long-term liabilities.

Other Assets

This represents assets that are considered *nonworking* capital and are not due for a relatively long period of time, usually more than one year. Notes receivable with maturity dates at least one year or more beyond the current balance sheet date are considered to be "noncurrent" assets. Select this account type if you are setting up assets such as deposits, organization costs, amortization expense, noncurrent notes receivable, and so on.

Other Current Assets

This represents those assets that are considered *nonworking* capital and are due within a short period of time, usually less than a year. Prepaid expenses, employee advances, and notes receivable with maturity dates of less than one year of the current balance sheet date are considered to be "current" assets. Select this account type if you are setting up assets such as prepaid expenses, employee advances, current notes receivable, and so on.

Other Current Liabilities

This represents debts that are due within a short period of time, usually less than a year. The payment of these debts usually requires the use of current assets. Select this account type if you are setting up accrued expenses from a vendor, extended lines of credit, short-term loans, sales tax payables, payroll tax payables, client escrow accounts, suspense (clearing) accounts, and so on.

THE TRIAL BALANCE

A trial balance is a list of accounts and their balances at a given time. Using a manual accounting system, a trial balance usually would be prepared at the end of an accounting period. However, Peachtree keeps a continual trial balance available for you. In a manual system, the primary purpose of a trial balance is to prove that the debits equal the credits after posting. Because Peachtree will not let you continue an entry unless it is in balance, the trial balance Peachtree generates will always be "in balance." As mentioned earlier, however, that does not mean your system is error free, that all transactions have been recorded, or that the ledger entries are correct.

The Working Trial Balance in Peachtree has a somewhat different purpose than in manual accounting. In Peachtree, the Working Trial Balance report prints the accounts and their balances, together with spaces to fill in information so you can have a "worksheet" to help make adjustments to account balances.

To see the Working Trial Balance in Peachtree:

Step 1: On the menu bar, click on Reports, and then click General Ledger.
Step 2: On the pull down menu, click on "Working Trial Balance"

The Working Trial Balance for Softbyte is shown in Figure 2.15.

Softbyte Computer Software
Working Trial Balance
As of Jan 31, 2002
Filter Criteria includes: Report order is by ID. Report is printed with Accounts having Zero Amounts and in Detail Format.

Account ID Account Description	Last FYE Bal	Current Bal	Debit Adj	Credit Adj	End Bal	Reference
101 Cash	0.00	8,050.00				
102 Accounts Receivable	0.00	1,400.00				
103 Supplies	0.00	1,600.00				
104 Equipment	0.00	7,000.00				
201 Accounts Payable	0.00	-1,600.00				
301 R. Neal, Capital	0.00	-15,000.00				
302 Owner's Drawing	0.00	1,300.00				
401 Service Revenue	0.00	-4,700.00				
501 Advertising Expense	0.00	250.00				
502 Rent Expense	0.00	600.00				
503 Salaries Expense	0.00	900.00				
504 Utilities Expense	0.00	200.00				
Total:	0.00	0.00				

Figure 2. 15 Working Trial Balance

Notice that under the Current Balance column, the Debit balances are positive amounts while the Credit balances have a negative sign or a negative balance.

Demonstration Problem

Bob Sample opened the Campus Laundromat on September 1, 2002. During the first month of operations the following transactions occurred.

Sept	1	Invested $20,000 cash in the business.
	2	Paid $1,000 cash for store rent for the month of September.
	3	Purchased washers and dryers for $25,000, paying $10,000 in cash and signing a $15,000, 6-month, 12% note payable.
	4	Paid $1,200 for one-year accident insurance policy.
	10	Received bill from the *Daily News* for advertising the opening of the Laundromat $200.
	20	Withdrew $700 cash for personal use.
	30	Determined that cash receipts for laundry services for the month were $6,200.

Load the company from student data disk.

Instructions:

a. Journalize in Peachtree's General Journal the September transactions. Use "Trans 1", "Trans 2", etc. as the reference number.

b. Print a copy of the General Journal, General Ledger and the General Ledger Trial Balance.

Solution to Demonstration Problem

General Journal

Campus Laundromat
General Journal
For the Period From Sep 1, 2002 to Sep 30, 2002
Filter Criteria includes: Report order is by Date. Report is printed with Accounts having Zero Amounts and with Truncated Transaction Descriptions and in Detail Format.

Date	Account ID	Reference	Trans Description	Debit Amt	Credit Amt
9/1/02	101	Trans 1	Initial investment in business	20,000.00	
	301		Initial investment in business		20,000.00
9/2/02	501	Trans 2	Paid store rent	1,000.00	
	101		Paid store rent		1,000.00
9/3/02	103	Trans 3	Purchased laundry equipment	25,000.00	
	201		Purchased laundry equipment		15,000.00
	101		Purchased laundry equipment		10,000.00
9/4/02	102	Trans 4	Paid Insurnace Premium	1,200.00	
	101		Paid Insurnace Premium		1,200.00
9/10/02	502	Trans 5	Advertising	200.00	
	202		Advertising		200.00
9/20/02	302	Trans 6	Withdrew money.	700.00	
	101		Withdrew money		700.00
9/30/02	101	Trans 7	Cash receipts for laundry	6,200.00	
	401		Cash receipts for laundry		6,200.00
		Total		54,300.00	54,300.00

General Ledger

Campus Laundromat
General Ledger
For the Period From Sep 1, 2002 to Sep 30, 2002
Filter Criteria includes: Report order is by ID. Report is printed with Truncated Transaction Descriptions and in Detail Format.

Account ID Account Description	Date	Referenc	Jrnl	Trans Description	Debit Amt	Credit Amt	Balance
101	9/1/02			Beginning Balance			
Cash	9/1/02	Trans 1	GEN	Initial investment in busi	20,000.00		
	9/2/02	Trans 2	GEN	Paid store rent		1,000.00	
	9/3/02	Trans 3	GEN	Purchased laundry equi		10,000.00	
	9/4/02	Trans 4	GEN	Paid Insurnace Premium		1,200.00	
	9/20/02	Trans 6	GEN	Withdrew money		700.00	
	9/30/02	Trans 7	GEN	Cash receipts for laundr	6,200.00		
				Current Period Change	26,200.00	12,900.00	13,300.00
	9/30/02			Ending Balance			13,300.00
102	9/1/02			Beginning Balance			
Prepaid Insurance	9/4/02	Trans 4	GEN	Paid Insurnace Premium	1,200.00		
				Current Period Change	1,200.00		1,200.00
	9/30/02			Ending Balance			1,200.00
103	9/1/02			Beginning Balance			
Laundry Equipment	9/3/02	Trans 3	GEN	Purchased laundry equi	25,000.00		
				Current Period Change	25,000.00		25,000.00
	9/30/02			Ending Balance			25,000.00
Notes Payable	9/3/02	Trans 3	GEN	Purchased laundry equi		15,000.00	
				Current Period Change		15,000.00	-15,000.00
	9/30/02			Ending Balance			-15,000.00
202	9/1/02			Beginning Balance			
Accounts Payable	9/10/02	Trans 5	GEN	Advertising		200.00	
				Current Period Change		200.00	-200.00
	9/30/02			Ending Balance			-200.00
301	9/1/02			Beginning Balance			
Bob Samples, Capital	9/1/02	Trans 1	GEN	Initial investment in busi		20,000.00	
				Current Period Change		20,000.00	-20,000.00
	9/30/02			Ending Balance			-20,000.00
302	9/1/02			Beginning Balance			
Bob Samples, Drawin	9/20/02	Trans 6	GEN	Withdrew money.	700.00		
				Current Period Change	700.00		700.00
	9/30/02			Ending Balance			700.00
401	9/1/02			Beginning Balance			
Service Revenue	9/30/02	Trans 7	GEN	Cash receipts for laundr		6,200.00	
				Current Period Change		6,200.00	-6,200.00
	9/30/02			Ending Balance			-6,200.00
501	9/1/02			Beginning Balance			
Rent Expense	9/2/02	Trans 2	GEN	Paid store rent	1,000.00		
				Current Period Change	1,000.00		1,000.00
	9/30/02			Ending Balance			1,000.00
502	9/1/02			Beginning Balance			
Advertising Expense	9/10/02	Trans 5	GEN	Advertising	200.00		
				Current Period Change	200.00		200.00
	9/30/02			Ending Balance			200.00

General Ledger Trial Balance

Campus Laundromat
General Ledger Trial Balance
As of Sep 30, 2002

Filter Criteria includes: Report order is by ID. Report is printed in Detail Format.

Account ID	Account Description	Debit Amt	Credit Amt
101	Cash	13,300.00	
102	Prepaid Insurance	1,200.00	
103	Laundry Equipment	25,000.00	
201	Notes Payable		15,000.00
202	Accounts Payable		200.00
301	Bob Samples, Capital		20,000.00
302	Bob Samples, Drawing	700.00	
401	Service Revenue		6,200.00
501	Rent Expense	1,000.00	
502	Advertising Expense	200.00	
	Total:	41,400.00	41,400.00

P2-1a

C.J. Sanculi started Frontier Park on April 1. The following events and transactions occurred during April.

April	1	Sanculi invested $40,000 cash in the business.
	4	Purchased land costing $30,000 for cash.
	8	Incurred advertising expense of $1,800 on account.
	11	Paid salaries to employees $1,500
	12	Hired park manager at a salary of $4,000 per month, effective May 1.
	13	Paid $1,500 cash for a one-year insurance policy.
	17	Withdrew $600 cash for personal use.
	20	Received $5,700 in cash for admission fees.
	25	Sold 100 coupon books for $25 each. Each book contains 10 coupons entitling the holder to one admission to the park.
	30	Received $5,900 in cash admission fees.
	30	Paid $900 on account for advertising incurred on April 8.

Instructions:

a. Load “Frontier Park” into Peachtree from your Student Data Disk.
b. Journalize the transactions in the General Journal using Peachtree Accounting.
c. Check your work by running a General Ledger Trial Balance.

P2-5a

Avtar Sandhu owns the Lake Theatre. All facilities were completed on March 31st. At that time, the ledger, in Peachtree Accounting showed: No. 101 Cash $6,000; No. 140 Land $10,000; No. 145 Building (concession stand, projection room, ticket booth and screen) $8,000; No. 157 Equipment $6,000; No. 201 Accounts Payable $2,000; No. 275 Mortgage Payable $8,000 and No.301 Avtar Sandhu, Capital $20,000. Lake Theatre, with the accounts and balances, can be loaded from your Student Data Disk. During April, the following events and transactions occurred.

April	2	Paid film rental of $800 on first movie.
	3	Ordered two additional films at $500 each.
	9	Received $1,800 cash from admissions.
	10	Made $2,000 payment on mortgage and $1,000 on Accounts Payable.
	11	Lake Theatre contracted with R. Thomas Company to operate the concession stand. Thomas is to pay 17% of gross concession receipts (payable monthly) for the right to operate the concession stand.
	12	Paid advertising expenses $300.
	20	Received one of the films ordered on April 3 and was billed $500. The film will be shown in April.
	25	Received $4,200 cash from admissions.
	29	Paid salaries $1,600.
	30	Received statement from R. Thomas showing gross concession receipts of $1,000 and the balance due to The Lake Theatre of $170 (17% of $1,000) for April. Thomas only paid half the balance due and will remit the remainder on May 5th.
	30	Prepaid rental on special film to be run in May.

In addition to the accounts identified above, add (create) the following accounts to the Chart of Accounts: No. 112 Accounts Receivable; No. 136 Prepaid Rentals; No. 405 Admission Revenue; No. 406 Concession Revenue; No. 610 Advertising Expense, No. 632 Film Rental Expense; and No. 726 Salaries Expense.

Instructions:

a.) In Peachtree, utilizing the General Journal, Journalize and post the April transactions. Transaction numbers may be used for the "Reference Number".

b.) Prepare an Income Statement, a Retained Earnings Statement and a Balance Sheet for The Lake Theater.

CHAPTER 3

Adjusting the Accounts

OBJECTIVES

- Explain why adjusting entries are needed.
- Prepare adjusting entries for prepaid and accrued accounts..
- Identify the major types of adjusting entries.
- Generate an adjusted trial balance.

SELECTING AN ACCOUNTING TIME PERIOD

In the previous chapter we looked at the General Journal recording process and how Peachtree keeps a running record of the trial balance and balance sheet. Before we can prepare the final set of financial statements there are some additional steps that must be taken.

What portion of our assets' costs, if any, should be recognized as an expense for the current accounting period? Those relevant account balances must be adjusted before we continue.

Because management usually wants *monthly* financial statements, and the Internal Revenue Service *requires* all businesses to file annual tax returns, accountants divide the economic life of a business into artificial time periods. This convenient assumption is referred to as the time period assumption.

Many business transactions affect more than one of these arbitrary time periods. For example a milking machine purchased by a farmer a couple years ago probably is still being used in active production today. Airplanes purchased by Delta Airlines two years ago most likely are still in use today. We must determine the relevance of each business transaction to specific accounting periods.

FISCAL AND CALENDAR YEARS

All companies prepare financial statements periodically in order to assess their financial condition and results of operations. Accounting time periods are generally a month, a quarter, or a year. Monthly and quarterly time periods are called interim periods. Many large companies are required to prepare both quarterly and annual financial statements.

An accounting time period that is a year in length is referred to as a fiscal year. A fiscal year usually begins with the first day of a month and ends 12 months later on the last day of a month. However, the accounting period used by most businesses coincides with the calendar year, January 1 to December 31. Some companies have a fiscal year that differs from the calendar year. For example, many educational institutes use a July 1 to June 30 fiscal year. The U.S. government uses October 1 to September 30 as a fiscal year.

Peachtree Accounting makes it easy to change from one accounting period to the next.

Changing Accounting Periods

Step 1: Launch Peachtree Accounting and load in "Softbyte Computer Software" from the previous chapter.

Step 2: From the Tasks menu, on the main menu bar, select System and then Change Accounting Period as shown in Figure 3.1.

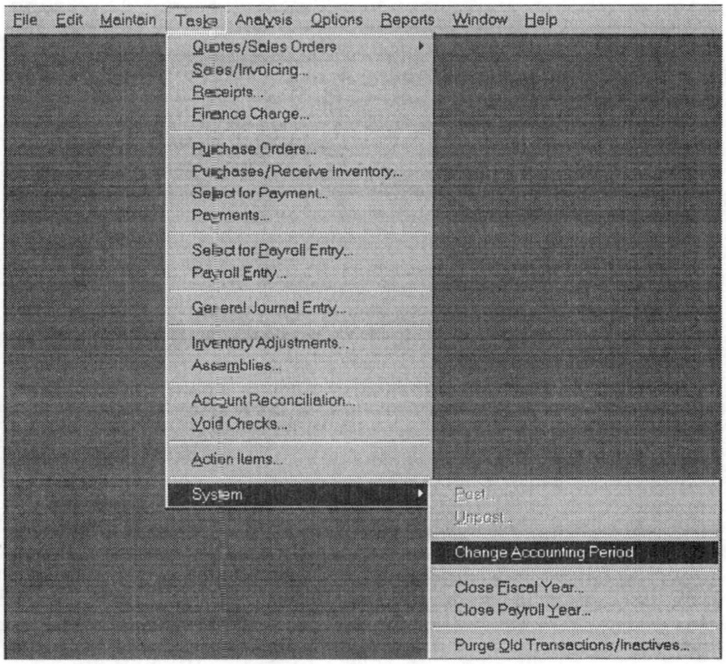

Figure 3. 1 Changing Accounting Periods

Step 3: Select the Accounting Period required from the Pull Down menu as shown in Figure 3.2

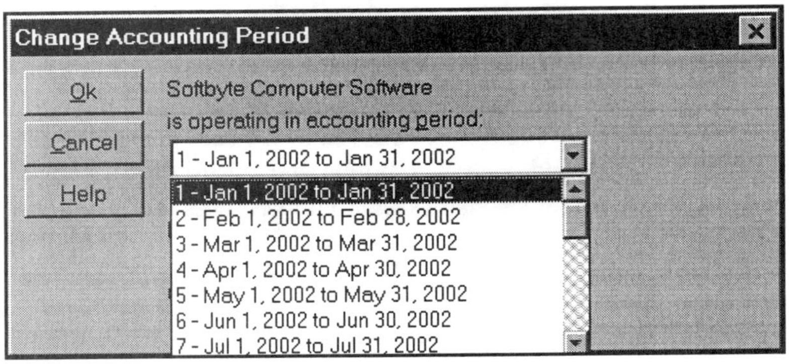

Figure 3. 2 Choosing a new accounting period.

Step 4: Change the period to your requirements and click OK.

Step 5: A message box appears asking if you would like to print reports before continuing. Select NO. If we were at the end of the accounting period for this company and wanted a full set of reports, then we would have selected the reports to be printed.

You can change the accounting period at will, moving back and forth in the fiscal year. The General Ledger will track balances as of the *current period date*. However, Peachtree Accounting selects the period in which to post a transaction by the transaction date. You can enter a transaction in the future but not in a prior accounting period.

BASICS OF ADJUSTING ENTRIES

In order for revenues to be recorded in the period in which they are earned and for expenses to be recognized in the period in which they are incurred, adjusting entries are made at the end of the accounting period. In short, adjusting entries are needed to ensure that the revenue recognition and matching principles are followed.

Adjusting entries make it possible to report on the balance sheet the appropriate assets, liabilities, and owner's equity at the statement date and to report on the income statement the proper net income (or loss) for the period.

Any prepaid asset account, such as Prepaid Insurance or Prepaid Rent (where more than a month has been paid), must be adjusted.

Supplies that have been used up will require an adjustment to the Supplies account. Depreciation on productive facilities, Fixed Assets, will have to be adjusted and expensed. Unearned revenue and accrued expenses, such as salaries and wages, must be adjusted.

These adjustments require General Journal entries, just like those you did in the first chapter.

Prepaid Assets (Insurance and Rent)

Most companies pay their insurance premiums in advance. Many insurance companies require that the entire year of premiums be paid ahead, and, many landlords require three months or more of rent to be paid in advance. As the month goes by, much of the insurance and rent payment becomes an expense instead of an asset.

Let's follow this through:

On January 1, Softbyte Computer Software pays the Phoenix Group $12,000 for office rent for the entire year, January 1 to December 31. This results in an initial debit to the asset account Prepaid Rent and a credit to cash. Starting January 31, and for each month following until December 31 we will expense $1,000 ($12,000 / 12 months) and deduct that from our prepaid asset called Prepaid Rent - a debit to Rent Expense and a credit to the asset Prepaid Rent. Because this is a prepaid expense, cash is not affected.

We follow the same logic for Insurance. On January 1, we pay J. Smith Lanier $6,000 for the insurance premium for a year's coverage - a debit to the asset Prepaid Insurance and a credit to cash. Each month during the year, we expense $500 as Insurance expense (a debit) and deduct that amount from the asset account Prepaid Insurance (a credit).

Let's make the entries:

Step 1: Launch Peachtree Accounting and open "Softbyte Computer Software" if it is not already open.

Step 2: . You will be required to create three new accounts. You learned how to create accounts in Chapter 2. Click on maintain, on the main menu Bar and then Chart of Accounts.

Step 3: Use account no. 105 for Prepaid Insurance, the Account Type is "Other Assets"; account no. 106 for Prepaid Rent, the Account Type is "Other Assets" and account no. 506 for Insurance Expense; the Account Type is "Expenses". (Rent Expense already exists.) The first account, Prepaid Insurance is shown in Figure 3.3.

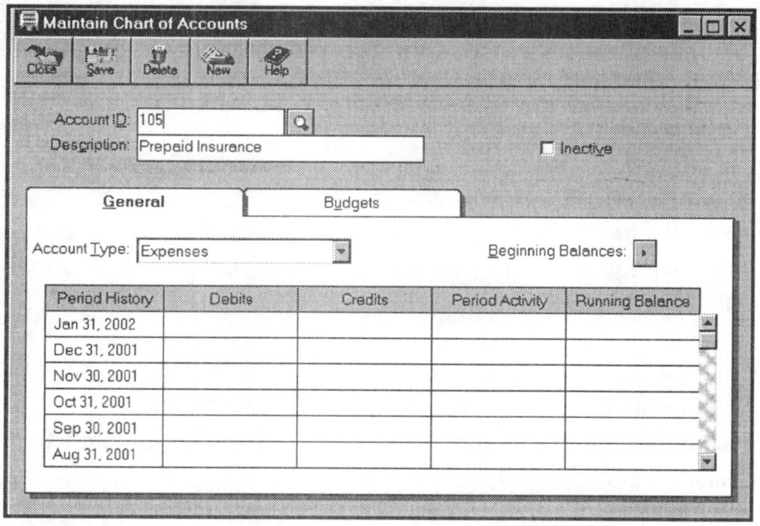

Figure 3. 3 New Account Creation - Prepaid Insurance

Step 4: After the accounts are created, use January 1 as the date and "5.1" as the transaction number in the reference box.

Step 5: Make the combination General Journal entry to record both the prepayment of Insurance for $12,000 and the prepayment of Rent for $6,000. The transaction is illustrated in Figure 3.4.

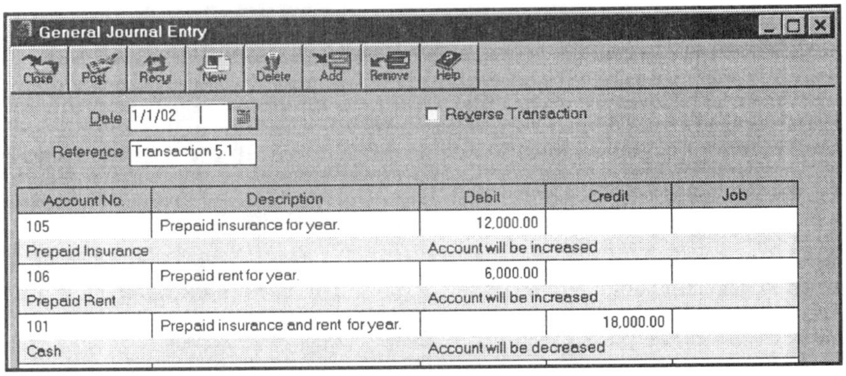

Figure 3. 4 Combination Journal Entry for prepaid assets.

A Special Note Before Continuing

We used "5.1" for the transaction number because we wanted the entry to "fit in" the order of General Journal entries that have already been created for "Softbyte." If you looked at the "Edit" command while you were in the General Journal entry section, you would see where this entry was made.

Also, if you look at the General Ledger Report or the Balance Sheet, you will notice that the Cash account (#101) now has a credit balance.

And, realize that because "Softbyte" is a new company, new accounts must be created along the way. You would only create the appropriate expense account once. You do not have to create new accounts every accounting period.

Making the Adjustments

On January 31 we must make the adjustment to recognize $500 of Prepaid Rent that was used up (expensed) and $1,000 of Prepaid Insurance that has expired (expensed). No cash was involved because the accounts were prepaid on January 1.

Step 1: Open the General Journal entry window.

Step 2: Change the date to read January 31. The transaction number is "11".

Step 3: Debit the expense account #506, Insurance Expense for $1,000 and Credit the asset account #105 Prepaid Insurance for $1,000

Step 4: Make sure your entry matches the one in Figure 3.5.

Step 5: Correct any errors and post your entry.

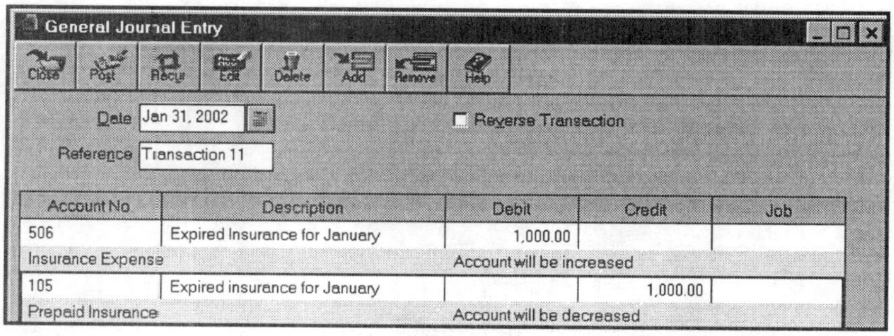

Figure 3. 5 Adjusting Journal entry for Prepaid Insurance

Follow the same procedure to post the adjusting entry for Prepaid Rent.

Step 1: Be sure the General Journal entry window is open and ready for the next transaction.

Step 2: Make sure the date reads January 31. The transaction number is "12".

Step 3: Debit the expense account no. 504, Rent Expense for $500 and Credit the asset account #106 Prepaid Rent for $500.

Step 4: Make sure your entry matches the one in Figure 3.6.

Step 5: If correct, post your entry.

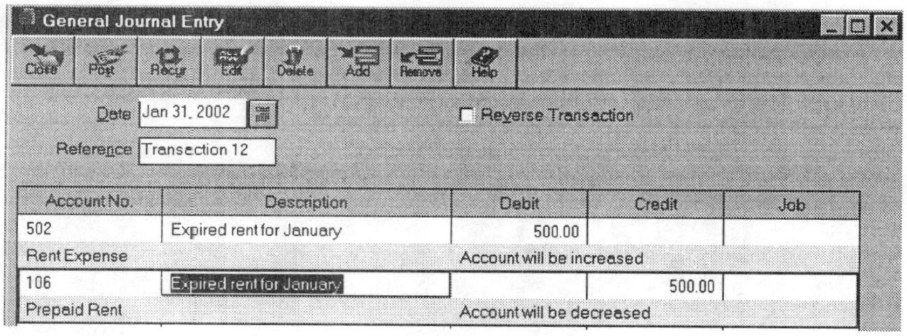

Figure 3. 6 Adjusting entry for Prepaid Rent

Supplies

In Chapter 1, one of the entries you made for Softbyte Computer Software was the purchase of Supplies on account for $1,600. It is ludicrous for someone to check the supply closet on a daily basis, take inventory, and record what supplies have been used. Normally, this is done once a month. In our example, when the inventory of the supplies has been taken, we find that there is $1,250 worth of supplies left in the supply closet. That means that $350 of our supplies has been used up, resulting in an expense.

An adjusting general journal entry needs to be made to reflect the correct balance of the asset Supplies for the beginning of February. The entry is simple: a debit (increasing) is made to the account Supplies Expense and a credit is made (decreasing) to the Supplies (asset) account.

Step 1: Create the Supplies Expense account, Account No. 507, Account Type is "Expense". The entry is shown in Figure 3.7.

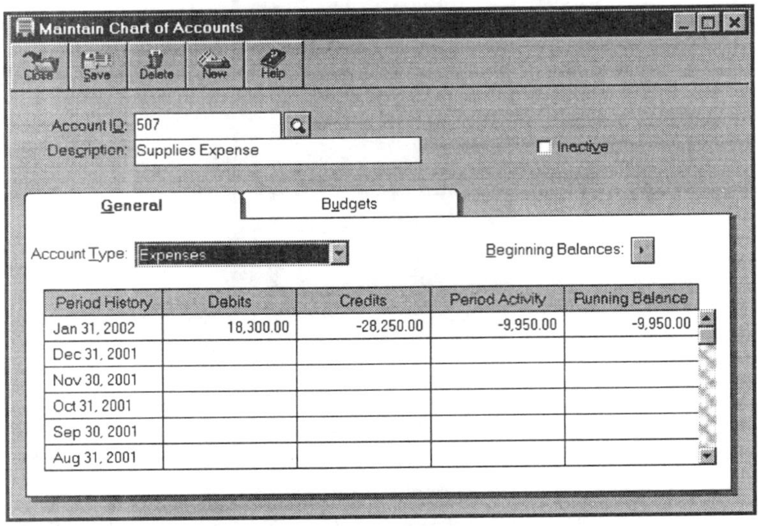

Figure 3. 7 New account - Supplies Expense

Step 2: January 31 is the date. You are now on Transaction 13. You are still in the January 2002 accounting period.

Step 3: Create a General Journal entry to debit (increase) the Supplies Expense account by \$350 and credit (decrease) the asset account Supplies by the same amount.

Step 4: The entry is shown in Figure 3.8. Make sure your work matches Figure 3.8 before posting the account.

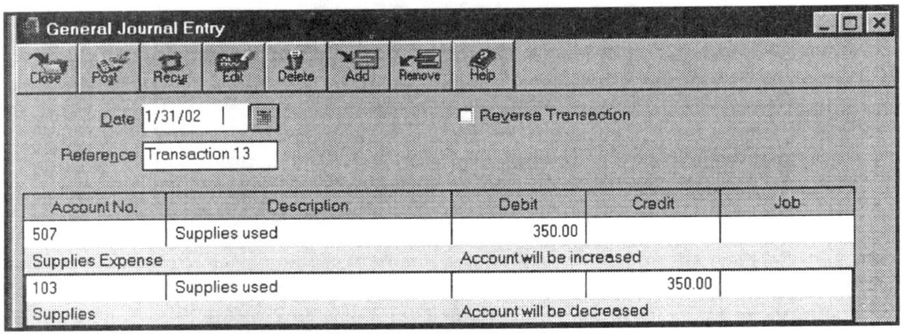

Figure 3. 8 General Journal entry adjusting supplies.

Depreciation

The theories and principles behind depreciation will be discussed in another chapter. Here, we just want to learn how to make the entry for depreciation expense and accumulated depreciation. In Chapter 1, Softbyte purchased \$7,000 worth of equipment. From an accounting standpoint, the equipment purchased is viewed as a long-term prepayment for services. The need for periodic adjustment for depreciation is similar to other prepaid entries. We need to recognize the cost that has expired during the period and to report the unexpired amount at the end of the accounting period.

Recognize depreciation as an estimate rather than a factual measurement of the cost that has expired. The asset may be useful for a longer or shorter period of time, depending on such factors as actual use, deterioration due to the elements or obsolescence.

A common procedure in computing depreciation expense is to divide the cost of the asset by its useful life. For example, the computer equipment the company purchased for $7,000 should last about four years before it becomes figuratively worthless. Therefore, the yearly depreciation for the equipment will be $1,750 a year or $146 a month with a slightly larger amount expensed the last month.

Two new accounts need to be created - Accumulated Depreciation – Equipment that will be a contra-asset account, and Depreciation Expense – Equipment, that will be an expense account.

Before making the entries, we must create the two new accounts.

Step 1: Since the Accumulated Depreciation – Equipment account is related to the asset account Equipment, use account number 104.1. The account type is "Accumulated Depreciation".

Step 2: Create the new account.

Step 3: The expense account, "Depreciation Expense – Equipment" is a regular expense account. Use account No. 508. And, the account type is "Expense".

Step 4: Create the new account.

Step 5: The new accounts are shown together in Figure 3.9.

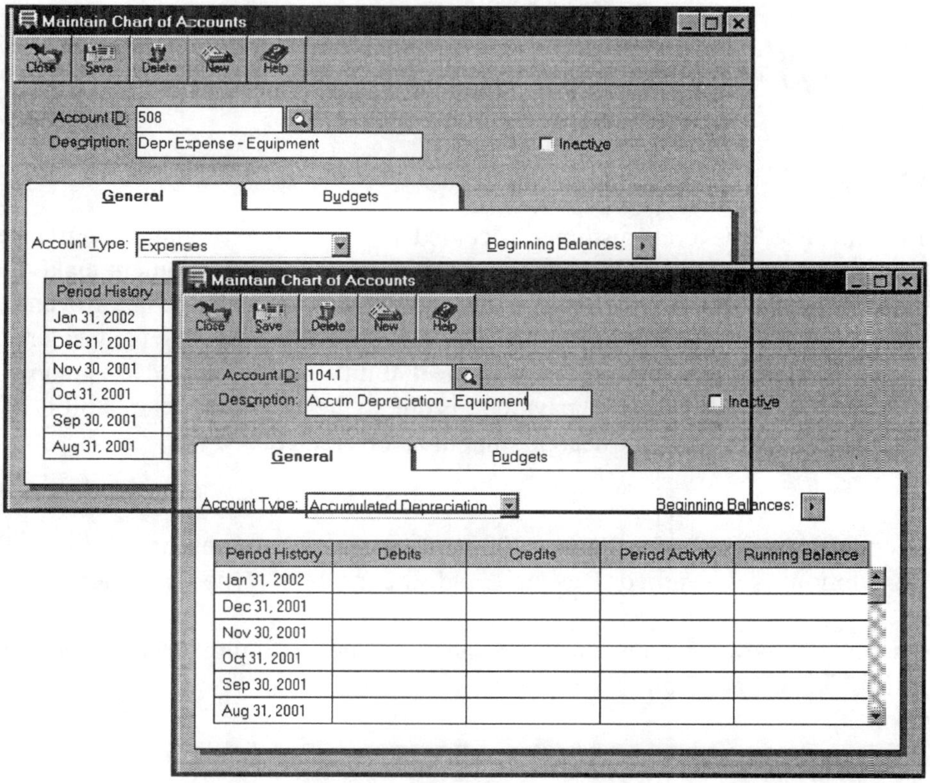

Figure 3. 9 New accounts to reflect accumulated depreciation and depreciation expense.

The entries to record depreciation expense are similar to ones you have done before.

Step 1: January 31 is still the date. You are now on Transaction 14. You are still in the January 2002 accounting period.

Step 2: Create a General Journal entry to debit (increase) the Depreciation Expense – Equipment account by $146 and credit (decrease) the contra asset account Accumulated Depreciation – Equipment by the same amount.

Step 3: The entry is shown in Figure 3.10. Make sure your work matches Figure 3.10 before posting the entry.

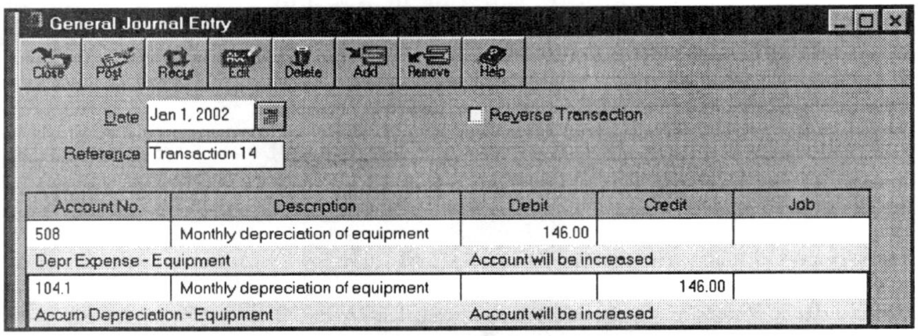

Figure 3. 10 Adjusting entry for depreciation of equipment

Unearned Revenue

In our example of "Softbyte," several customers decided to enter into a contract agreement where they will pay $600 up front for six months of on site service. Five customers make their $600 payment, a total of $3,000. "Softbyte" recognizes the total amount as Unearned Revenue, a liability. When cash is received for a service not yet rendered the amount is considered a liability. Only after service has been performed will the liability be recognized as income or revenue. The service, represented by the $600 payment, is due to the client, thus the liability. The Unearned Revenue account is the only new account that must be created.

Create the account:

Step 1: Use Account No. 202. Remember the 200 level of accounts represent liabilities. The account description is Unearned Revenue and the account type is Other Current Liabilities.

Step 2: Make sure your new account entry matches the one in Figure 3.11. Correct any errors and save the new account.

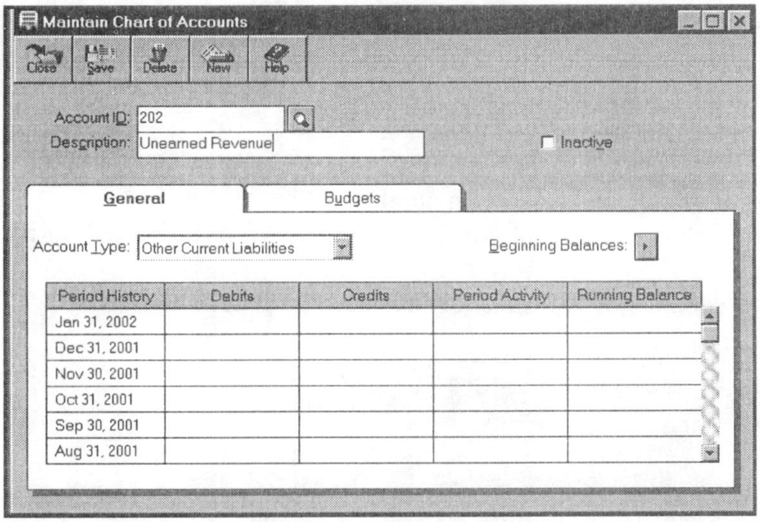

Figure 3. 11 Creation of the Unearned Revenue account

Because cash was received for services yet to be rendered, we now must make a General Journal entry recognizing the $3,000. (Five Customers @ $600/ea = $3,000).

Step 1: Open the General Journal window.
Step 2: On January 1, the contracts were each signed and each customer wrote a check to "Softbyte" for $600. Since we are inserting another transaction, the transaction number will be 1.1 (putting the transaction near the top of the edit list).
Step 3: The Cash account, No. 101 will be debited (increased) by $3,000. Be sure to add the explanation.
Step 4: The Unearned Revenue account, No. 202 will be credited (also increased) by the same amount.
Step 5: Make sure your entries match the ones in Figure 3.12.
Step 6: Correct any mistakes and post your entry.

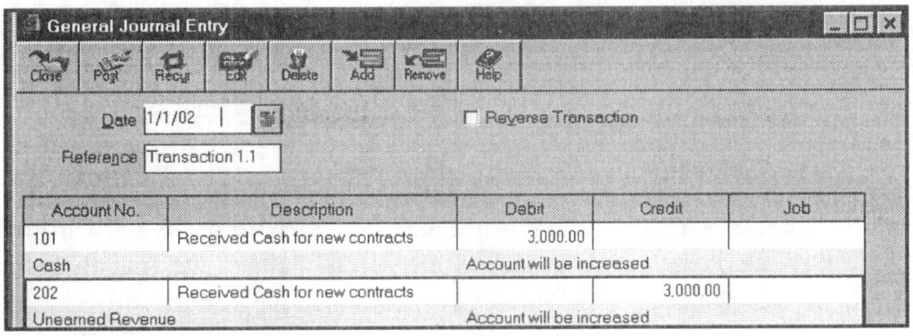

Figure 3. 12 Entry for receiving cash and recognizing unearned income.

At the end of January, "Softbyte" must make an adjusting entry to the revenue account recognizing the monies earned.

Make the entries:

Step 1: Change the date to January 31. Your transaction number is "15".
Step 2: The Unearned Revenue account, Account No. 201 must be debited (decreased) by $500.
Step 3: The Revenue account, Account No. 401, must be increased (credited) by $500.
Step 4: Check your entry with Figure 3.13.

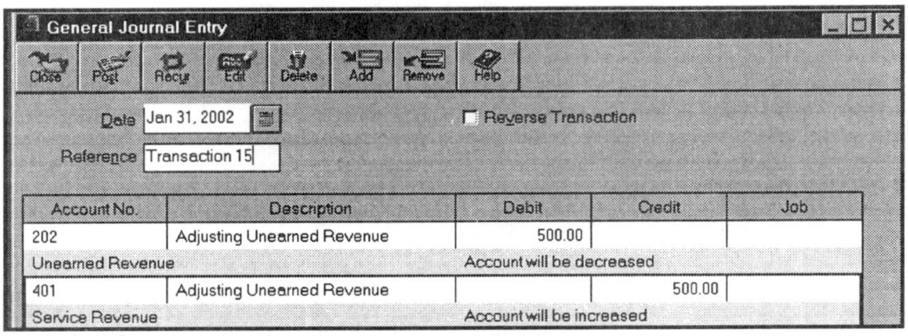

Figure 3. 13 Adjusting entry for Unearned Income

There is one other adjusting entry to be considered before we wrap up Chapter 3.

Accrued Salaries

Most companies pay their employees every week or every two weeks. For accounting purposes it would be helpful if we paid our employees on Friday and the last day of every month ended on a Friday. But, it rarely happens that way. In fact, the last day of the month often falls in the middle of the week. To keep accurate accounting and payroll records (payroll will be covered in another chapter) we must recognize the payroll expenses when they occur even though we are not issuing a paycheck at that time. We recognize what is due as a liability. When the actual payroll is paid, the liability is wiped out and the total payroll is paid.

To illustrate:

Looking at the calendar for January 2002, the last payday for Pioneer Advertising was Friday, January 25, 2002. The next payday will be in two weeks on Friday, February 8, 2002. The total payroll for Pioneer is $12,600 for a seven-day workweek. Of course, many of Pioneer's employees only work five days. There are 14 total days in the pay period with 6 days left in the pay period for January. If we divide the total payroll, $12,600, by the 14 days, we find that the daily payroll equals $900. Multiply the $900 by the 6 days left in January we get $5,400. That is the amount that must be expensed in January and recognized as a payable in February until it is paid on the next payday, February 8, 2002.

Let's make the entries:

Step 1: Open Pioneer Advertising on your Student Data Disk.
Step 2: For the General Journal entry, use the date January 31, 2002. Leave the transaction reference blank. On January 31, the salaries for the last 6 days of the month represent an accrued expense and a related liability. Although we call these entries *accruals* we do not put *accrual* in any of the account titles.
Step 3: The adjusting entry will be a debit to Account No. 501, Salaries Expense for $5,400.
Step 4: The corresponding credit will be to the liability Account No. 201, Salaries Payable for $5,400.
Step 5: The entry is shown below in Figure 3.14. Make sure your entry matches Figure 3.14.
Step 6: Correct any errors and post the entry.

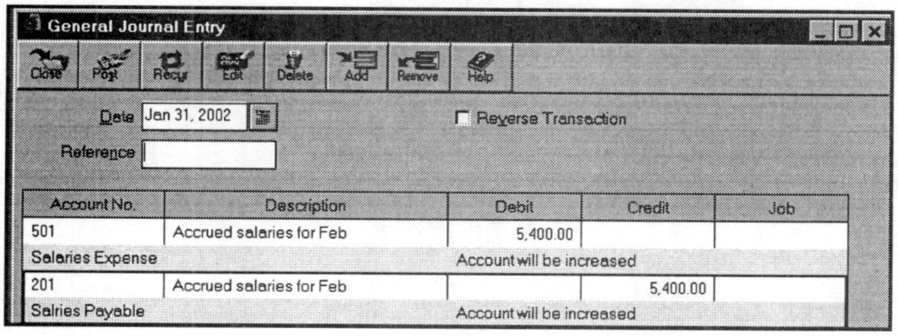

Figure 3. 14 Adjusting entry to recognize accrued payroll.

Since payroll for Pioneer is paid every two weeks, on February 8, 2002 employees will receive their paychecks. On that date, an entry will be made to debit (decrease) Salaries Payable by $5,400, debit (increase) Salaries Expense by $7,200 and credit (decrease) cash by $12,600.

Let's make the entry:

Step 1: Change the date to February 8, 2002. Ignore the entry for the transaction reference at this point.
Step 2: Make a compound General Journal entry:
a. Debiting (decrease) Salaries Payable by $5,400
b. Debiting (increase) Salaries Expense by $7,200
c. Crediting (decrease) cash by $12,600.

Make sure your entries match those in Figure 3.15. Correct any errors and post your entry.

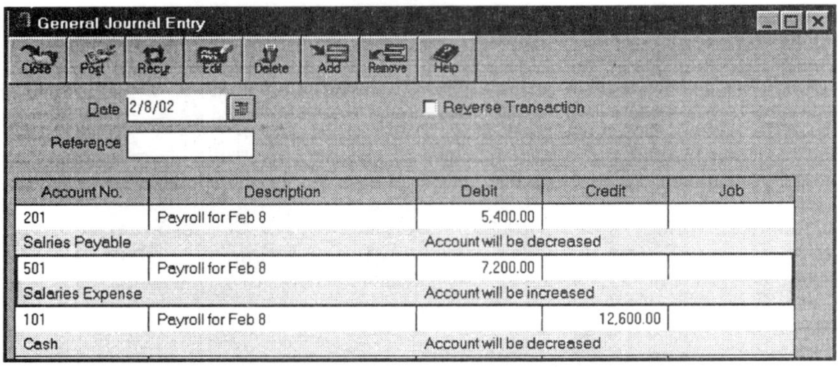

Figure 3. 15 Paying payroll Feb. 8, 2002

In Peachtree accounting, payroll is an automated process you will learn in a later chapter.

Demonstration Problem

Terry Thomas opened the Green Thumb Lawn Care Company on the First of April. On April 30th, the General Ledger Trial Balance reflected the following balances for selected accounts:

No. 103	Prepaid Insurance	$3,600
No. 105	Equipment	28,000
No. 207	Notes Payable	20,000
No. 210	Unearned Revenue	4,200
No. 401	Service Revenue	1,800

End of the month analysis reveals the following additional data:

1. Prepaid insurance is the cost of a 2-year insurance policy, effective April 1.
2. Depreciation on the equipment is $500 per month.
3. The note payable is dated April 1st. It is a 6-month, 12% note.
4. Seven customers paid for the company's 6-month lawn service package of $600 beginning in April. These customers were also serviced in April.
5. Lawn services provided other customers but not billed on April 30th totaled $1,500.

Instructions:

a.) Load Green Thumb Lawn Care from your Student Data Disk into Peachtree.
b.) Journalize in the General Journal the adjusting entries for the month of April. Use "ADJUSTING" as the reference.

Solution to Demonstration Problem

Date Apr 30, 2002   ☐ Reverse Transaction

Reference Adjusting

Account No.	Description	Debit	Credit	Job
520	Prepaid Insurance Expired	150.00		
Insurance Expense		Account will be increased		
102	Prepaid Insurance Expired		150.00	
Prepaid Insurance		Account will be decreased		
505	Monthly Depreciation	500.00		
Depr Exp - Equipment		Account will be increased		
115	Monthly Depreciation		500.00	
Accum Depr - Equipment		Account will be increased		
525	Interest on Note Payable	200.00		
Interest Expense		Account will be increased		
220	Interest on Note Payable		200.00	
Interest Payable		Account will be increased		
230	Service Revenue	700.00		
Unearned Revenue		Account will be decreased		
401	Service Revenue		700.00	
Service Revenue		Account will be increased		

P3-2a

Muddy River Resort opened for business on June 1st with eight air-conditioned units. Its trial balance before adjustments on August 31st is as follows:

Muddy River Resort

Trial Balance
August 31, 2002

Account No.		Debit	Credit
101	Cash	$19,600	
126	Supplies	3,300	
130	Prepaid Insurance	6,000	
140	Land	25,000	
143	Cottages	125,000	
149	Furniture	26,000	
201	Accounts Payable		6,500
208	Unearned Rent		7,400
275	Mortgage Payable		80,000
301	P. Javorek, Capital		100,000
302	P. Javorek, Drawing	5,000	
429	Rent Revenue		80,000
622	Repair Expense	3,600	
726	Salaries Expense	51,000	
732	Utilities Expense	9,400	
		$273,900	$273,900

Instructions:

a. Journalize the adjusting entries for the month of August in the General Journal using Peachtree Accounting.
b. Run an Income Statement, Statement of Retained Earnings and a Balance Sheet as of August 31st.

P3-5a

On September 1, 2002, the account balances of Rijo Equipment Repair were as follows:

No.	Debits		No.	Credits	
101	Cash	4,880	154	Accumulated Depreciation	1,500
112	Accounts Receivable	3,520	201	Accounts Payable	3,400
126	Supplies	2,000	209	Unearned Service Revenue	1,400
153	Store Equipment	15,000	212	Salaries Payable	500
			301	J. Rijo, Capital	18,600
		$25,400			$25,400

During September the following summary transactions were completed:

Sept. 8 Paid $1,100 for salaries due employees, of which $600 is for September.
10 Received $1,200 cash fro customers on account.
12 Received $3,400 cash fro services performed in September.
15 Purchased store equipment on account $3,000.
17 Purchased supplies on account $1,500.
20 Paid creditors $4,500 on account.
22 Paid September rent $500.
25 Paid salaries $1,050.
27 Performed services on account and billed customers for services rendered $700.
29 Received $650 from customers for future service.

Adjustment data consists of:

1. Supplies on hand $1,700
2. Accrued salaries payable $400
3. Depreciation is $200 per month
4. Unearned service revenue of $1,450 is earned

Instructions:

a. Open Rijo Equipment Repair in Peachtree from your Student Data Disk.
b. Create the accounts as shown in the trial balance along with their beginning balances. Note that Account 301 J. Rijo, Capital and its balance has been created for you.
c. Create the additional accounts: No. 407 Service Revenue, No. 615 Depreciation Expense, No. 631 Supplies Expense, No. 726 Salaries Expense and No. 729 Rent Expense.
d. Journalize in Peachtree's General Ledger the adjusting entries for September.
e. Run an Income Statement, a Retained Earnings Statement and a balance sheet for Rijo Equipment Repair as of September 30th.

CHAPTER 4

Completion of the Accounting Cycle

OBJECTIVES

- State the required steps in the accounting cycle.
- Describe the content and purpose of a post closing trial balance
- Explain the process of changing the accounting period
- Explain the process of closing the books.

USING A WORK SHEET

Two somewhat different but similar trial balance reports are available in Peachtree. The General Ledger Trial Balance, Figure 4.2, shows each account and its balance as of the date or period you select. The Working Trial Balance, Figure 4.4, provides blank spaces so you can fill in any adjusting trial balance information. This is designed to help you make adjustments to account balances.

These reports are simply devices used to make it easier to prepare adjusting entries and to guide you in the process of preparing your financial statements. These work sheets probably would not be used in small companies, such as our sample company, Softbyte Computer Software, which has just few a accounts and adjustments.

In the "manual" accounting process, financial statements are prepared directly from the worksheets prepared by the bookkeeper. The account balances of these worksheets are gathered directly from the General Ledger and the postings from the General Journal. In an automated system, such as Peachtree, the balances of the General Ledger accounts are continually updated as entries are made resulting in statement balances being continually updated. At the end of the accounting period however, general journal adjusting entries must be made as you did in the previous chapter.

THE GENERAL LEDGER TRIAL BALANCE

Step 1: Click on Reports on the Menu Bar, then General Journal. You will be presented with the Select A Report menu screen.

Step 2: General Ledger should be highlighted on the left side under Report Area by default. If not, make sure it is highlighted before selecting General Ledger Trial Balance as illustrated in Figure 4.1.

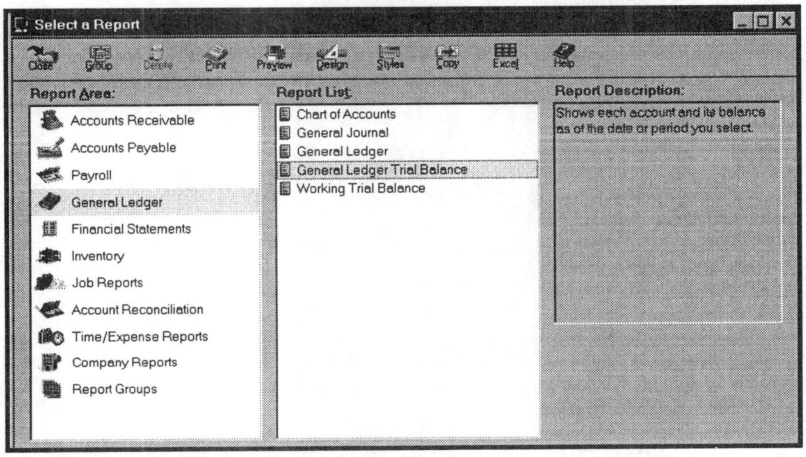

Figure 4. 1 Select a report menu screen.

Step 3: You may click the "Preview" icon on the tool bar to read the report on the screen or click the "Print" icon on the tool bar to produce a paper copy of the report.

The General Ledger Trial Balance for Softbyte Computer Company is shown in Figure 4.2.

Softbyte Computer Software
General Ledger Trial Balance
As of Jan 31, 2002

Filter Criteria includes: Report order is by ID. Report is printed in Detail Format.

Account ID	Account Description	Debit Amt	Credit Amt
101	Cash		6,950.00
102	Accounts Receivable	1,400.00	
103	Supplies	1,250.00	
104	Equipment	7,000.00	
104.1	Accum Depreciation - Equi		146.00
105	Prepaid Insurance	11,000.00	
106	Prepaid Rent	5,500.00	
201	Accounts Payable		1,600.00
202	Unearned Revenue		2,500.00
301	R. Neal, Capital		15,000.00
302	Owner's Drawing	1,300.00	
401	Service Revenue		5,200.00
501	Advertising Expense	250.00	
502	Rent Expense	1,100.00	
503	Salaries Expense	900.00	
504	Utilities Expense	200.00	
506	Insurance Expense	1,000.00	
507	Supplies Expense	350.00	
508	Depr Expense - Equipment	146.00	
	Total:	31,396.00	31,396.00

Figure 4. 2 The General Ledger Trial Balance.

THE WORKING TRIAL BALANCE

Step 1: Click on Reports on the Menu Bar, then General Journal. You will be presented with the "Select A Report" menu screen.

Step 2: General Ledger should be highlighted on the left side under Report Area by default. If not, make sure it is highlighted before selecting General Ledger Trial Balance as illustrated in Figure 4.3.

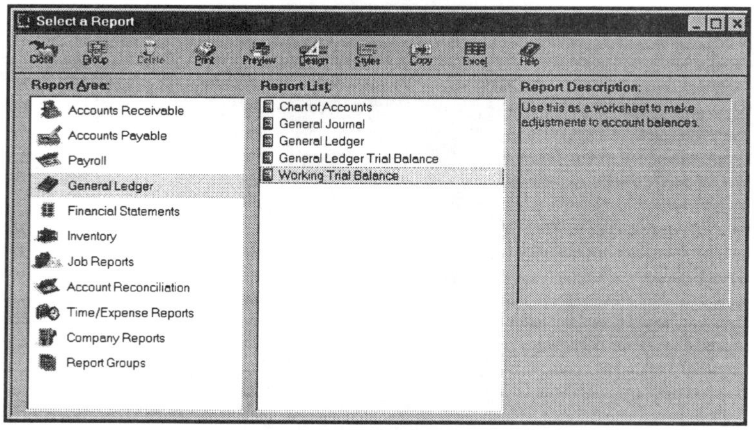

Figure 4. 3 Select a Report menu screen.

Step 3: You may click the "Preview" icon on the tool bar to read the report on the screen or click the "Print" icon on the tool bar to produce a paper copy of the report.

A portion of The Working Trial Balance for Softbyte Computer Company is shown below in Figure 4.4 below.

Softbyte Computer Software
Working Trial Balance
As of Jan 31, 2002
Filter Criteria includes: Report order is by ID. Report is printed with Accounts having Zero Amounts and in Detail Format.

Account ID Account Description	Last FYE Bal	Current Bal	Debit Adj	Credit Adj	End Bal	Reference
101 Cash	0.00	-6,950.00	______	______	______	______
102 Accounts Receivable	0.00	1,400.00	______	______	______	______
103 Supplies	0.00	1,250.00	______	______	______	______
104 Equipment	0.00	7,000.00	______	______	______	______
104.1 Accum Depreciation - Equi	0.00	-146.00	______	______	______	______
105 Prepaid Insurance	0.00	11,000.00	______	______	______	______

Figure 4. 4 Portion of the Working Trial Balance for Softbyte Computer Software.

CHANGING ACCOUNTING PERIODS

In Peachtree Accounting, accounting periods are set up when you create a new company. Once you have set up accounting periods, you cannot change the structure of the periods. You must wait until the end of a fiscal year, year-end closing before those changes can be made. In other words, you can only change the current accounting period within the established structure.

There are 26 accounting periods that can be open in Peachtree. For example, you may have last year's history available for editing or adjusting throughout the current year. Or, you can be in the next year without closing this year. The current period is shown in the status bar at the bottom right of the Peachtree window as shown in Figure 4.5.

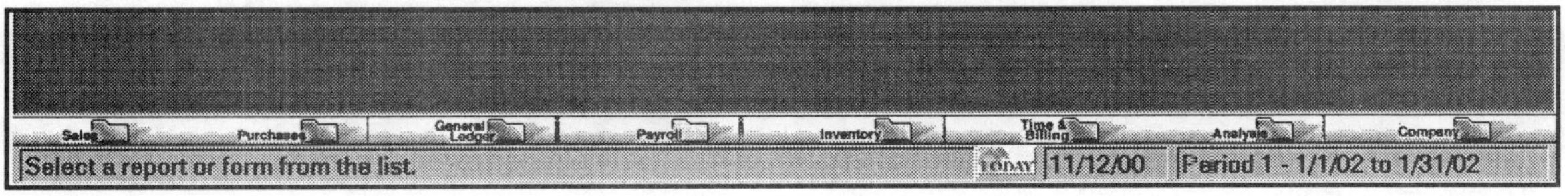

Figure 4. 5 Bottom of the Peachtree window showing the Current Accounting Period on the far right.

Step 1: From the Tasks menu, select System, and then Change Account Period from the submenu as illustrated in Figure 4.6.

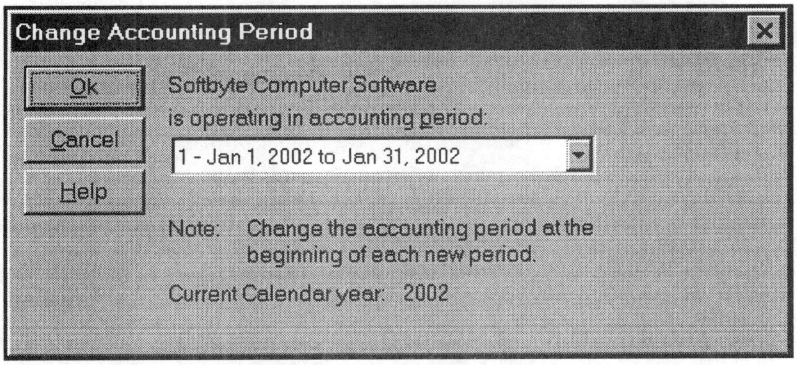

Figure 4. 6 Change Accounting Period submenu.

Step 2: Select the accounting you want to change to, and select OK.

Step 3: A message box will appear asking if you would like to print reports before continuing. Select "YES".

Step 4: A Print Reports window appears with the listing of suggested reports that you may wish to have printed paper copies. The window is shown in Figure 4.7.

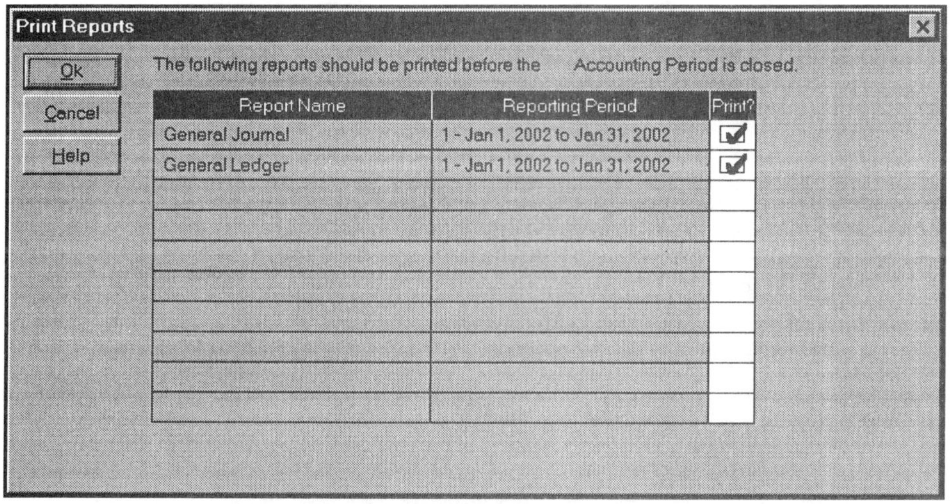

Figure 4. 7 The Print Reports menu.

In our sample company, Softbyte, only two reports are shown.

> **Step 5:** Select the "Print?" checkbox to uncheck (or check) any of the reports that you do not want printed.
> **Step 6:** Select OK when you have chosen all the reports you want to print.

This is important, and requires repeating: You can change the accounting period at will, anytime you want, by moving back and forth in the fiscal year. The General Ledger will track your balances as of the current period dates. Peachtree Accounting also will select the correct period in which to post a transaction by the *transaction date*. For example, you may enter a transaction in the future, but – you must change accounting periods to enter a "past" transaction.

> **Step 7:** Select OK to change the current accounting period.

AN ADDITIONAL WORD ABOUT CHANGING ACCOUNTING PERIODS

In the manual accounting process, it is necessary to distinguish between temporary and permanent accounts. Temporary (or nominal) accounts relate only to a given accounting period. For example, all income statement accounts, income or revenue accounts with account numbers in the 400 – 499 range and expense accounts with account numbers in the 500+ range, in a manual system would be closed. Their balances would be "zeroed out". The Owner's Drawing account, which in Peachtree is considered an equity account "that closes" also falls into that category – one that is closed each month in a manual system.

In contrast, in a manual system, permanent or real accounts, ones that can and will relate to one or more future accounting periods, in a manual system would stay open – their balances would carry over to the next period. Those accounts consist of all balance sheet accounts including Owner's Capital. Again, in a manual system, those accounts are not closed. The balances are carried over to the next period.

As discussed earlier, Peachtree keeps a "running" balance of all accounts. However, in many of the Peachtree reports, account balances are shown both as cumulative balances – those where the totals are added together month after month and a current period balance.

Let's look at an example:

Step 1: Open the company "Bellwether Garden Supply" found on your data disk. Bellwether Garden Supply is a generic company that Peachtree Accounting uses for demonstration purposes.

Step 2: The company should open in the default accounting period of "Period 3 – March 1, 2003 – March 31, 2003. Make sure the accounting period is correct before continuing.

Step 3: Make a printed copy of "Bellwether's Income Statement. A portion, the revenue section, is shown in Figure 4.8 below.

Bellwether Garden Supply
Income Statement
For the Three Months Ending March 31, 2003

		Current Month			Year to Date	
Revenues						
Sales	$	5,000.00	16.99	$	8,075.95	18.20
Sales - Aviary		3,508.41	11.92		4,608.19	10.38
Sales - Books		89.85	0.31		3,594.70	8.10
Sales - Ceramics		0.00	0.00		0.00	0.00
Sales - Equipment		2,249.78	7.64		7,011.40	15.80
Sales - Food/Fert		349.62	1.19		679.26	1.53
Sales - Furntiture		15,000.00	50.96		15,000.00	33.80
Sales - Hand Tools		199.92	0.68		801.64	1.81
Sales - Landscape Services		1,179.72	4.01		1,899.58	4.28
Sales - Miscellaneous		0.00	0.00		0.00	0.00
Sales - Nursery		782.58	2.66		1,020.44	2.30
Sales - Pots		504.59	1.71		574.54	1.29
Sales - Seeds		223.17	0.76		766.24	1.73
Sales - Soil		351.48	1.19		365.46	0.82
Sales - Statuary		0.00	0.00		0.00	0.00
Sales - Topiary		0.00	0.00		0.00	0.00
Interest Income		0.00	0.00		0.00	0.00
Other Income		0.00	0.00		0.00	0.00
Finance Charge Income		0.00	0.00		0.00	0.00
Sales Returns and Allowances		0.00	0.00		0.00	0.00
Sales Discounts		<5.80>	<0.02>		<19.52>	<0.04>
Total Revenues		29,433.32	100.00		44,377.88	100.00

Figure 4. 8 Income Statement for Bellwether Garden Supply.

In the first column, each of the income sources for Bellwether is listed. The next columnar heading is for the current month, which is the 3rd accounting period ending on March 31, 2003. Each figure, going down the first column, is the monthly balance of that particular account. The second column shows the percentage of the total of that month.

The second set of columns, Year To Date, shows the balances of the accounts from January 1, 2003 up to when the statement was requested. If a previous accounting period had been selected, each of the columns would reflect balances based on that particular date.

Account balances are continually updated and carried over to Peachtree's balance sheet. A carry over of the previous month's balances is not needed for the balance sheet.

There is one section on a Peachtree balance sheet that required discussion. Look at the capital section of Bellwether's Balance sheet. It is illustrated below in Figure 4.9.

Capital		
Common Stock	5,000.00	
Paid-in Capital	100,000.00	
Retained Earnings	189,037.60	
Net Income	10,377.36	
Total Capital		304,414.96

Figure 4. 9 The Capital portion of Bellwether Garden Supply's balance sheet.

Bellwether is a corporation, which requires a section for Common Stock and Paid In Capital. Corporate accounting will be covered later. The Retained Earnings account is the amount of Net Income that has been reinvested back into the company. The Net Income figure represents the current net income which is the same net income figure shown on your print out of the income statement in the previous exercise. The figure will get added to the Retained Earnings figure in the next accounting period.

DEMONSTRATION PROBLEM

Open Watson Answering Service on your Student Data Disk. Run a General Ledger Trial Balance. You will be presented with the following unadjusted General Ledger Trial Balance.

Watson Answering Service
General Ledger Trial Balance
As of Aug 31, 2002

Filter Criteria includes: Report order is by ID. Report is printed in Detail Format.

Account ID	Account Description	Debit Amt	Credit Amt
101	Cash	5,400.00	
102	Accounts Receivable	2,800.00	
103	Prepaid Insurance	2,400.00	
104	Supplies	1,300.00	
105	Equipment	60,000.00	
201	Accounts Payable		2,400.00
204	Notes Payable		40,000.00
301	Ray Watson, Capital		30,000.00
302	Ray Watson, Drawing	1,000.00	
400	Service Revenue		4,900.00
501	Salaries Expense	3,200.00	
502	Utilities Expense	800.00	
503	Advertising Expense	400.00	
	Total:	77,300.00	77,300.00

Other data consists of the following:

1. Insurance expires at the rate of $200 per month.
2. There is $1,000 of supplies on hand at August 31.
3. Monthly depreciation is $900 the equipment.
4. Interest of $500 has accrued during August on the notes payable

Instructions:

a) Based on the above data, enter the necessary General Journal transactions to adjust the month end balances assuming $35,000 of the notes payable is long term.
b) Check your work by printing a General Ledger Trial Balance.
c) Print an Income Statement, a Retained Earnings Statement and a Classified Balance Sheet for the month ended August 31, 2002.
d) Change the accounting period to the next period.
e) Print an Income Statement as of the new current period. Nctice the zero balances for the current month (September) and the carry over balances from the previous month (August).

Solution To Demonstration Problem

General Journal Entries for Expenses.

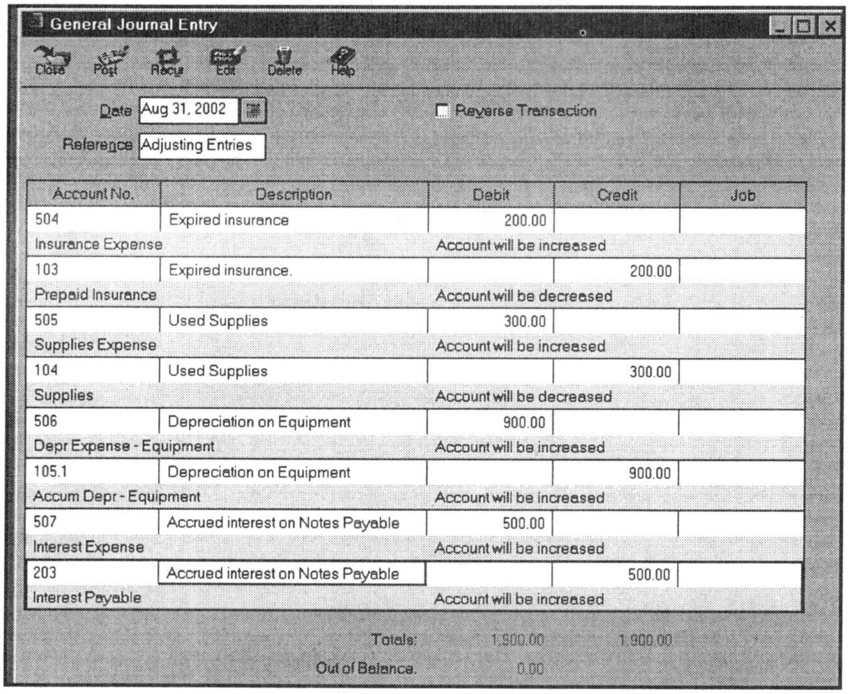

General Journal Entry

Close Post Recur Edit Delete Help

Date Aug 31, 2002

Reference Adjusting Entries

Reverse Transaction

Account No.	Description	Debit	Credit	Job
504 Insurance Expense	Expired insurance	200.00		
	Account will be increased			
103 Prepaid Insurance	Expired insurance.		200.00	
	Account will be decreased			
505 Supplies Expense	Used Supplies	300.00		
	Account will be increased			
104 Supplies	Used Supplies		300.00	
	Account will be decreased			
506 Depr Expense - Equipment	Depreciation on Equipment	900.00		
	Account will be increased			
105.1 Accum Depr - Equipment	Depreciation on Equipment		900.00	
	Account will be increased			
507 Interest Expense	Accrued interest on Notes Payable	500.00		
	Account will be increased			
203 Interest Payable	Accrued interest on Notes Payable		500.00	
	Account will be increased			
	Totals:	1,900.00	1,900.00	
	Out of Balance.	0.00		

General Journal entry transferring $5,000 of Notes Payable from the Long Term Liability classification to the Notes Payable account classified as a Current Liability. This transaction makes $5,000 of Notes Payable a current liability, payable within a year.

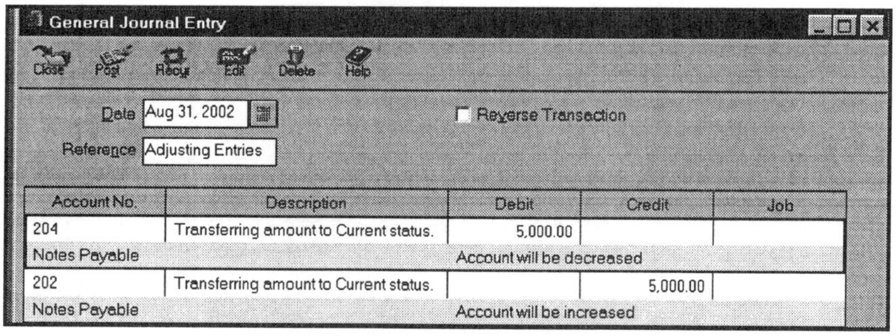

General Journal Entry

Close Post Recur Edit Delete Help

Date Aug 31, 2002

Reference Adjusting Entries

Reverse Transaction

Account No.	Description	Debit	Credit	Job
204 Notes Payable	Transferring amount to Current status.	5,000.00		
	Account will be decreased			
202 Notes Payable	Transferring amount to Current status.		5,000.00	
	Account will be increased			

General Ledger Trial Balance

Watson Answering Service
General Ledger Trial Balance
As of Aug 31, 2002

Filter Criteria includes: Report order is by ID. Report is printed in Detail Format.

Account ID	Account Description	Debit Amt	Credit Amt
101	Cash	5,400.00	
102	Accounts Receivable	2,800.00	
103	Prepaid Insurance	2,200.00	
104	Supplies	1,000.00	
105	Equipment	60,000.00	
105.1	Accum Depr - Equipment		900.00
201	Accounts Payable		2,400.00
202	Notes Payable		45,000.00
203	Interest Payable		500.00
204	Notes Payable	5,000.00	
301	Ray Watson, Capital		30,000.00
302	Ray Watson, Drawing	1,000.00	
400	Service Revenue		4,900.00
501	Salaries Expense	3,200.00	
502	Utilities Expense	800.00	
503	Advertising Expense	400.00	
504	Insurance Expense	200.00	
505	Supplies Expense	300.00	
506	Depr Expense - Equipment	900.00	
507	Interest Expense	500.00	
	Total:	83,700.00	83,700.00

The Income Statement

Watson Answering Service
Income Statement
For the One Month Ending August 31, 2002

		Current Month			Year to Date	
Revenues						
Service Revenue	$	4,900.00	100.00	$	4,900.00	100.00
Total Revenues		4,900.00	100.00		4,900.00	100.00
Cost of Sales						
Total Cost of Sales		0.00	0.00		0.00	0.00
Gross Profit		4,900.00	100.00		4,900.00	100.00
Expenses						
Salaries Expense		3,200.00	65.31		3,200.00	65.31
Utilities Expense		800.00	16.33		800.00	16.33
Advertising Expense		400.00	8.16		400.00	8.16
Insurance Expense		200.00	4.08		200.00	4.08
Supplies Expense		300.00	6.12		300.00	6.12
Depr Expense - Equipment		900.00	18.37		900.00	18.37
Interest Expense		500.00	10.20		500.00	10.20
Total Expenses		6,300.00	128.57		6,300.00	128.57
Net Income	$	<1,400.00>	<28.57>	$	<1,400.00>	<28.57>

The Retained Earnings Statement

Watson Answering Service
Statement of Retained Earnings
For the One Month Ending August 31, 2002

Beginning Retained Earnings	$	30,000.00
Adjustments To Date		0.00
Net Income		<1,400.00>
Subtotal		28,600.00
Ray Watson, Drawing		<1,000.00>
Ending Retained Earnings	$	27,600.00

The Balance Sheet

Watson Answering Service
Balance Sheet
August 31, 2002

ASSETS

Current Assets				
Cash	$	5,400.00		
Accounts Receivable		2,800.00		
Prepaid Insurance		2,200.00		
Supplies		1,000.00		
Total Current Assets				11,400.00
Property and Equipment				
Equipment		60,000.00		
Accum Depr - Equipment		<900.00>		
Total Property and Equipment				59,100.00
Other Assets				
Total Other Assets				0.00
Total Assets			$	70,500.00

LIABILITIES AND CAPITAL

Current Liabilities				
Accounts Payable	$	2,400.00		
Notes Payable		45,000.00		
Interest Payable		500.00		
Total Current Liabilities				47,900.00
Long-Term Liabilities				
Notes Payable		<5,000.00>		
Total Long-Term Liabilities				<5,000.00>
Total Liabilities				42,900.00
Capital				
Ray Watson, Capital		30,000.00		
Ray Watson, Drawing		<1,000.00>		
Net Income		<1,400.00>		
Total Capital				27,600.00
Total Liabilities & Capital			$	70,500.00

Changing the Accounting Period

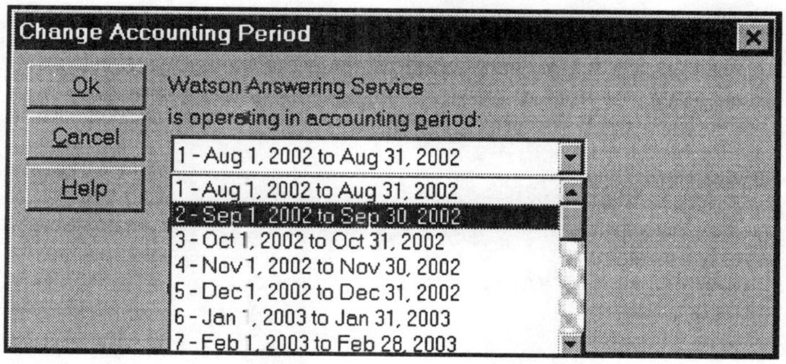

Income Statement reflecting the new accounting period

Watson Answering Service
Income Statement
For the Two Months Ending September 30, 2002

	Current Month		Year to Date	
Revenues				
Service Revenue	$ 0.00	0.00	$ 4,900.00	100.00
Total Revenues	0.00	0.00	4,900.00	100.00
Cost of Sales				
Total Cost of Sales	0.00	0.00	0.00	0.00
Gross Profit	0.00	0.00	4,900.00	100.00
Expenses				
Salaries Expense	0.00	0.00	3,200.00	65.31
Utilities Expense	0.00	0.00	800.00	16.33
Advertising Expense	0.00	0.00	400.00	8.16
Insurance Expense	0.00	0.00	200.00	4.08
Supplies Expense	0.00	0.00	300.00	6.12
Depr Expense - Equipment	0.00	0.00	900.00	18.37
Interest Expense	0.00	0.00	500.00	10.20
Total Expenses	0.00	0.00	6,300.00	128.57
Net Income	$ 0.00	0.00	$ <1,400.00>	<28.57>

P4-2a

The adjusted trial balance of the "work sheet" for Shmi Skywalker Company is as follows:

Shmi Skywalker Co.
Work Sheet
For the year ended, December 31, 2002

Account No.	Account Titles	Adjusted Trial Balance Dr.	Adjusted Trial Balance Cr.
101	Cash	20,800	
112	Accounts Receivable	15,400	
126	Supplies	2,300	
130	Prepaid Insurance	4,800	
151	Office Equipment	44,000	
152	Accumulated Depreciation – Office Equipment		18,000
200	Notes Payable		20,000
201	Accounts Payable		8,000
212	Salaries Payable		3,000
230	Interest Payable		1,000
301	S. Skywalker, Capital		36,000
306	S. Skywalker, Drawing	12,000	
400	Service Revenue		79,000
610	Advertising Expense	12,000	
631	Supplies Expense	3,700	
711	Depreciation Expense	6,000	
722	Insurance Expense	4,000	
726	Salaries Expense	39,000	
905	Interest Expense	1,000	
		165,000	165,000

Create the accounts and their balances based on the above chart. When "Shmi Skywalker Co." is opened, you find that the capital account has already been created for you.

Instructions:

a. Run a General Ledger Balance Sheet to check the accuracy of your entries.
b. Run an Income Statement, Retained Earnings Statement and a Balance Sheet for the current period.
c. Change accounting periods and run another Balance Sheet.
d. Run another income statement and notice how the current month is "zeroed" out and the previous balances have moved over to the next column.

P4-5a

Ewok-Ackbar opened Ewok's Carpet Cleaners on March 1, 2002. During March, the following transactions were completed:

March	1	Invested $10,000 cash in the business.
	1	Purchased used truck for $6,000, paying $4,000 cash and the balance on account.
	3	Purchased cleaning supplies for $1,200 on account.
	5	Paid $1,800 cash on one-year insurance policy effective March 1.
	14	Billed customers $2,800 for cleaning services.
	18	Paid $1,500 cash on amount owed on truck and $500 on amount owed on cleaning supplies.
	20	Paid $1,500 cash for employee salaries.
	21	Collected $1,600 cash from customers billed on March 14.
	28	Billed customers $2,500 for cleaning services.
	31	Paid gas and oil for month on truck $200.
	31	Withdrew $700 cash for personal use.

Create the Chart of Accounts for Ewok's Carpet Cleaners: No. 112 Accounts Receivable, No. 128 Cleaning Supplies, No. 130 Prepaid Insurance, No. 157 Equipment, No. 158 Accumulated Depreciation – Equipment, No. 201 Accounts Payable, No. 212 Salaries Payable, No. 306 A. Ewok, Drawing, No. 400 Service Revenue, No. 633 Gas & Oil Expense, No. 634 Cleaning Supplies Expense, No. 711 Depreciation Expense, No. 722 Insurance Expense, No. 726 Salaries Expense.

The Cash Account and the Capital Account, along with the first entry have been done for you.

Instructions:

a. Journalize and post the March transactions as presented above.
b. Prepare a General Ledger Trial Balance as of March 31st.
c. Enter the following adjusting entries:
    1. Earned but unbilled revenue at March 31st was $600.
    2. Depreciation on equipment for the month was $250.
    3. One-twelfth of the insurance expired.
    4. An inventory count shows $400 of cleaning supplies on hand at March 31st.
    5. Accrued, but unpaid employee salaries were $500.
d. Prepare an Income Statement, Retained Earnings Statement and a Balance Sheet as of March 31st.
e. Change accounting periods.

CHAPTER 5

Accounting for Merchandising Operations

OBJECTIVES

- Identify the differences between a service enterprise and a merchandiser.
- Explain the entries for purchases under a perpetual inventory system.
- Explain the entries for sales revenues under a perpetual inventory system.
- Explain the steps in the accounting cycle for a merchandiser.
- Distinguish between a multiple step and a single step income statement.
- Explain the computation and the importance of gross profit.

MERCHANDISING OPERATIONS

Merchandisers are companies that purchase and sell directly to consumers. There are two types of merchandisers, retailers and wholesalers. Kmart, Safeway, and Toys "R" Us are retailers. On the other hand, merchandisers that sell to retailers are known as wholesalers. Walgreen's might buy goods from McKesson & Robbins, which is a wholesaler. The wholesaler United Stationers might sell office supplies to Office Depot. Walgreen's and Office Depot sell their goods to the consumer.

The steps in the accounting cycle for a merchandising company are the same as for a service enterprise with the addition of several additional accounts and entries.

Measuring net income for a merchandiser is similar as a service enterprise. For example, net income results from the matching of expenses with revenue. The primary source of revenue for a merchandiser is often referred to as sales revenue or just plain sales. There are two different expense categories in a merchandising enterprise: (1) The cost of goods sold and (2) operating expenses.

The cost of goods sold is the total cost of merchandise sold during the period. This expense is directly related to the revenue recognized when goods are sold. Sales revenue less cost of goods sold is called gross profit on sales. For example, when a calculator that costs $15 is sold for $25, the gross profit would be $10 on that item. Gross profit for a merchandise company is reported on the income statement. After gross profit is calculated, operating expenses are deducted to determine net income or loss. Then operating expenses, those that are incurred in the process of earning sales revenue, are totaled and subtracted.

In Peachtree Accounting, following some preliminary effort, most of the work is done for you.

ENTERING VENDOR INFORMATION

A vendor is the seller, the merchant, the retailer, or the manufacturer that has goods, products or merchandise that you plan to buy, increase the price, and resale to your customers. In Peachtree Accounting, before we can enter any merchandise to be sold, we must have a record of our vendors.

Step 1: Open the company "Beyer Video" on your Student Data Disk.
Step 2: Click on "Maintain" from the menu bar and then click on "Vendors" from the pull down menu. You should see the "Maintain Vendors" screen as shown in Figure 5.1 below.

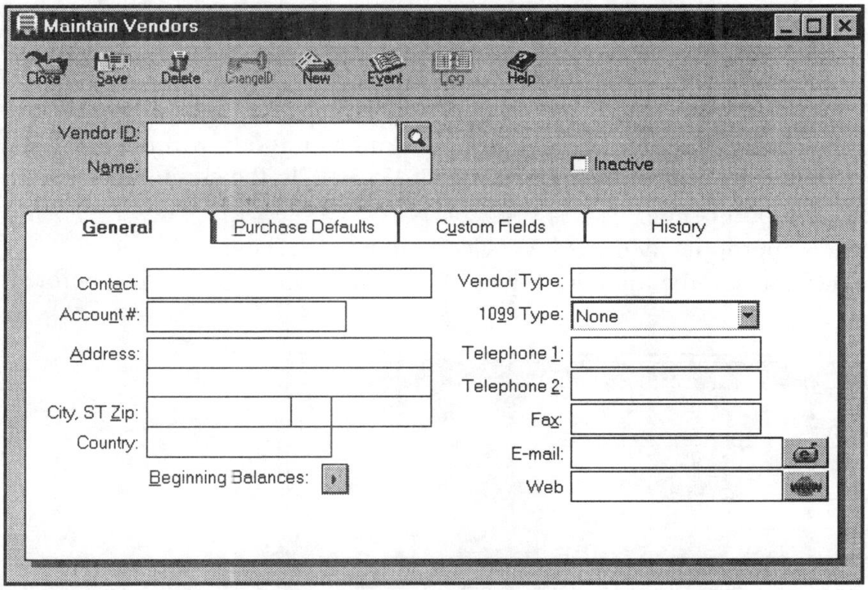

Figure 5. 1 Maintain Vendors window.

Each vendor selling to your company should be listed by Vendor ID and their company name.

Step 3: Enter the following information in the appropriate boxes. The first Vendor ID is V101. The vendor's name is Columbus Import Company.

The next set of text boxes on the left side of the form under the "General" tab include a contact name, usually your salesperson, a resource person you can talk with at the company, your account number, and the address information of the vendor.

Step 4: Enter the following information on the left side of the form: Alyce Merchant is your contact person, your account number at Columbus Import is 1347, Columbus Import's address is 1492 Queen Isabella Way in Madrid, GA 30341.

On the right side of the form, under the "General" tab include any additional information you may feel is necessary.

You may assign a "type" to your vendors. Some companies will "type" vendors such as the phone company or the electric company as utilities, and so on. Merchants, on the other hand, can be "typed" as merchants.

Next, it is particularly important to check to see if the vendor requires a Form 1099. An outside contractor earning more than $600 would require a 1099. Columbus Import is not an outside contractor.

Phone numbers, fax numbers, e-mail, and Web page information follows. Note the icon by the e-mail and Web page blanks. Once you enter the information you may then click on the icon to send e-mail to a vendor or visit their Web site.

Step 5: Enter the following additional information on the left side of the form: the vendor type is "Wholesaler." You may abbreviate it as "whlsler." Make sure every other wholesaler listed uses exactly the same abbreviation. Columbus Imports will not receive a 1099. The phone number for Columbus Imports is (770)555-1029; the e-mail address is a_merchant@columbusimport.com.

The web site is appropriately named www.columbusimport.com.

Step 6: Your entry should match the one in Figure 5.2. Make any corrections before continuing.

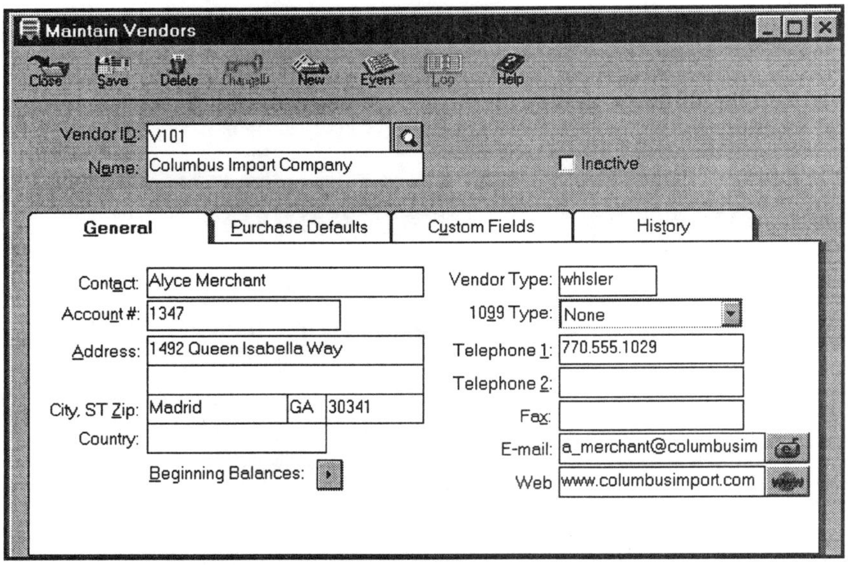

Figure 5. 2 The completed Maintain Vendors window.

Before continuing to enter additional information, you must assign a purchasing account to the vendor. Because our vendors are only wholesalers, we will assign the "Cost of Goods Sold," account no. 508 to the vendor.

Step 7: Click on the "Purchase Defaults" tab and enter account number 508 in the "Purchase Account" text box as shown in Figure 5.3.

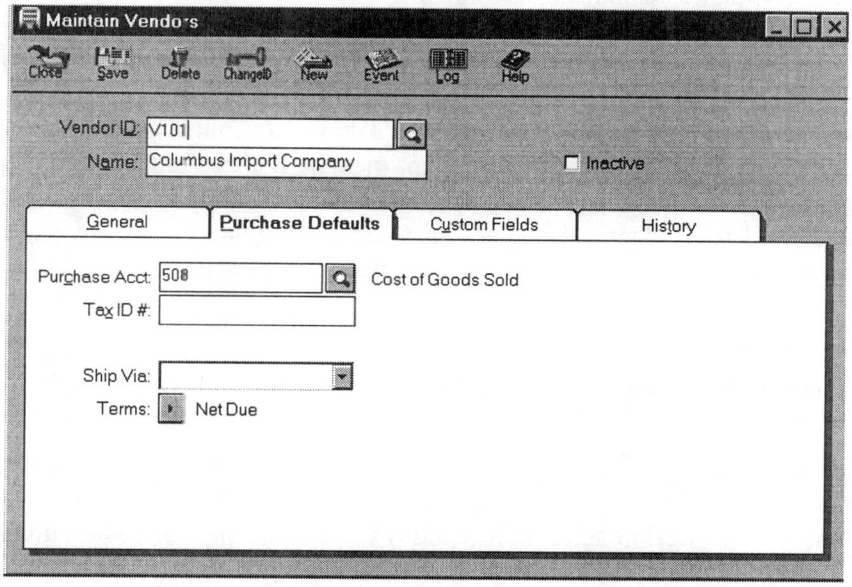

Figure 5. 3 Assigning a purchase account to the vendor.

Step 8: Click the "Save" icon on the toolbar to save your work.
Step 9: Using the information in Table 5.1, continue entering the three additional vendors.

Table 5. 1 Data for Vendors

Vendor ID	V102	V103	V104
Company	Southern Video	Atlanta Television	Ivory Group
Contact	John Pack	Peter Bell	Larry Ivory
Account #	1397	5812	9174
Address	753 Northside Dr.	99 Spring St.	23 Tuxedo Dr.
City/State/Zip	Atlanta, GA 30340	Alpharetta, GA 30041	Buckhead, GA 30300
Vendor Type	whlsler	whlsler	whlsler
1099?	N/A	N/A	N/A
Telephone	770.555.4900	770.555.9713	770.555.3732
Email	jp@mindspring.com	pbell@atltv.com	larry@ivory.com
Web Site	www.sovid.com	www.atltv.com	www.ivory.com

Step 10: When finished, run a vendor's report from the Accounts Payable report group to check for errors. Make any corrections before continuing.

THE PERPETUAL INVENTORY SYSTEM

The merchandise company keeps track of its inventory to determine what is available for sale and what has been sold. Most companies using an automated system such as Peachtree will very likely use a perpetual inventory system – one that is maintained continuously. For example, an antique store such as Great Gatsby's in Atlanta will keep individual inventory records for each item, its cost and its retail price, either on their showroom floor or in their warehouse.

Under a perpetual inventory system, the cost of goods sold is determined each time a sale occurs. This system provides much better control over inventories than other systems such as the Periodic System, which is also discussed in your text. In a perpetual system, the inventory records show the quantities that should be on hand, the goods that can be counted at any time to see whether the amount of goods actually on hand agrees with the inventory records.

MAINTAINING INVENTORY ITEMS FOR SALE

Beyer Video sells several different electronic items such as: 19," 25", and 32" color televisions, DVD players, stereo VCRs, standard home stereo component units, surround/sound entertainment units, computer monitors, 52" projection televisions, and 74" flat screen wall entertainment centers. They also sell furniture for the three smaller models of color televisions. Each of these inventory items will have a specific inventory identification number and each is sold to Beyer Video through the vendors entered earlier. All of these items are considered stock items, meaning that Beyer Video carries these items on a continuous basis. Occasionally there will be some special items sold, but let's keep it simple for now.

Also notice that we are concerned here only with the sales price of an item and not the actual cost. We will concern ourselves with cost when an actual purchase has been made.

As we continue, each inventory item above must be documented in the system.

Step 1: On the menu bar, click on "Maintain," and then click "Inventory Items" on the pull down menu. You will be presented with the screen as shown in Figure 5.4 on the next page.

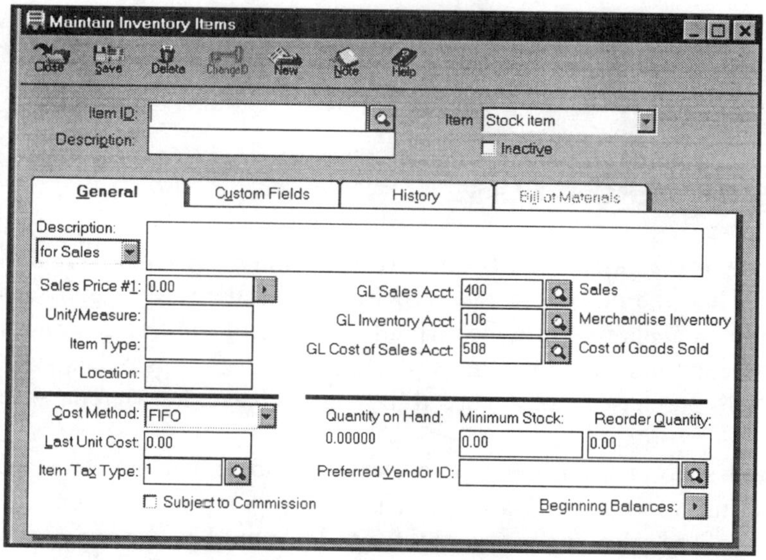

Figure 5. 4 Maintain Inventory Items window.

Step 2: The first item to be entered is the 19" Color TV. Enter TV19 as the Item ID. The description would be, of course, 19" Color TV. Leave the larger description box blank for now.

Step 3: In Peachtree, your items for retail may have five different pricing levels. In our example we will use only one. The sales price for the 19" Color TV is $225.

Step 4: Leave the units of measurement, item type and location blank. Those data are not needed at this time. Notice on the right side of the form, above the bar line, the sales account, merchandise inventory, and the cost of goods sold account numbers have been filled in for you.

Step 5: Leave everything below the bar in its default state.

Step 6: Use Table 5.2 to continue entering inventory items. You have already completed the first entry,

Table 5.2 Inventory Items

Inventory Item	*ID Number*	*Description*	*Sales Price*
19" Color TV	TV19	19" Color TV	$225
25" Color TV	TV25	25" Color TV	$275
32" Color TV	TV32	32" Color TV	$325
DVD Player	DV01	DVD Player	$199
Stereo VCR	VC23	Stereo VCR	$299
Home Stereo	ST61	Home Stereo	$750
Surround Sound	SU85	Surround Sound	$950
Computer Monitor	MO17	Computer Monitor	$345
Projection System	PROJ	Projection System	$999
Flat Screen System	FLAT	Flat Screen System	$999
19" Cabinet	CAB19	19" Cabinet	$35
25" Cabinet	CAB25	25" Cabinet	$45
32" Cabinet	CAB32	32" Cabinet	$32

Step 7: Check your work for errors by running an "Item Price List" under the "Inventory Reports" heading.

RECORDING PURCHASES OF MERCHANDISE

Purchases of inventory may be made for cash or on account (credit minus accounts payable). Purchases are normally recorded when the goods are received from the seller. Every purchase should be supported by business documents that provide written evidence of the transaction. A canceled check or a cash register receipt indicating the items purchased and amounts paid should support each cash purchase. Cash purchases are recorded by an increase in Merchandise Inventory and a decrease in Cash.

A purchase invoice should support each credit purchase. This document indicates the total purchase price and other relevant information, but the purchaser does not prepare a separate purchase invoice. Instead, the copy of the sales invoice sent by the seller is used by the buyer as a purchase invoice.

To enter the purchase of inventory items:

Step 1: At the bottom of the Peachtree Accounting window screen is a row of "navigator" icons, click "Inventory" (Figure 5.5) to obtain the pop-up screen shown in Figure 5.6.

Figure 5. 5 Inventory Icon at bottom of Peachtree screen.

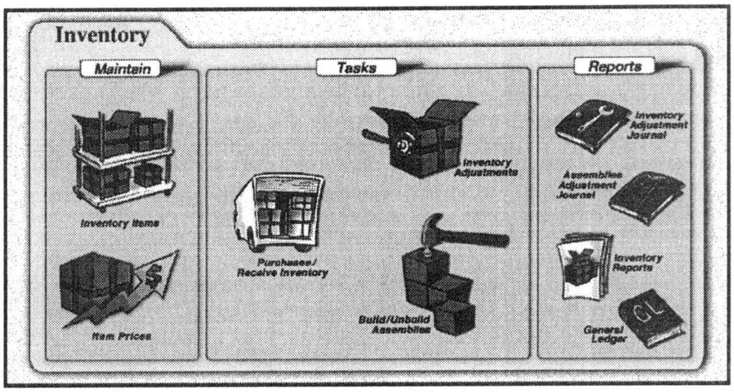

Figure 5. 6 Inventory Navigator icons

Step 2: Click on the "Purchases/Receive Inventory" icon (the back of the truck) in the middle section. You will then be presented with the form pictured in Figure 5.7 on the next page.

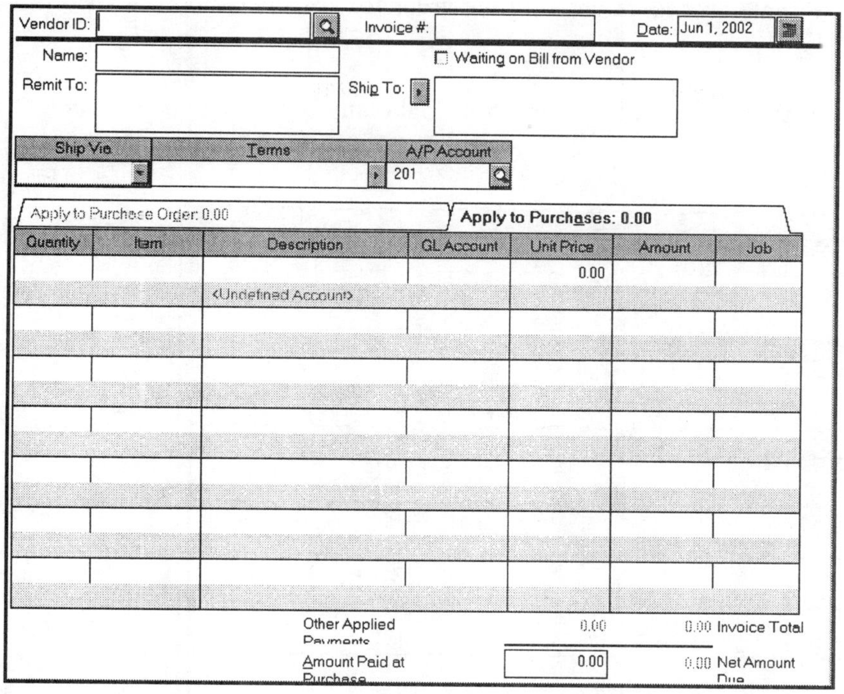

Figure 5. 7 Inventory form maintaining cost of items purchased.

On June 3, 2002, Beyer Video purchased: two “19 Color TV's for $175/ea, six 25” Color TV's for $225/ea and four 32” color TV's for $300/ea from Southern Video. The Invoice Number is 0603a and the GL Account is the Merchandise Inventory Account No. 106. The Accounts Payable Account No. 201 has been defaulted for you.

Step 1: Referring to Figure 5.7, click on the magnifying glass at the vendor ID text box to get a pull-down listing of all of the available vendors. This is the list you composed earlier.

Step 2: Find and double click on vendor V102, Southern Video. Notice all of the information that has now been entered on the form for you, including billing and shipping addresses.

Step 3: Enter 0603a as the invoice number. Note that this is the invoice to be issued from the vendor.

Step 4: You will enter the purchasing information on the main body of the form. We'll be ordering three items from Southern Video. Under “quantity” enter 2.0. Again, the decimal must be entered.

Step 5: Tab to the next space, “Item,” and click on the magnifying glass. The pull-down menu is a listing of all of the items available for our company, Beyer Video, to purchase and sell. Find and click on ID No. TV19, which is the 19” color TV. The General Ledger account number for Merchandise Inventory will be automatically entered for you. However, because the cost may change at will by the vendor, you must enter the individual item cost $175.00. The extended cost will be figured for you.

Step 6: Repeat the same procedure entering the order for six 25" Color Televisions and four 32" color TV's.

Step 7: Your entry should look like Figure 5.8. Make any necessary changes before saving your order.

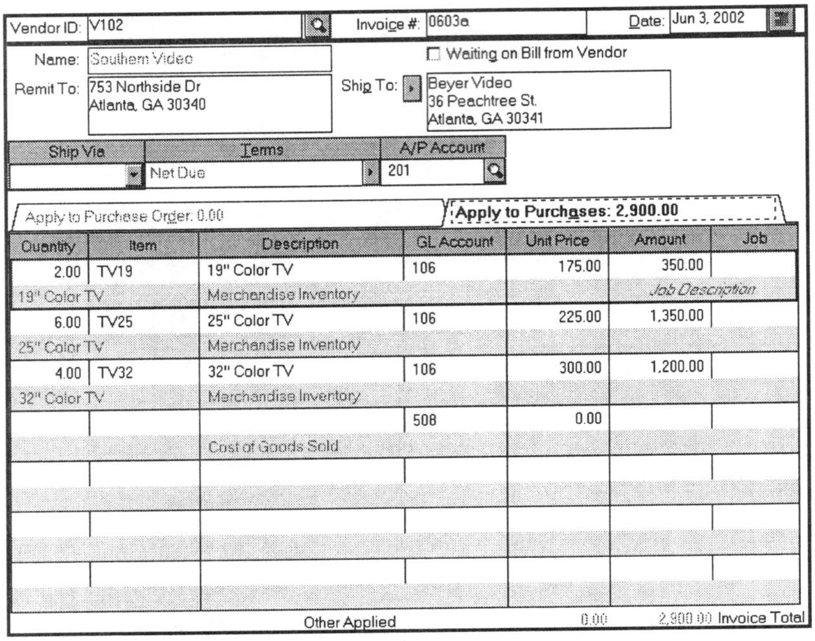

Figure 5. 8 Purchase Inventory form.

Some of the prices that Beyer will pay for items will change. When you enter cost information into the system, it will be automatically default to that cost the next time you enter the item. If it is the same, no changes are needed. If the price (cost) does change, however, the new price must be entered for accurate accounting.

Table 5.3 Additional inventory purchases

			Additional Purchases			
Date Purchased	*Invoice Number*	*Cost*	*Inventory Item*	*Quantity*	*ID No.*	*Vendor*
June 10	0610	$145	DVD Player	30	DV01	Ivory
		$200	Stereo VCR	30	VC23	Ivory
		$500	Home Stereo	10	ST61	Ivory
		$500	Surround Sound	25	SU85	Ivory
		$200	Computer Monitor	5	MO17	Ivory
June 15	0615	$750	Projection System	1	PROJ	Atlanta TV
		$750	Flat Screen System	1	FLAT	Atlanta TV
June 18	0618	$ 10	19" Cabinet	5	CAB19	Columbus Imports
		$ 20	25" Cabinet	10	CAB25	Columbus Imports
		$ 22	32" Cabinet	5	CAB32	Columbus Imports
June 19	0619	$165	19" Color TV	3	TV19	Southern Video
		$230	25" Color TV	2	TV25	Southern Video
		$275	32" Color TV	1	TV32	Southern Video

June 21	0621	$150	DVD Player	5	ST61	Ivory
		$225	Stereo VCR	2	VC23	Ivory
June 27	0627	$ 10	19" Cabinet	3	CAB19	Columbus
		$ 20	25" Cabinet	2	CAB25	Columbus
		$ 30	32" Cabinet	1	CAB32	Columbus

In order to check your work, run an inventory valuation report. A portion of the report is shown in Figure 5.9.

Beyer Video
Inventory Valuation Report
As of Jun 30, 2002

Filter Criteria includes: 1) Stock/Assembly. Report order is by ID. Report is printed with Truncated Long Descriptions.

Item ID Item Class	Item Description	Unit	Cost Met	Qty on Hand	Item Value	Avg Cost	% of Inv Valu
CAB19 Stock item	19" TV Cabinet		FIFO	8.00	80.00		0.25
CAB25 Stock item	25" TV Cabinet		FIFO	12.00	240.00		0.74
CAB32 Stock item	32" TV Cabinet		FIFO	6.00	140.00		0.43
DV01 Stock item	DVD Player		FIFO	3.00	435.00		1.35
FLAT Stock item	Flat Screen System		FIFO	1.00	750.00		2.33
MO17 Stock item	Computer Monitor		FIFO	5.00	1,000.00		3.10
PROJ Stock item	Projection System		FIFO	1.00	750.00		2.33
ST61 Stock item	Home Stereo		FIFO	15.00	5,750.00		17.84
SU85 Stock item	Surround Sound		FIFO	25.00	12,500.00		38.79
TV19 Stock item	19" Color TV		FIFO	5.00	845.00		2.62
TV25 Stock item	25" Color TV		FIFO	8.00	1,810.00		5.62

Figure 5. 9 Inventory Summary Valuation Report

ENTERING INVENTORY ADJUSTMENTS

Occasionally, you may need to record adjustments to on-hand quantities of inventory items. The inventory adjustment task makes it easy to make and track these adjustments

There are two types of inventory adjustments, increases in quantity and decreases in quantity. For an adjustment up, you will enter a positive quantity and can also enter a unit cost. This will increase your quantity on hand and total inventory value much as a purchase would. If you previously miscounted your inventory and now have more units on hand than you realized, you could adjust up.

For an adjustment down, you will enter a negative quantity, but you can't enter a unit cost. Peachtree will figure out the cost value that these units are being removed at, much like a sale. An inventory adjustment down will decrease the quantity on hand as well as the total value. For example, if something was stolen or broken or if inventory was previously miscounted, you would adjust down.

When you make an adjustment, the Cost of Goods Sold, Inventory Total Value, and Inventory G/L accounts are all updated.

To record an inventory adjustment

Step 1: From the Tasks menu, select Inventory Adjustments. Peachtree displays the inventory adjustment window as shown in Figure 5.10.

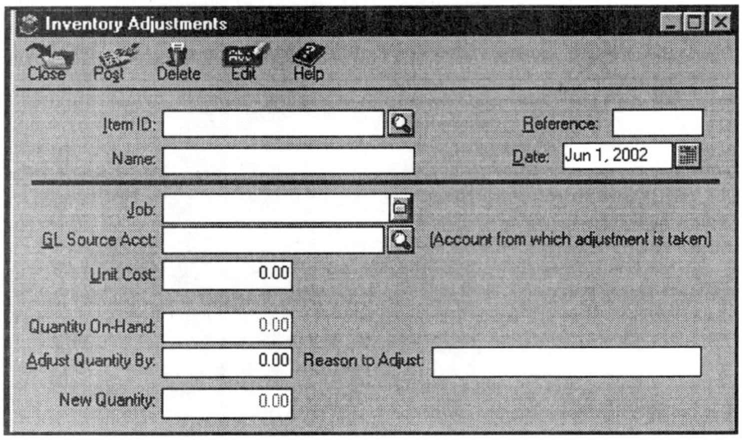

Figure 5. 10 Inventory Adjustment Window.

Step 2: Enter or select the item ID you want to adjust. To display a list of existing items, type **?** in the field, or select the Lookup button (magnifying glass). This can only be done if an item is classified as a stock item.

Step 3: The Reference Field is for internal use. However, the text is limited to 20 alphanumeric characters.

Step 4: Enter the date that the change in inventory occurred (or the date of the physical inventory count).

Step 5: The default GL Source Account is the Cost of Goods Sold Account. The other account affected by adjustments will probably be the Inventory Account (Merchandise Inventory). Both of these account numbers are defaulted on the form.

Step 6: The Unit Cost default is the current cost of the item and must be positive.

Step 7: Enter the amount by which to adjust the quantity. The Quantity on Hand is already filled in, and Peachtree Accounting calculates the New Quantity after you enter the adjustment.

Step 8: If you know the reason for the adjustment, enter it. For example, Found in warehouse or Theft. Post or Save the adjustment by selecting the appropriate button.

If you made entries in the previous section, do not post your work. *Cancel* the form and continue to the next activity.

ENTER AND APPLY A VENDOR CREDIT MEMO

Occasionally, a vendor may issue you credit. This happens when the purchaser is dissatisfied with the merchandise received, or if the goods are damaged or defective. When this occurs, the purchaser may return the goods to the seller. The purchaser is then granted credit if the sale was made on credit or a cash refund if the purchase was for cash. This transaction is known as a purchase return. Sometimes the purchaser may choose to keep the merchandise if the seller is willing to grant an allowance (deduction) from the purchase price. This is known as a purchase allowance.

To record these types of transaction, use the Purchases/Receive Inventory form.

In our example, we will return the Projection System, on June 29, to Atlanta TV for a credit on our account.

Step 1: From the Tasks menu, select purchase/receive inventory form. The vendor ID for Atlanta Television is V103.

Step 2: If the credit memo resulted from a reduction in your inventory, enter a negative number in front of the quantity. If the credit memo doesn't affect your inventory, enter a negative number in front of the amount.

Step 3: In our example, since we are returning the projection system, a negative amount will be entered for both the quantity (to remove it from inventory) and the amount (to remove it from accounts payable). Enter "-1" in the quantity column.

Step 4: Select the item to be returned, "PROJ" and the cost "- $750" will be generated by the system into the amount column.

Step 5: Check your work for any errors with the completed form shown in Figure 5.11.

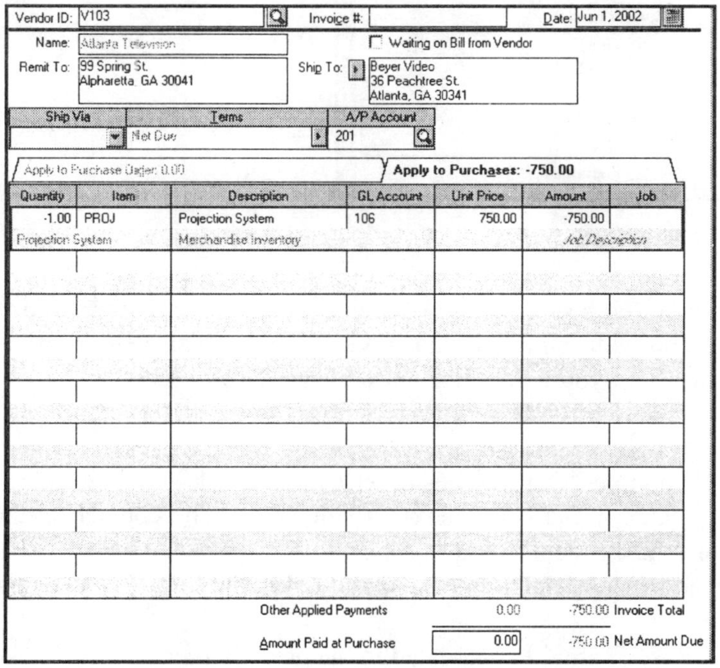

Figure 5. 11 Completed "Credit Memo" returning goods to the supplier for credit on account.

Step 6: Click the "Save" button to save the transaction.

RECORDING THE SALES OF MERCHANDISE

Sales revenue, like service revenues are recorded when earned. This is in accordance with the revenue recognition principle. Typically, sales revenues are earned when the goods are transferred from the seller to the buyer. At this point the sales transaction is completed and the sales price has been established.

Sales may be made on credit or for cash. Every sales transaction should be supported by a business document that provides written evidence of the sale. Cash register tapes provide evidence of cash sales. A sales invoice, such as the one shown in Figure 5.11 provides support for a credit sale. The original copy of the invoice goes to the customer. A copy is kept by the seller for use in recording the sale. The invoice shows the date of sale, customer name, total sales price, and other relevant information.

Companies that sell goods on credit keep a listing of their customers, their addresses, contact information, credit limits, etc. Those entries are made in Peachtree using the "Maintain Customer Form" as shown in Figure 5.12.

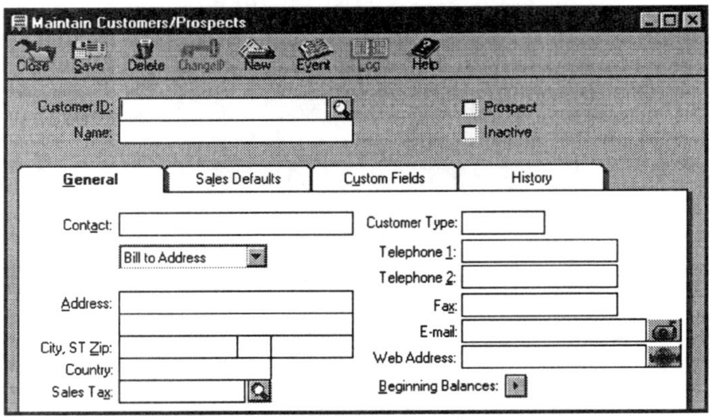

Figure 5. 12 Maintain Customers Form

Use the Maintain Customers/Prospects window to enter, change, and store information about companies and people to whom you sell goods and services. You can also enter information about companies and people with whom you would like to do business (prospects).

Step 1: Enter the customer ID number. Our first customer's ID is C101.
Step 2: Enter the customer's name in the Name box: Adam Zoula. The contact, in the next box is the same as the customer, Adam Zoula.
Step 3: Enter Mr. Zoula's address in the proper boxes: 347 Appling Dr., Atlanta, GA 30300.
Step 4: Ignore the Sales Tax box. That will be updated in the next chapter.
Step 5: For the sake of time and typing, we will leave the phone numbers, beginning balances, e-mail, Web sites and fax numbers blank for now.
Step 6: Click on the Sales Default tab and change the GL/Sales Account to Acct # 400/Sales.
Step 7: At the bottom of the form, click on the "Terms" button to get the window shown in Figure 5.13.
Step 8: Delete the check mark at "Use Standard Terms." Click on "Due in # days" and enter 30 in the net due days box.
Step 9: Change the credit limit to $5000.

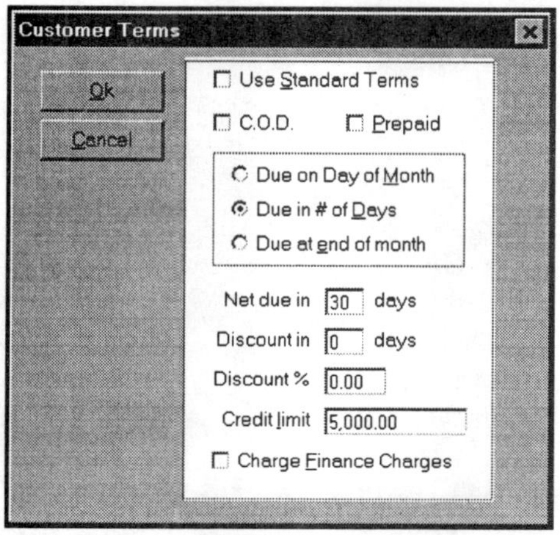

Figure 5. 13 Customer terms

Step 10: Check your work with the completed forms below in Figure 5.14 before continuing with the remaining three customers in Table 5.4. Remember to change the terms and the credit limit under the "Sales Default" tab.

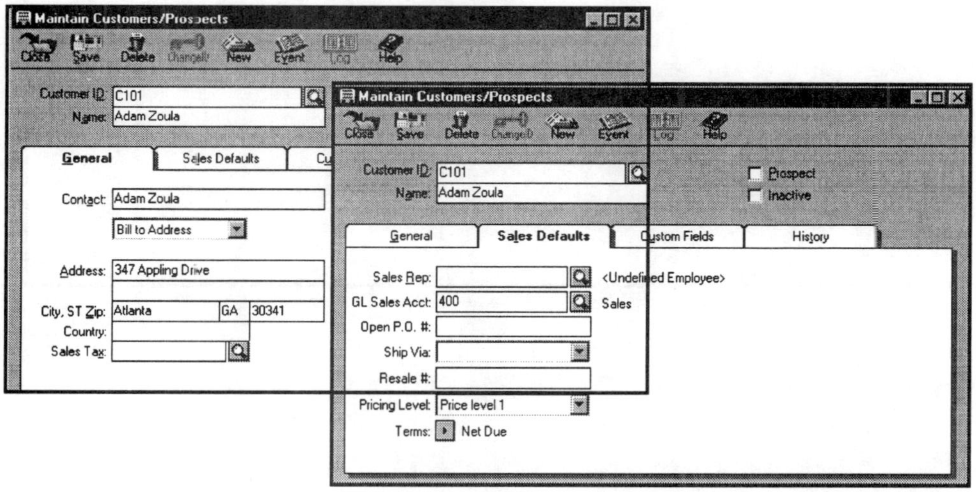

Figure 5. 14 Completed Customer entry.

Table 5.4 Additional customers to be included on client list.

	Additional Customers		
Customer ID	*C102*	*C103*	*C104*
Name	Betty Young	Cathy Xao	Donald Walace
Contact	Betty Young	Cathy Xao	Donald Walace
Address	347 Appling Dr. Atlanta, GA 30300	513 Lake Cir. Atlanta, GA 30340	1397 Toyta Dr. Atlanta, GA 30302

After entering the customers above, run the Customer Master File list. The report is shown in Figure 5.15 below. The sales invoice can be found in the "Sales" section of the Navigation bar located at the bottom of the Peachtree Main screen.

Beyer Video
Customer Master File List

Filter Criteria includes: Report order is by ID.

Customer ID **Customer**	**Address line 1** **Address line 2** **City ST ZIP**	**Contact** **Telephone 1** **Telephone 2** **Fax Number**	**Tax Code** **Resale No** **Terms** **Cust Since**
C101 Adam Zoula	347 Appling Drive Atlanta, GA 30341	Adam Zoula	 Net Due 11/16/00
C102 Betty Young	513 Lake Circle Atlanta, GA 30300	Betty Young	 Net Due 11/16/00
C103 Cathy Xao	1397 Toyta Drive Hoyta, GA 30300	Cathy Xao	 Net Due 11/16/00
C104 Donald Wallace	1400 Barnes Drive Noble, GA 30041	Donald Wallace	 Net Due 11/16/00

Figure 5. 15 Master Customer List Report

Step 1: Click on the "Sales" icon on the navigation bar to get the "Sales" navigation activities. They are shown below in Figure 5.16.

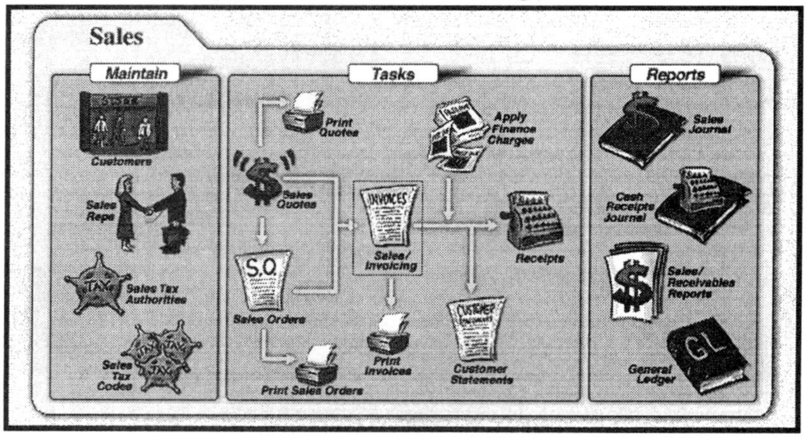

Figure 5. 16 Sales Activities.

Click on Sales Invoicing in the “Tasks” section to get the sales invoice as shown in Figure 5.16. The form should look familiar. It is similar to the form used to enter inventory items into the system.

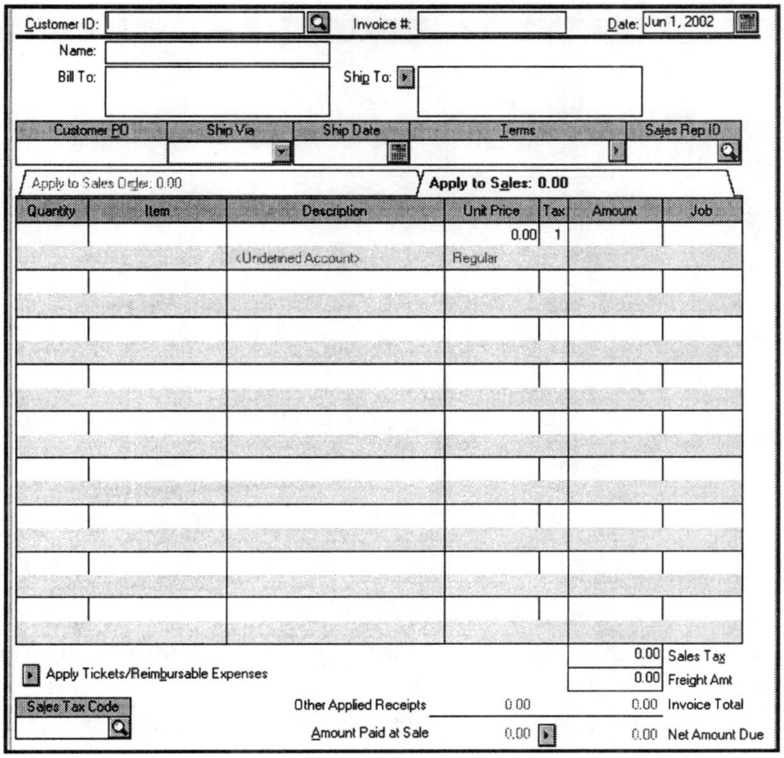

Figure 5. 17 The Sales Invoice

Step 2: Enter the customer ID number for “Adam Zoula.” C101 is the number. The invoice number is 0612. Information such as billing address will be entered by the default information entered earlier in the Customer Entry procedure.

Step 3: Mr. Zoula is buying a 25” Color TV with the matching cabinet and a VCR. Enter the information on the form. It is correctly filled out in Figure 5.18. Suggestion: take advantage of the magnifying glass that gives you the drop down list of required information.

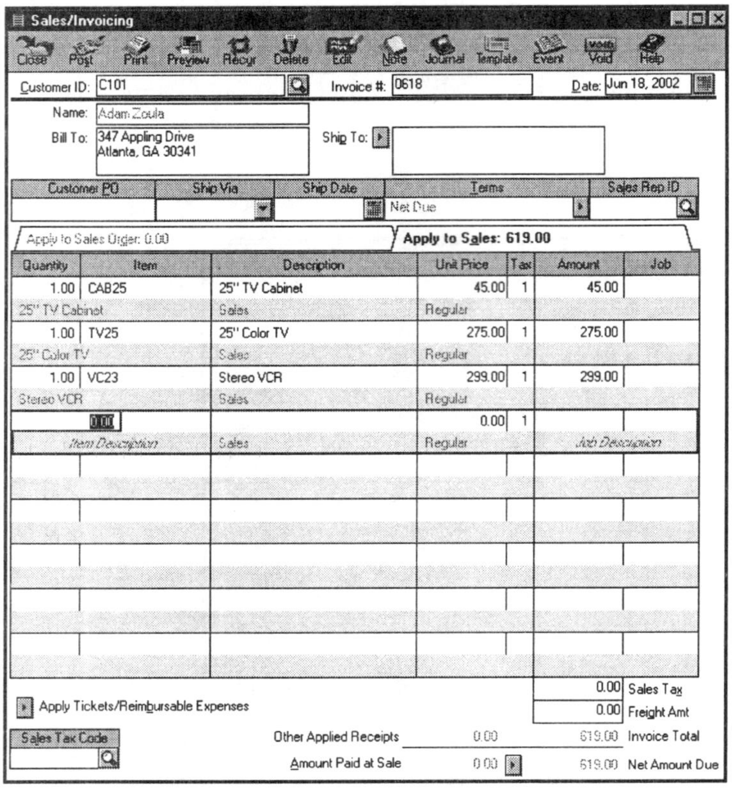

Figure 5. 18 Completed Sales Invoice.

Table 5.5 lists the other items customers purchased during this accounting period. Make the entries for each customer following the previous instructions.

Table 5. 5 Additional Customer Purchases

Customer ID	*Customer Name*	*Date of Purchase*	*Invoice Number*	*Items Purchased*
C102	Betty Young	6/21/02	0621	1. Home Stereo System (ST61) 2. 25" Color TV (TV25) 3. Stereo VCR (VC23)
C103	Cathy Xao	6/14/02	0614	1. DVD Player (DV01) 2. 32" Color TV (TV32) 3. 32" Color TV Cabinet (CAB32) 4. Surround Sound System (SU85)
C104	Donald Wallace	6/27/02	0627	1. 25" Color TV (TV25) 2. Stereo VCR (VC23) 3. DVD Player (DV01)

Run a "Items Sold to Customers" report under the "Accounts Receivable" report list to check your work. A portion of the report is shown in Figure 5.19.

Beyer Video
Items Sold to Customers
For the Period From Jun 1, 2002 to Jun 30, 2002
Filter Criteria includes: Report order is by Customer ID, Item ID. Report is printed in Detail Format.

Customer ID Name	Item ID	Qty	Amount	Cost of Sales	Gross Profit	Gross Margi
C101	CAB25	1.00	45.00	20.00	25.00	55.56
Adam Zoula	TV25	1.00	275.00	225.00	50.00	18.18
	VC23	1.00	299.00	200.00	99.00	33.11
		3.00	619.00	445.00	174.00	28.11
C102	ST61	1.00	750.00	500.00	250.00	33.33
Betty Young	TV25	1.00	275.00	225.00	50.00	18.18
	VC23	1.00	299.00	200.00	99.00	33.11
		3.00	1,324.00	925.00	399.00	30.14
C103	CAB32	1.00	32.00		32.00	100.00
Cathy Xao	DV01	1.00	199.00	145.00	54.00	27.14
	SU85	0.01	9.50	5.00	4.50	47.37
	TV32	1.00	325.00	300.00	25.00	7.69
		3.01	565.50	450.00	115.50	20.42

Figure 5. 19 Portion of "Items Sold to Customers" report.

Notice the information given on the report including: Quantity of Items Sold, the Total Amount (revenue), the Cost of Goods Sold (an expense), the Gross Profit on the item(s) sold, and the Gross Profit Margin. Managers are always interested in those figures.

MULTIPLE STEP INCOME STATEMENT

The multiple step income statement is so named because it shows the steps in determining net income (or net loss). Two steps are shown, (1.) Cost of Goods Sold which is subtracted from net sales and results in Gross Profit, and (2.) Operating Expenses which are deducted from the Gross Profit and results in Net Income.

The top portion of the multiple step income statement, Cost of Goods Sold, for the data entered thus far in this chapter, is shown on 5.20.

Beyer Video
Income Statement
For the One Month Ending June 30, 2002

		Current Month			Year to Date	
Revenues						
Sales	$	3,281.50	100.00	$	3,281.50	100.00
Total Revenues		3,281.50	100.00		3,281.50	100.00
Cost of Sales						
Cost of Goods Sold		2,412.00	73.50		2,412.00	73.50
Freight		0.00	0.00		0.00	0.00
Total Cost of Sales		2,412.00	73.50		2,412.00	73.50
Gross Profit		869.50	26.50		869.50	26.50

Figure 5. 20 Top portion of Income Statement showing Sales and Cost of Goods Sold

Demonstration Problem

The General Ledger Trial Balance for January 2002 for Dykstra Co. is shown below. Open the company on your Student Data Disk.

Dykstra Company
General Ledger Trial Balance
As of Jan 31, 2002

Filter Criteria includes: Report order is by ID. Report is printed in Detail Format.

Account ID	Account Description	Debit Amt	Credit Amt
10100	Cash on Hand	14,500.00	
11000	Accounts Receivable	11,100.00	
12000	Product Inventory	29,000.00	
14000	Prepaid Expenses	2,500.00	
15100	Equipment	95,000.00	
17100	Accum. Depreciation - Equi		18,000.00
20000	Accounts Payable		10,600.00
27000	Notes Payable-Noncurrent		25,000.00
39005	Retained Earnings		81,000.00
39007	Owner's Draw	12,000.00	
40000	Sales-Merchandise		536,800.00
40600	Interest Income		2,500.00
48000	Sales Returns and Allowan	6,700.00	
49000	Sales Discounts	5,000.00	
50000	Cost of Goods Sold	363,400.00	
57500	Cost of Sales-Freight	7,600.00	
60100	Advertising Expense	12,000.00	
64000	Depreciation Expense	9,000.00	
67000	Insurance Expense	4,500.00	
67500	Interest Expense	3,600.00	
74000	Rent or Lease Expense	24,000.00	
77000	Salaries Expense	56,000.00	
78000	Utilities Expense	18,000.00	
	Total:	673,900.00	673,900.00

Instructions:

a. Prepare an Income Statement based on the above data.
b. Prepare an Income/Retained Earnings Statement.

Solution to Demonstrtion Problem

Income/Retained Earnings Statement

Dykstra Company
Statement of Income and Retained Earnings
For the One Month Ending January 31, 2002

	Current Month		Year to Date	
Revenues				
Sales-Merchandise	536,800.00	101.74	536,800.00	101.74
Interest Income	2,500.00	0.47	2,500.00	0.47
Sales Returns and Allowances	<6,700.00>	<1.27>	<6,700.00>	<1.27>
Sales Discounts	<5,000.00>	<0.95>	<5,000.00>	<0.95>
Total Revenues	527,600.00	100.00	527,600.00	100.00
Cost of Sales				
Cost of Goods Sold	363,400.00	68.88	363,400.00	68.88
Cost of Sales-Freight	7,600.00	1.44	7,600.00	1.44
Total Cost of Sales	371,000.00	70.32	371,000.00	70.32
Gross Profit	156,600.00	29.68	156,600.00	29.68
Expenses				
Advertising Expense	12,000.00	2.27	12,000.00	2.27
Depreciation Expense	9,000.00	1.71	9,000.00	1.71
Insurance Expense	4,500.00	0.85	4,500.00	0.85
Interest Expense	3,600.00	0.68	3,600.00	0.68
Rent or Lease Expense	24,000.00	4.55	24,000.00	4.55
Salaries Expense	56,000.00	10.61	56,000.00	10.61
Utilities Expense	18,000.00	3.41	18,000.00	3.41
Total Expenses	127,100.00	24.09	127,100.00	24.09
Net Income	29,500.00	5.59	29,500.00	5.59
Beginning Retained Earnings	0.00		0.00	
Adjustments To Date	81,000.00		81,000.00	
Owner's Draw	<12,000.00>		<12,000.00>	
Ending Retained Earnings	$ 98,500.00		98,500.00	

Income Statement

Dykstra Company
Income Statement
For the One Month Ending January 31, 2002

		Current Month			Year to Date	
Revenues						
Sales-Merchandise	$	536,800.00	101.74	$	536,800.00	101.74
Interest Income		2,500.00	0.47		2,500.00	0.47
Sales Returns and Allowances		<6,700.00>	<1.27>		<6,700.00>	<1.27>
Sales Discounts		<5,000.00>	<0.95>		<5,000.00>	<0.95>
Total Revenues		527,600.00	100.00		527,600.00	100.00
Cost of Sales						
Cost of Goods Sold		363,400.00	68.88		363,400.00	68.88
Cost of Sales-Freight		7,600.00	1.44		7,600.00	1.44
Total Cost of Sales		371,000.00	70.32		371,000.00	70.32
Gross Profit		156,600.00	29.68		156,600.00	29.68
Expenses						
Advertising Expense		12,000.00	2.27		12,000.00	2.27
Depreciation Expense		9,000.00	1.71		9,000.00	1.71
Insurance Expense		4,500.00	0.85		4,500.00	0.85
Interest Expense		3,600.00	0.68		3,600.00	0.68
Rent or Lease Expense		24,000.00	4.55		24,000.00	4.55
Salaries Expense		56,000.00	10.61		56,000.00	10.61
Utilities Expense		18,000.00	3.41		18,000.00	3.41
Total Expenses		127,100.00	24.09		127,100.00	24.09
Net Income	$	29,500.00	5.59	$	29,500.00	5.59

P5-2a

Hubbs Distributing Co. completed the following merchandising transactions in the month of April. At the beginning of April, the ledger of Hubbs showed Cash of $9,000 and M. Hubbs, Capital of $9,000.

April 2 Purchased merchandise on account, 100 pieces of material at $59 each from Leshner Supply Co. $5,900 total, terms 2/10,n/30.

4 Sold merchandise on account 20 pieces of material at $260 each, $5,200 total, terms 2/10,n/30. To Lulu's Bait and Tackle Shop (make up address, etc.)

5 Paid $200 freight on April 4th sale.

6 Received credit from Leshner Supply Co. for 15 pieces of material returned.

11 Paid Leshner Supply Co. in full, less discount.

13 Received collections in full, less discounts, from customer billed on April 4.

April 14 Purchased additional merchandise for cash, 44 pieces of material at $100 each, $4,400 total.

16 Received refund from supplier on cash purchase of April 14, $500. 5 pieces of material were returned.

18 Purchased merchandise from Testa Distributors, 60 pieces of material at $70 each, $4,200 total, terms 2/10,n/30

20 Paid freight on April 18th purchase $100

23 Sold merchandise for cash, 25 pieces of material at $240 each, $6,000 total.

26 Purchased merchandise for cash $2,300. 23 pieces of material at $100 each.

27 Paid Testa Distributors in full, less discount

29 Made refunds to cash customers for defective merchandise $240. 10 pieces of material were returned. The returned merchandise had a scrap value of $30.

30 Sold merchandise 370 pieces of material on account to Piedmont Crash Club, $3,700 total, terms n/30. (Again, make up the address etc.)

Hubbs Co.'s chart of accounts includes the following: No. 101 Cash, No. 112 Accounts Receivable, No. 120 Merchandise Inventory, No. 201 Accounts Payable, No. 301 M. Hubbs, Capital, No. 401 Sales, No. 412 Sales Returns and Allowance, No. 414 Sales Discounts, No. 505 cost of Goods Sold and No. 644 Freight Out.

Instructions:

a. Create the needed accounts. The capital account and the cash account have been created for you.
b. Create the sales and receipts invoices assigning each transaction to its specific account.
c. Prepare an Income Statement, Retained Earnings Statement and a Balance Sheet as of the end of April for Hubbs Co.

P5-4a

Mike Young, a former professional tennis star, Operates Mike's Tennis Shop at Jackson Lake Resort. At the beginning of the current season, the ledger of Mike's Tennis Shop showed Cash $2,500, Merchandise Inventory $1,700 and M. Young, Capital $4,200. The following transactions were completed during April.

April 4 Purchased 80 racquets at $8 each from Sampras Co. $640, total

6 Paid freight on purchase from Sampras Co. $40

8 Sold 20 of the newly purchased racquets to club members for S90 each, terms n/30.

10 Received credit from Sampras for two of the racquets that were not strung right. They were returned.

11 Purchased 300 pairs of tennis shoes from Alan Sports for cash, $1 each.

13 Paid Sampras in full.

14 Purchased 70 sets of shirts and matching shorts from Tiger's Sportsware, $10 per set, $700 total.

April	17	Paid freight on Tiger's Sportsware purchase of $30.
	18	Sold 20 sets of the shirts and matching shorts to club members for $50 per set on account.
	20	Received $500 from various members on their accounts.
	21	Paid Tiger's Sportsware in full
	30	Received an additional $750 from various members on their accounts.

Mike's chart of accounts includes the following: No. 101 Cash, No. 112 Accounts Receivable, No. 120 Merchandise Inventory, No. 201 Accounts Payable, No. 301 M. Young, Capital, No. 401 Sales, No. 412 Sales Returns and Allowance, No. 414 Sales Discounts, No. 505 cost of Goods Sold and No. 644 Freight Out.

Instructions:

d. Create the needed accounts. The capital account and the cash account have been created for you.
e. Create the sales and receipts invoices assigning each transaction to its specific account.
f. Prepare an Income Statement, Retained Earnings Statement and a Balance Sheet as of the end of April for Mike's Tennis Shop.

CHAPTER 6

Inventories

OBJECTIVES

- Be able to determine the various cost methods involved in inventory valuation: LIFO, FIFO and Average Cost.
- Explain the advantages of using an automated inventory system.
- Be able to recognize inventory default information
- Understand cost of goods sold, including Freight, tax and shipping
- Be able to prepare a history of inventory items; "what has come in and what has gone out."
- Be able to make Inventory adjustments in an automated system.
- Be able to prepare the various Inventory reports

ADVANTAGES OF USING THE PEACHTREE INVENTORY SYSTEM

Peachtree Accounting automatically keeps track of each of the inventory items bought and sold. The quantities are updated after each posted purchase and sale. The three-step process in tracking inventory in Peachtree involves:

1. Entering the item information, which includes the Sales account, the Inventory account, and the Cost of Sales account.
2. Using the "item codes" whenever a purchase or a sale is made.
3. Entering adjustments to the inventory, through the Inventory Adjustments Task.

The inventory navigation aid, found at the bottom of the main Peachtree window can be used to complete many of those tasks. It is shown in Figure 6.1.

As you saw in the previous chapter, through Maintain Inventory items you can set up your system with the goods and/or services you sell. A unit price (or a different pricing scale) can be set up and adjusted. When you enter a purchase or a sale of an item, everything is automatically updated for you. All totals are computed on the sales invoice.

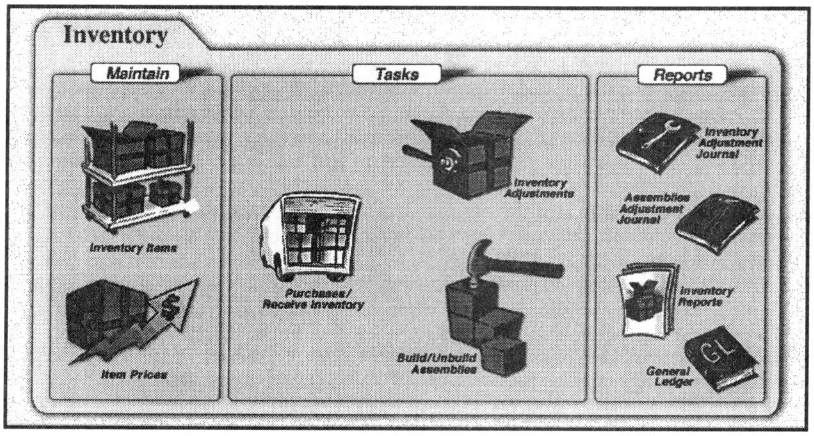

Figure 6. 1 The Inventory Navigation Aid

COST METHODS

Three different cost methods for inventory are available to use as shown in Figure 6.2. The cost methods, shown on the pull-down menu, are:

- Average Cost
- LIFO (Last In, First Out)
- FIFO (First In, First Out)

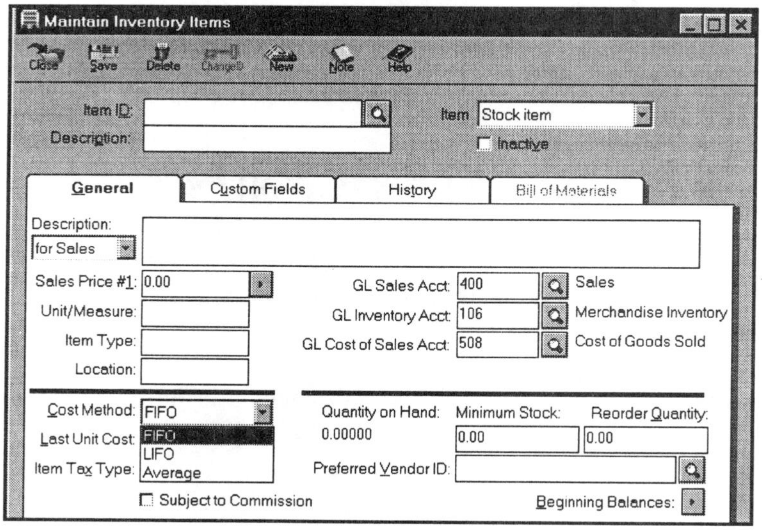

Figure 6. 2 The Maintain Inventory Items form.

Average Cost

The average cost method keeps track of the cost for each stock-type item. Each time you make a purchase, the average cost for that item is recalculated.

Whenever you sell an inventory item that has an average cost type, Peachtree Accounting uses the average cost it has been tracking to compute the Cost of Goods Sold. The Cost of Goods Sold is the average cost times the quantity of the item sold. On a daily basis, an entry is made to the Cost of Goods Sold account that encompasses the sales for the day.

Please refer back to your text for additional details and examples.

Example – Average Cost

The company, Average Sales Company, on January 1, 2002 buys three AVGUNITS for $2/ea. On January 15, 2002 three more are purchased for $1/each. The average cost thus far would be $1.50 ($9 divided by 6 Average Units)

Run a purchase journal report:

Step 1: On your student data disk, open the company: "Average Sales Company."

Step 2: From the reports menu, select "Accounts Payable," then double click on "Purchase Journal."

Look at the Purchase Journal shown in Figure 6.3 to see how the two purchases affected the Accounts Payable (liability) account and the Merchandise Inventory (asset) account.

Average Sales Company
Purchase Journal
For the Period From Jan 1, 2002 to Jan 31, 2002
Filter Criteria includes: Report order is by Date. Report is printed in Detail Format.

Date	Account ID Account Description	Invoice #	Line Description	Debit Amoun	Credit Amount
1/1/02	110 Merchandise Inventory	010202	Average Inventory Unit for Retail	6.00	
	205 Accounts Payable		Average Wholesale Company		6.00
1/15/02	110 Merchandise Inventory	011502	Average Inventory Unit for Retail	3.00	
	205 Accounts Payable		Average Wholesale Company		3.00
				9.00	9.00

Figure 6. 3 The Purchase Journal.

Example – Adjustments to Inventory

Peachtree Accounting makes it easy to conduct a physical inventory count by providing a form listing all of the inventory items and providing blanks to the side for an employee to write in the specific count of an inventory item.

Run an inventory item list report:

Step 1: From the reports area menu, choose "Inventory."

Step 2: From the reports list click on "Physical Inventory." It is a short list, since we have only one inventory item. The report is shown in Figure 6.4 below with the inventory count already completed.

Average Sales Company
Physical Inventory List
As of Jan 31, 2002
Filter Criteria includes: 1) Stock/Assembly. Report order is by ID. Report is printed with Truncated Long Descriptions.

Item ID	Item Description	Unit	Location	Count	By
AVGUNIT	Average Inventory Unit	Each	Atlanta	3	Brad

Figure 6. 4 Physical Inventory List

Based on Brad's report (Figure 6.4) it appears that three Average Units are missing from the warehouse. To account for the missing items, an inventory adjustment must be made. This can be done through the "Tasks" menu.

Step 1: From the "Tasks" menu, click on "Inventory Adjustments." The completed entry window is shown in Figure 6.5.
Step 2: In the blank window, enter the Item ID. Once the Item ID is entered the cost information is automatically generated.
Step 3: The reference number is "0125." Change the date to January 25, 2002.
Step 4: Make sure $2.00 appears in the "Unit Cost" text box. Make the change if it does not.

A new window is generated for each cost factor; meaning that if you change the "Unit Cost" the inventory count corresponding to that cost will appear in the window.

Brad said in his report, that three of the units have disappeared. We believe they are $2.00 cost units (Step 4).

Step 5: Enter "-3" (a negative number) in the "Adjust Quantity By" text box.
Step 6: Click "Post" to save your work.

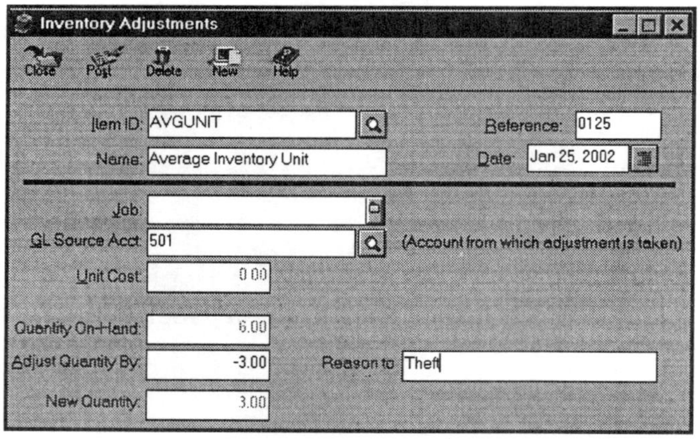

Figure 6. 5 Inventory Adjustments window.

The average cost of our units will still be $1.50 because the cost will not change even though units might be missing. The cost will not change even though your inventory has been adjusted down.

Example – Cost of Goods Sold
On January 30, 2002, Cindy Customer buys the remaining three average inventory units for $6/each. The cost of goods sold would be $4.50 (Average Cost * Quantity Sold) or ($1.50 * 3).

Record Cindy's Purchase:

Step 1: Click on the Sales navigation aid. Click on "Sales Invoicing" in the middle section.

Step 2: Complete the invoice (refer back to Chapter 5, if necessary). Cindy purchases three units at $6/each.

Step 3: Check your work for errors before continuing. The completed invoice is illustrated in Figure 6.6.

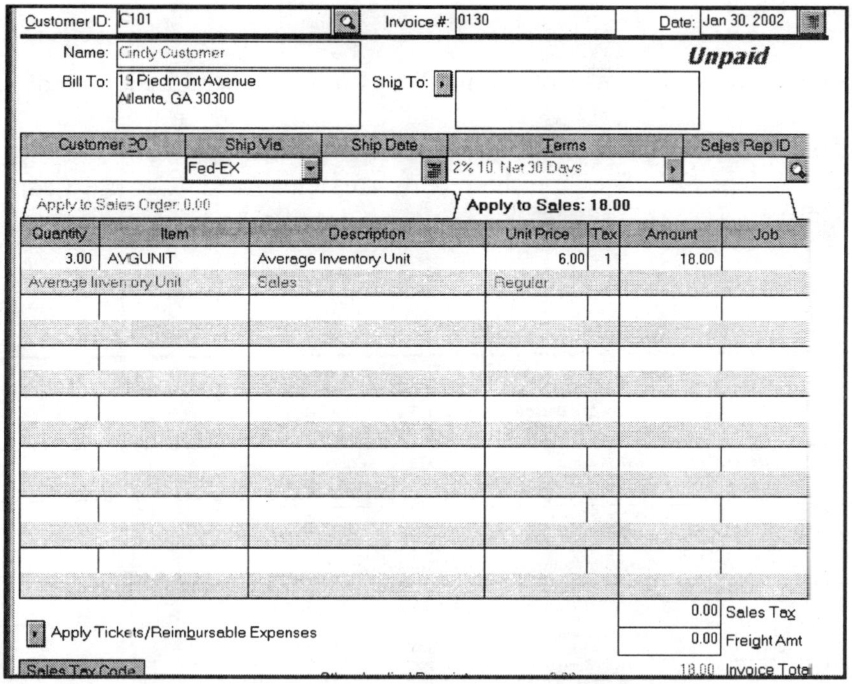

Figure 6. 6 Cindy Customer's invoice.

To see how accounts are affected, run an "Item Costing Report."

Step 1: Click on the reports menu and then click on "Inventory." Click on "Item Costing Report." The report is shown in Figure 6.7. Notice on the report each affect each transaction has on the inventory value.

Average Sales Company
Item Costing Report
For the Period From Jan 1, 2002 to Dec 31, 2003
Filter Criteria includes: Report order is by ID.

Item ID Item Description	Date	Qty Receive	Item Cost	Actual Cost	Assembly Qt Assembly ($)	Adjust Qt Adjust ($)	Quantity So	Cost of Sale	Remaining Qt	Remain Value
AVGUNIT Average Inventory Unit										
	1/1/02	3.00	2.00	6.00					3.00	6.00
	1/15/02	3.00	1.00	3.00					6.00	9.00
	1/25/02					-3.00 -4.50			3.00	4.50
	1/30/02						3.00	4.50		

Figure 6. 7 Item Costing Report

To see the "Big Picture" and how accounts have been affected, run a General Ledger Report.

Step 1: Click on the reports menu and then click on "General Ledger."
Step 2: Click on "General Ledger" on the reports area menu and "General Ledger" on the reports list.

A portion of the report is shown in Figure 6.8.

Average Sales Company
General Ledger
For the Period From Jan 1, 2002 to Jan 31, 2002
Filter Criteria includes: Report order is by ID. Report is printed with Truncated Transaction Descriptions and in Detail Format.

Account ID Account Description	Date	Referenc	Jrnl	Trans Description	Debit Amt	Credit Amt	Balance
105	1/1/02			Beginning Balance			
Accounts Receivable	1/30/02	0130	SJ	Cindy Customer	18.00		
				Current Period Change	18.00		18.00
	1/31/02			Ending Balance			18.00
110	1/1/02			Beginning Balance			
Merchandise Invento	1/1/02	010202	PJ	Average Wholesale Co	6.00		
	1/15/02	011502	PJ	Average Wholesale Co	3.00		
	1/25/02	0125	INAJ	Average Inventory Unit		4.50	
	1/30/02	0130	COG	Cindy Customer - Item:		4.50	
				Current Period Change	9.00	9.00	
	1/31/02			Ending Balance			
205	1/1/02			Beginning Balance			
Accounts Payable	1/1/02	010202	PJ	Average Wholesale Co		6.00	
	1/15/02	011502	PJ	Average Wholesale Co		3.00	
				Current Period Change		9.00	-9.00
	1/31/02			Ending Balance			-9.00

Figure 6. 8 General Ledger report.

Last In, First Out (LIFO)

The LIFO method keeps track of the price you paid for each group of units you receive at the same time at the same unit cost. LIFO costs your sales and values your inventory as if the items you sell are the ones you have received most recently (and remain unsold).

Select the LIFO method when you charge the most recent inventory costs against revenue. LIFO yields the lowest possible amount of net income in periods of constantly rising costs because the cost of the most recently acquired item more closely approximates the replacement cost of the item. Of course, in periods of declining costs, the effect is reversed.

Please refer back to your text for additional explanation and examples.

Example – LIFO

LIFO Sales Company, on January 1, 2002, buys 10 LIFO Units for $10/each. On January 5, 2002, 10 more are purchased for $12/each and on January 10, 2002 and additional 10 units were purchased at $13/each.

Run a Purchase Journal Report:

Step 1: On your student data disk, open the company: "LIFO Sales Company."

Step 2: From the reports menu, select "Accounts Payable," then double click on "Purchase Journal."

Look at the purchase journal in Figure 6.9 to see how the three purchases affected the Accounts Payable (liability) account and the Merchandise Inventory (asset) account.

LIFO Sales Company
Purchase Journal
For the Period From Jan 1, 2002 to Jan 31, 2002
Filter Criteria includes: Report order is by Date. Report is printed in Detail Format.

Date	Account ID Account Description	Invoice #	Line Description	Debit Amoun	Credit Amount
1/1/02	110 Merchandise Inventory	010103	LIFO Sales Units for Retail	100.00	
	205 Accounts Payable		LIFO Wholesale Company		100.00
1/5/02	110 Merchandise Inventory	010502	LIFO Sales Units for Retail	120.00	

Figure 6. 9 Purchase Journal for LIFO

On January 30, 2002, Cindy Customer buys 15 LIFO units; the first 10 units purchased cost $13/each, the next 5 units purchased cost the company $12/each.

We sold a total of 15 units:

(10 units @ $13/each = $130 and 5 units @ $12/each = $60 or a total cost of $190.)

Record Cindy's Purchase:

Step 1: Click on the Sales Navigation aid. Click on "Sales Invoicing" in the middle section.

Step 2: Complete the invoice. Cindy buys 15 units from us. Her price is $15/per unit.

Step 3: Check your work before continuing. The completed invoice is illustrated in Figure 6.10.

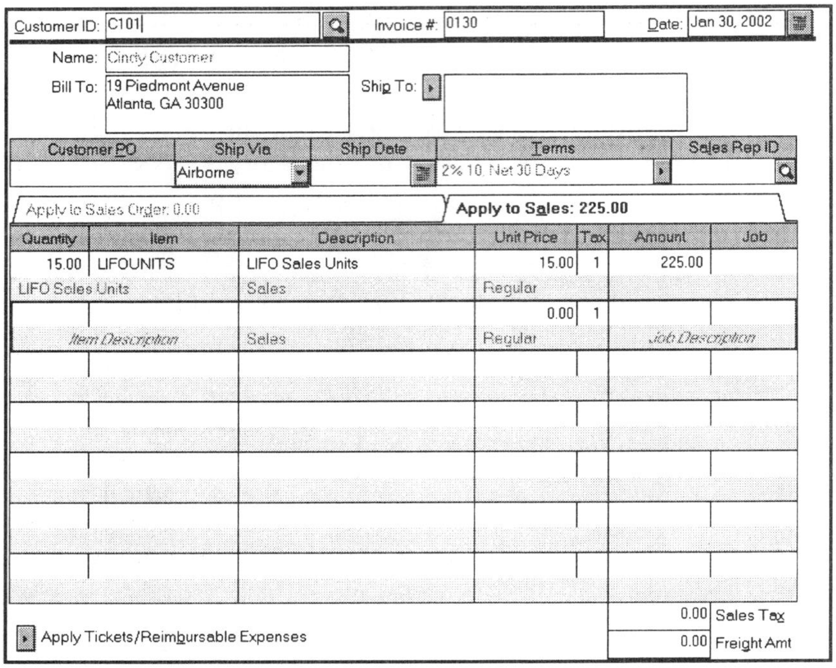

Figure 6. 10 Cindy's Customer Invoice (LIFO)

To see how accounts are affected, run an "Item Costing Report."

Step 1: Click on the reports menu and then click on "Inventory."

Step 2: Click on "Item Costing Report." The report is shown in Figure 6.11.

LIFO Sales Company
Item Costing Report
For the Period From Jan 1, 2002 to Dec 31, 2003
Filter Criteria includes: Report order is by ID.

Item ID Item Description	Date	Qty Receive	Item Cost	Actual Cost	Assembly Qt Assembly ($)	Adjust Qt Adjust ($)	Quantity So	Cost of Sale	Remaining Qt	Remain Value
LIFOUNITS LIFO Sales Units										
	1/1/02	10.00	10.00	100.00					10.00	100.00
	1/5/02	10.00	12.00	120.00					20.00	220.00
	1/10/02	10.00	13.00	130.00					30.00	350.00
	1/30/02						15.00	190.00	15.00	160.00

Figure 6. 11 Item Costing Report (LIFO)

Notice on the report how the transaction affected each of the cost items.

Let's look at the effect on our income and profits. Run a copy of the "Income Statement." The Income Statement is shown below in Figure 6.12. Notice how the costs have been reflected in Cost of Goods Sold and in Revenue. Hold on to this report because in the next section you will want to compare these totals with those obtained using the FIFO method of inventory tracking.

LIFO Sales Company Income Statement For the One Month Ending January 31, 2002						
		Current Month			Year to Date	
Revenues						
Sales	$	225.00	100.00	$	225.00	100.00
Total Revenues		225.00	100.00		225.00	100.00
Cost of Sales						
Purchases		190.00	84.44		190.00	84.44
Total Cost of Sales		190.00	84.44		190.00	84.44
Gross Profit		35.00	15.56		35.00	15.56
Expenses						
Theft		0.00	0.00		0.00	0.00
Total Expenses		0.00	0.00		0.00	0.00
Net Income	$	35.00	15.56	$	35.00	15.56

Figure 6. 12 LIFO Income Statement

Here is how we got the amounts shown in Figure 6.12.

Revenue:
Sales or Revenue was obtained by multiplying the number of units Cindy bought (15) by the unit price ($15) or $225.

Cost of Sales (Purchases):
Cost of Sales (Purchases) were obtained by the cost of the first 10 units that were purchased last (10 * $13) plus the cost of the next 5 units purchased (5 * $12) or $190.

Gross Profit:
Gross Profit was obtained by subtracting Purchases ($190) from Total Revenue ($225) or $35. Because, in our example, no other expenses were incurred our net income was $35.

First In, First Out (FIFO)

The FIFO method is similar to LIFO and keeps track of the price you paid for each group of units received at the same time at the same unit cost. However, FIFO costs your sales and values your inventory as if the items you sell are those you have had in stock for the longest time.

Select FIFO when you charge costs against revenue in the order in which costs occur. This method generally yields the highest possible amount of net income during periods of constantly rising costs because costs increase regardless of whether you may receive merchandise prior to the cost increase. In periods of declining cost, the effect is reversed.

Example – FIFO

The company, FIFO Sales Company, on January 1, 2002 buys 10 FIFO Units for $10/ea. On January 15, 2002, 10 more FIFO units were purchased at a cost of $12/each and 10 more were purchased on January 20, 2002 for $13/each.

Run a Purchase Journal Report:

Step 1: On your student data disk, open the company: "FIFO Sales Company."

Step 2: From the reports menu, select "Accounts Payable," then double click on "Purchase Journal."

Look at the Purchase Journal in Figure 6.13 to see how the three purchases affected the Accounts Payable (liability) account and the Merchandise Inventory (asset) account.

FIFO Sales Company
Purchase Journal
For the Period From Jan 1, 2002 to Jan 31, 2002
Filter Criteria includes: Report order is by Date. Report is printed in Detail Format.

Date	Account ID / Account Description	Invoice #	Line Description	Debit Amoun	Credit Amount
1/1/02	110 Merchandise Inventory	010102	FIFO Unit for Retail	100.00	
	205 Accounts Payable		FIFO Wholesale Company		100.00
1/15/02	110 Merchandise Inventory	011502	FIFO Unit for Retail	120.00	
	205 Accounts Payable		FIFO Wholesale Company		120.00
1/20/02	110 Merchandise Inventory	012002	FIFO Unit for Retail	130.00	
	205 Accounts Payable		FIFO Wholesale Company		130.00
				350.00	350.00

Figure 6. 13 FIFO Purchase Journal

On January 30, 2002 Cindy Customer buys 15 FIFO units for $15 each.

Record Cindy's purchase:

Step 1: Click on the Sales Navigation Aid. Click on "Sales Invoicing in the middle section.

Step 2: Complete the invoice as shown below in Figure 6.xx. Cindy purchases 15 FIFO units for $15/each.

Step 3: Check your work for errors before going on. The completed invoice is shown below in Figure 6.14.

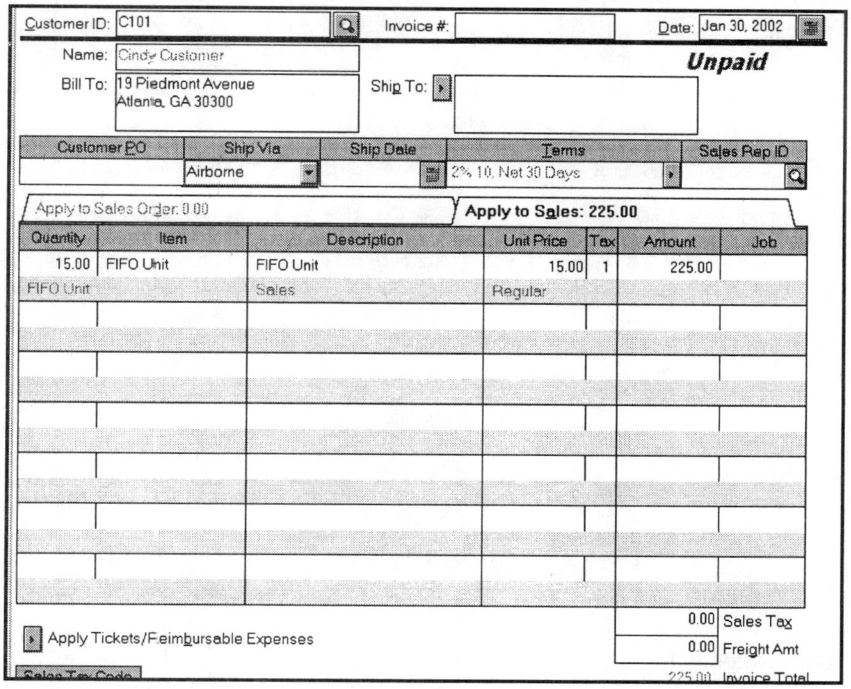

Figure 6. 14 Cindy Customer's invoice for FIFO units.

To see how accounts are affected, run an "Item Costing Report."

Step 1: Click on the reports menu and then click on "Inventory."

Step 2: Click on "Item Costing Report." The report is shown in Figure 6.15

FIFO Sales Company
Item Costing Report
For the Period From Jan 1, 2002 to Dec 31, 2003
Filter Criteria includes: Report order is by ID.

Item ID Item Description	Date	Qty Receive	Item Cost	Actual Cost	Assembly Qt Assembly ($)	Adjust Qt Adjust ($)	Quantity So	Cost of Sale	Remaining Qt	Remain Value
FIFO Unit FIFO Unit										
	1/1/02	10.00	10.00	100.00					10.00	100.00
	1/15/02	10.00	12.00	120.00					20.00	220.00
	1/20/02	10.00	13.00	130.00					30.00	350.00
	1/30/02						15.00	160.00	15.00	190.00

Figure 6. 15 Item Costing Report

Notice on the report how the transaction affected each of the cost items.

Let's look at the effect on our income and profits. Run a copy of the Income Statement.Which is shown in Figure 6.16. Notice how the costs have been reflected in Cost of Goods Sold and in Revenue. Compare the FIFO income statement with the one previously generated from LIFO sales.

FIFO Sales Company
Income Statement
For the One Month Ending January 31, 2002

		Current Month			Year to Date	
Revenues						
Sales	$	225.00	100.00	$	225.00	100.00
Total Revenues		225.00	100.00		225.00	100.00
Cost of Sales						
Purchases		160.00	71.11		160.00	71.11
Total Cost of Sales		160.00	71.11		160.00	71.11
Gross Profit		65.00	28.89		65.00	28.89
Expenses						
Theft		0.00	0.00		0.00	0.00
Total Expenses		0.00	0.00		0.00	0.00
Net Income	$	65.00	28.89	$	65.00	28.89

Figure 6. 16 FIFO Income Statement

How did we get the figures shown in Figure 6.16?

Revenue:
Sales or Revenue was obtained by multiplying the number of units Cindy bought (15) by the unit price ($15) or $225.

Cost of Sales (Purchases):
Cost of Sales (Purchases) were obtained by the cost of the first 10 units that were purchased first (10 * $10) plus the cost of the next 5 units purchased (5 * $12) or $160.

Gross Profit:
Gross Profit was obtained by subtracting Purchases ($160) from Total Revenue ($225) or $65. Because, in our example, no other expenses were incurred our net income was $65.

INVENTORY DEFAULT INFORMATION

Peachtree Accounting lets you set up default information for inventory items. This feature is like a template or model in which you "build" your inventory item records. You enter the most common information; then, when you set up new inventory items and enter transactions, the default information is automatically included.

To set up or review inventory item defaults

Step 1: Select Default Information from the Maintain menu and choose Inventory Items.
Step 2: You have a choice of three tabs, as shown in Figure 6.17. Let's look at GL Accounts/Costing first.

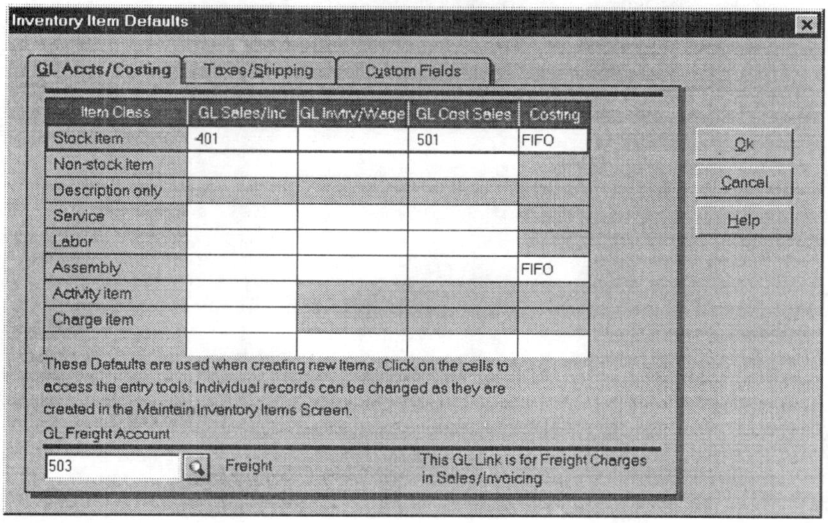

Figure 6. 17 Inventory Items Default

Step 3: Enter "401" for the General Ledger Sales account and "501" for the Cost of Sales (Purchases) account and "503" at the bottom, for Freight.
Step 4: Click on the "Taxes/Shipping" tab to get the form shown below in Figure 6.18

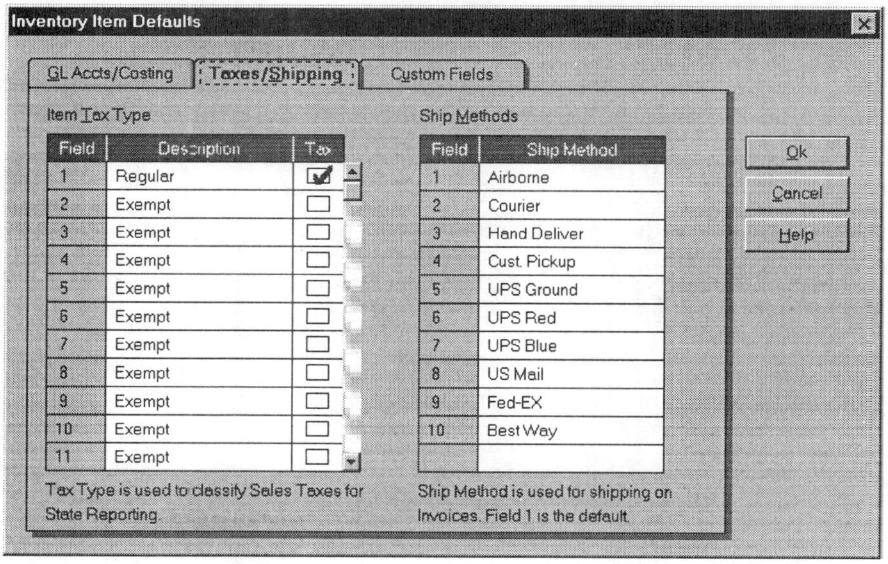

Figure 6. 18 Taxes/Shipping defaults.

Step 5: Leave these defaults as they are.
Step 6: Click on the "Custom Fields" tab. The form is shown in Figure 6.19.

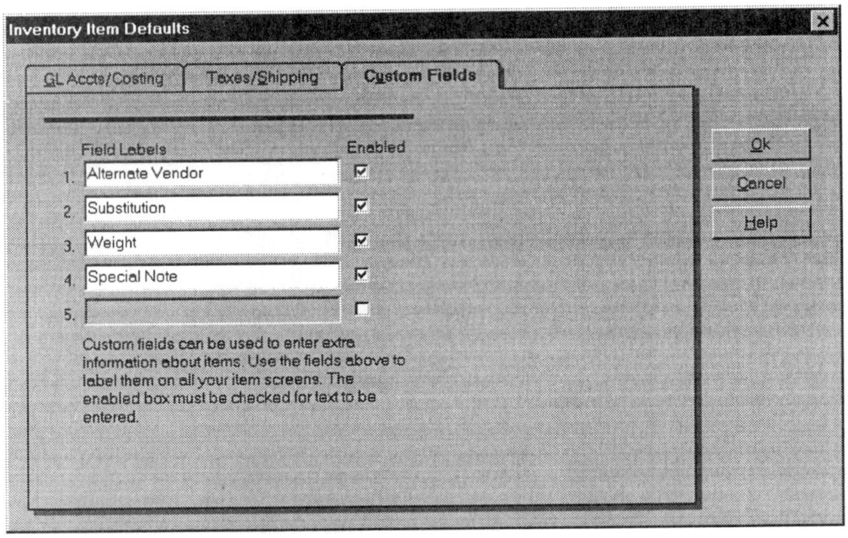

Figure 6. 19 Inventory Items Defaults - Custom Field Labels.

Step 7: You may change these fields to meet your needs. For now, we'll leave them as they are.

Step 8: Click "OK" to return to the main screen.

INVENTORY REPORTS

Peachtree Accounting provides you with a variety of default reports for organizing and monitoring the inventory process. These reports include listing inventory items, cost, quantity on hand, assembly components, adjustments, and general ledger activity.

To obtain Inventory Reports:

Step 1: Under the "Reports" heading on the menu bar, click on "Inventory."

Step 2: You are presented with the "Inventory" reports selection menu as shown in Figure 6.20.

Step 3: Select the report required.

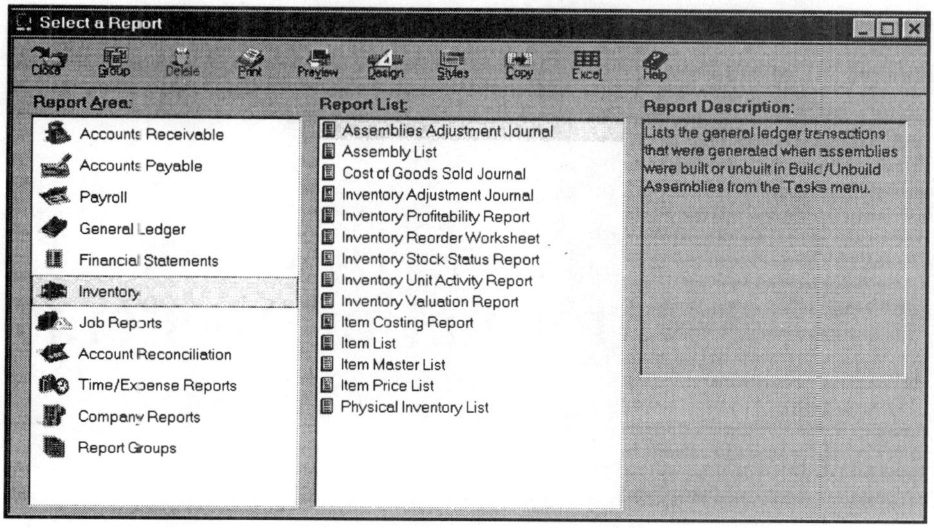

Figure 6. 20 Available Inventory reports.

CHAPTER 7

Accounting Information Systems

OBJECTIVES

- Identify the basic principles of accounting information systems.
- Explain the major phases in the development of an accounting system.
- Describe the nature and purpose of a subsidiary ledger.
- Explain how special journals are used in journalizing.
- Indicate how a multicolumn journal is posted.

BASIC CONCEPTS OF ACCOUNTING INFORMATION SYSTEMS

The accounting information system is the system of collecting and processing transaction data and distributing financial information to interested parties. An Accounting Information System (AIS for short) includes each of the steps in the accounting cycle you have studied in your text. The documents providing evidence of the transactions and events and the records, trial balances, worksheets and financial statements are a result of a solid Accounting Information System. It may be either manual or computerized.

An efficient and effective accounting information system is based on certain principles:

- Cost effectiveness
- Usefulness
- Flexibility

In a manual accounting system, the debits and credits for each transaction were first entered in a book called a *journal*. The journal record for each transaction is called a *journal entry*, or simply an *entry*. Later on, in this "manual system" the journal entries are copied, or *posted*, to another book called the *ledger*.

The journal lists the transactions in the order in which they occur, somewhat like a diary; the ledger contains a page for each account and a running balance total. In a manual system, the journal tells the bookkeeper which accounts are to be debited and which credited, and in what amounts. The bookkeeper carries out these instructions by posting these journal entries to the ledger.

In Peachtree Accounting, most of this is done for you.

MANUAL VERSUS COMPUTERIZED SYSTEMS

In a manual accounting system, each of the steps in the accounting cycle is performed by hand. For example, each accounting transaction is entered manually in a journal and each is posted manually to the ledger. To obtain a ledger account balance or to prepare a trial balance and financial statements, manual computations must be made.

In a computerized accounting system, there are programs for performing the steps in the accounting cycle such as journalizing, posting, and preparing trial balances. In addition, there is software for business functions such as billing customers, preparing the payroll, and budgeting.

The first step is to decide which accounts should be debited or credited for a given transaction, and the amounts of the debits and credits.

In the automated system, just as in the manual system, each account has an identifying number – an account number and a description or title. When reports are generated in Peachtree, names (or descriptions) of the accounts are used rather than numbers, which makes the procedure easier to follow. In the journal in Chapter 1, you entered each account number; the title/description was automatically generated for you and the amounts that affected each transaction, and whether it is a debit or a credit. And, you made certain that debits equaled credits.

SUBSIDIARY LEDGERS AND PEACHTREE REPORTS

Imagine a business that has several thousand charge (credit) customers and shows the transactions with these customers using only one general ledger account – accounts receivable. It would be impossible to determine the balance owed by a single customer at any specific time. Similarly, the amount we need to pay to a creditor would also be difficult to locate quickly from a single Accounts Payable account in the general ledger. This is why companies use subsidiary ledgers to keep track of individual balances.

A subsidiary ledger, or reports as they are called in Peachtree, is a group of accounts with a common characteristic. For example, all accounts receivable (money owed to us by our customers) are contained in one report. The subsidiary ledger frees the general ledger from the details of individual balances. A subsidiary ledger simply is an addition to a second volume or an expansion of the general ledger.

The two most common subsidiary ledgers in Peachtree are as follows:

- The Accounts Receivable Ledger - contains information about the transactions affecting the company's customers. A listing of who owes the company money.
- The Accounts Payable Ledger - contains information about the transactions affecting the company's creditors. A listing of those to whom the company owes money.

THE ACCOUNTS RECEIVABLE LEDGER

The Accounts Receivable Ledger is found under the Reports heading of the menu bar.

Run a copy of the Accounts Receivable Ledger for "Bellwether Garden Supply."
Step 1: Open "Bellwether Garden Supply" on your student disk.
Step 2: Click on "Reports" on the reports menu and then click on "Accounts Receivable." You will be presented with the complete listing of reports pertaining to "Accounts Receivable" as shown in Figure 7.1.

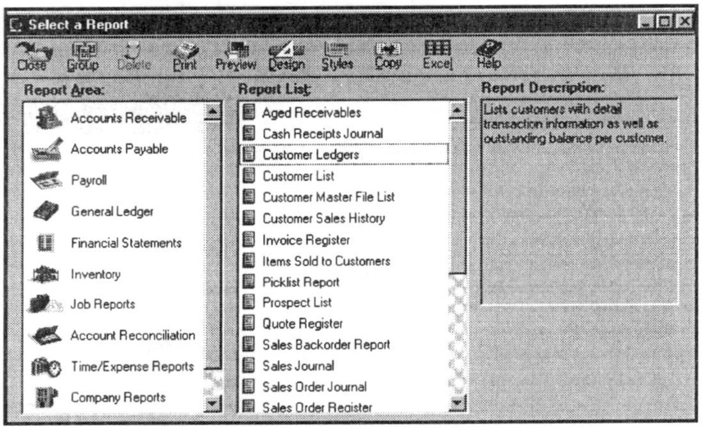

Figure 7. 1 Select A Report window (Accounts Receivable)

Step 3: Click on "Customer Ledgers" under the Report List to obtain a listing of "Bellwether's" customers and balances, and such. A portion of the report is shown in Figure 7.2.

Bellwether Garden Supply
Customer Ledgers
For the Period From Mar 1, 2003 to Mar 31, 2003
Filter Criteria includes: Report order is by ID. Report is printed in Detail Format

Customer ID Customer	Date	Trans No	Typ	Debit Amt	Credit Amt	Balance
CHAPMAN-MURPHY-01		No Activity				0.00
Chapman-Murphy Law Office						
COLEMAN-01	3/1/03	Balance Fwd				57.20
Coleman Realty	3/3/03	10303	SJ	99.56		156.76
	3/4/03	3114	CRJ	1.99	1.99	156.76
	3/4/03	3114	CRJ		99.56	57.20
	3/11/03	10306	SJ	184.29		241.49
CUNNINGHAM-01	3/13/03	10307	SJ	180.18		180.18
Cunningham Construction						
ERTLEY-01	3/1/03	Balance Fwd				756.35
Ertley Bulldog Sports	3/3/03	10301	SJ	190.69		947.04
	3/5/03	2231	CRJ	3.81	3.81	947.04
	3/5/03	2231	CRJ		190.69	756.35
FREEMAN-01	3/1/03	Balance Fwd				381.56
Freeman Enterprises	3/3/03	10302	SJ	588.72		970.28
	3/7/03	10302V	SJ		588.72	381.56
HARDING-01		No Activity				0.00
Harding Consulting						
HENSLEY-01	3/1/03	Balance Fwd				449.29
Hensley Park Apartments	3/15/03	10310	SJ	845.23		1,294.52
HOLT-01	3/1/03	Balance Fwd				2,650.00
Holt Properties, Inc.	3/4/03	10304	SJ	168.96		2,818.96

Figure 7. 2 Portion of Customer Ledgers for "Bellwether Garden Supply"

Look at the information provided for "Coleman Realty." Each date on which business was conducted with "Coleman" is listed, including sales for $99.56 and $184.29 and a payment for $99.56, leaving a balance due of $241.49. The $1.99 is a discount that was taken by "Coleman."

THE ACCOUNTS PAYABLE LEDGER

The Accounts Payable Ledger is also found under the Reports heading of the menu bar.

Run a copy of the Accounts Payable Ledger for "Bellwether Garden Supply."

Step 1: Open "Bellwether Garden Supply" on your student disk if it is not already open.

Step 2: Click on "Reports" on the reports menu bar and then click on "Accounts Payable." You will be presented with the complete listing of reports pertaining to "Accounts Payable" as shown in Figure 7.3.

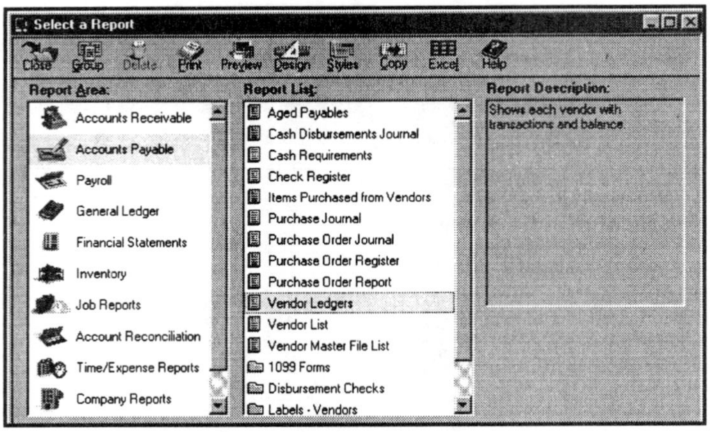

Figure 7. 3 Report listing for Accounts Payable

Step 3: Click on "Vendor Ledgers" under the Report List to obtain a listing of "Bellwether's" creditors and balances, and such. A portion of the report is shown in Figure 7.4.

Bellwether Garden Supply
Vendor Ledgers
For the Period From Mar 1, 2003 to Mar 31, 2003

Filter Criteria includes: Report order is by ID.

Vendor ID Vendor	Date	Trans No	Type	Paid	Debit Amt	Credit Amt	Balance
ANDERSON-01	3/17/03		CDJ		1,000.00	1,000.00	0.00
Anderson Distribution							
ARBOR-01	3/1/03	Balance Fwd					2,663.00
Arbor Wholesale Suppliers	3/10/03	22113	PJ			64.80	2,727.80
	3/13/03	AR1303	PJ			1,192.50	3,920.30
BRENNAMAN-01	3/1/03	Balance Fwd					124.68
Brennaman Chemical Supply	3/12/03	10201	CDJ		124.68		0.00
	3/12/03	116655	PJ			297.60	297.60
CORCORAN-01							0.00
Corcoran Consulting Compan							
DUFFEY-01	3/7/03	45541	PJ			75.00	75.00
Duffey Lawn Pro, Inc.	3/12/03	10204	CDJ		335.50	335.50	75.00
GAREVENUE-01	3/31/03		CDJ		73.42	73.42	0.00
Georgia Department of Reven							

Figure 7. 4 Portion listing of Vendor Ledger (Accounts Payable)

Look at the information provided for "Arbor Wholesale Suppliers." Each date business was conducted with "Arbor" is listed, including purchases for $64.80 and $1,192.50. No payments to "Arbor" were made during the period. A balance is due of $3,920.30

SPECIAL JOURNALS

In addition to the two subsidiary ledgers we looked at in the preceding exercises, there are four companion special journals: the sales journal, the cash receipts journal, the purchases journal, and the cash payments journal.

Sales Journal

The sales journal is used to record sales of merchandise on account. Cash sales would be entered in the cash receipts journal. Credit sales of assets other than merchandise would be entered through a General Journal entry. Credit sales are automatically entered into the Sales Journal as an invoice is completed for each customer.

Run a copy of the Sales Journal:

Step 1: Continue to use the Peachtree demo company, "Bellwether Garden."
Step 2: Click on "Reports" and "Accounts Payable."
Step 3: On the Report listing, click on (highlight) the sales journal. A portion of the journal is shown in Figure 7.5.

Bellwether Garden Supply
Sales Journal
For the Period From Mar 1, 2003 to Mar 31, 2003
Filter Criteria includes: Report order is by Invoice Date. Report is printed in Detail Format.

Date	Account ID	Invoice No	Line Description	Debit Amnt	Credit Amnt
3/3/03	23100	10301	GEORGIA: Georgia State Sales Tax		7.19
	23100		GWINNETT: Gwinnett County Sales		3.60
	40000-EQ		Bell-Gro Impulse Sprinkler		59.98
	50000-EQ		Cost of sales	23.90	
	12000		Cost of sales		23.90
	40000-FF		Bell-Gro Lawn Fertilizer 5 lb. Bag;		59.94
	50000-FF		Cost of sales	23.70	
	12000		Cost of sales		23.70
	40000-HT		Bell-Gro Long-Handled Tined Garden		19.99
	50000-HT		Cost of sales-prong	7.95	
	12000		Cost of sales		7.95
	40000-EQ		Bell-Gro Fertilizer Compression		39.99
	50000-EQ		Cost of salesSprayer - 3 Gallon	15.95	
	12000		Cost of sales		15.95
	11000		Ertley Bulldog Sports	190.69	
3/3/03	23100	10302	GEORGIA: Georgia State Sales Tax		11.27
	23100		GWINNETT: Gwinnett County Sales		5.64
	40000-LS		Weekly Landscaping Service		249.95
	40000-EQ		Bell-Gro Impulse Sprinkler		179.94
	50000-EQ		Cost of sales	71.70	
	12000		Cost of sales		71.70
	40000-NU		Yellow Rose Starter Bush		101.94
	57200-NU		Cost of sales	30.60	
	12000		Cost of sales		30.60
	40000-LS		Planting Service		39.98
	11000		Freeman Enterprises	588.72	

Figure 7. 5 Sales Journal for Bellwether Garden Supply.

Look at the entries made on March 3, 2003. The Cost of Sales, an expense, is listed on the debit side. The actual sales made appear on the credit side. Because this is a journal there is no a "running" balance, just the journal entry as it was entered on the invoice under the "Sales" icon on the "Sales" navigation aid.

The Cash Receipts Journal

All receipts of cash are recorded in the cash receipts journal. This is done automatically for you as a payment is entered through the payments icon under the "Sales" navigation aid. The most common types of cash received are cash sales of merchandise and collections of accounts receivable. A portion of Peachtree's cash receipts journal is shown in Figure 7.6 for "Bellwether Garden Supply."

Step 1: The Cash Receipts Journal is obtained just like the sales journal above.
Step 2: Click on "Cash Receipts Journal" to get a journal page like that shown in Figure 7.6.

Bellwether Garden Supply
Cash Receipts Journal
For the Period From Mar 1, 2003 to Mar 31, 2003
Filter Criteria includes: Report order is by Check Date. Report is printed in Detail Format.

Date	Account ID	Transaction Ref	Line Description	Debit Amnt	Credit Amnt
3/3/03	23100	4452	GEORGIA: Georgia State Sales Tax		8.23
	23100		FULTON: Fulton County Sales Tax		4.12
	23100		MARTA: Transportation Tax		2.06
	40000-HT		Bell-Gro Wheelbarrow - Green Metal;		49.99
	50000-HT		Cost of sales: feet	19.95	
	12000		Cost of sales		19.95
	40000-EQ		Bell-Gro Heavy Duty Garden Hose -		39.99
	50000-EQ		Cost of salesn. hose	15.95	
	12000		Cost of sales		15.95
	40000-PO		Bell-Gro Cedar Window/Trough Box		79.98
	50000-PO		Cost of sales5 in. long x 11.5 in. wide	31.90	
	12000		Cost of salesgh w/brackets		31.90
	40000-FF		Bell-Gro Azalea and Evergreen Food 4		35.94
	50000-FF		Cost of sales	14.10	
	12000		Cost of sales		14.10
	10200		Williamson Industries	220.31	
3/4/03	49000	3114	Discounts Taken	1.99	
	11000		Invoice: 10303		99.56
	10200		Coleman Realty	97.57	
3/5/03	49000	2231	Discounts Taken	3.81	
	11000		Invoice: 10301		190.69
	10200		Ertley Bulldog Sports	186.88	

Figure 7. 6 Portion of Cash Receipts Journal for Bellwether Garden Supply

Notice that the layout is similar to a checkbook. Cash received is debited, paid out is credited.

The Purchases Journal

All purchases of merchandise on account for resale purposes are recorded in the purchases journal and are automatically entered through the system whenever a purchase order is placed through the "Purchases" section of Peachtree. Whenever an item was purchased for "Beyer Video", that purchase would have appeared on the company's purchase journal. A portion of the purchases journal is shown in Figure 7.7.

Step 1: The purchases journal is found by double clicking "Reports" and then "Accounts Payable."

Step 2: Click on "Purchases" under the selection menu. A portion of the journal is shown in Figure 7.7

Bellwether Garden Supply
Purchase Journal
For the Period From Mar 1, 2003 to Mar 31, 2003
Filter Criteria includes: Report order is by Date. Report is printed in Detail Format.

Date	Account ID Account Description	Invoice #	Line Description	Debit Amount	Credit Amount
3/3/03	61000 Auto Expenses	26171	radial tires for landscape truck	274.56	
	20000 Accounts Payable		Jones Auto Repair		274.56
3/3/03	74000 Rent or Lease Expense	LS-6341	Landscape Equipment Rental	550.00	
	20000 Accounts Payable		Miller Leasing Corp.		550.00
3/4/03	60000 Advertising Expense	2456-D22	Design spring flyers	650.00	
	20000 Accounts Payable		Wills Advertising Company		650.00

Figure 7. 7 Portion of Purchases Journal.

Notice the amounts in both the debit column and the credit column.

Cash Payments Journal

All payouts from the cash account are automatically entered in the cash payments journal. Entries are made through a system of prenumbered checks. In Peachtree Accounting this report is also known as the Cash Disbursements Journal, which is shown in Figure 7.8.

To run a copy of the Cash Disbursements Journal:

Step 1: The Cash Disbursements journal is found by double clicking reports and then Accounts Payable.
Step 2: Click on Cash Disbursements Journal under the selection menu. A portion of the journal is shown in Figure 7.8.

Bellwether Garden Supply
Cash Disbursements Journal
For the Period From Mar 1, 2003 to Mar 31, 2003
Filter Criteria includes: Report order is by Date. Report is printed in Detail Format.

Date	Check #	Account ID	Line Description	Debit Amou	Credit Amo
3/12/03	10201	20000	Invoice: 33112	124.68	
		10200	Brennaman Chemical Supply		124.68
3/12/03	10202	20000	Invoice: 44555	360.00	
		10200	Gunter, Wilson, Jones, & Smith		360.00
3/12/03	10203	20000	Invoice: LS-6211	550.00	
		10200	Miller Leasing Corp.		550.00
3/12/03	10204	57300-LS	Ground Prep: Chapman	215.70	
		57300-LS	Lawn Prep: Hensley Job	119.80	
		10200	Duffey Lawn Pro, Inc.		335.50
3/14/03	10205	89500	Discounts Taken		3.00
		20000	Invoice: 3445574	150.00	
		10200	Gwinnett County License Board		147.00
3/14/03	10206	20000	Invoice: 26171	274.56	
		10200	Jones Auto Repair		274.56
3/14/03	10207	20000	Invoice: LS-6341	550.00	
		10200	Miller Leasing Corp.		550.00

Figure 7. 8 Portion of the Cash Disbursements Journal.

Notice the various sections of the cash disbursements journal including the date, check number; the account ID, the debit and credit amounts.

Demonstration Problem

Celine Dion opened her company, appropriately named The Celine Dion Company, in June 2002. The General Ledger Balance Sheet is shown below.

Celine Dion Company
General Ledger Trial Balance
As of Jun 30, 2002

Filter Criteria includes: Report order is by ID Report is printed in Detail Format

Account ID	Account Description	Debit Amt	Credit Amt
101	Cash	15,000.00	
110	Accounts Receivable	5,800.00	
115	Merchandise Inventory	1,740.00	
200	Accounts Payable		5,220.00
301	Celine Dion, Capital		15,000.00
401	Sales		5,800.00
405	Cost of Sales	3,480.00	
	Total:	26,020.00	26,020.00

Cash Receipts transactions for the month of July 2002 are as follows:

July	3	Cash sales totaled 100 pieces of material sold for $58/each for a cash total of $5,800. (Cost will be automatically figured by the system.)
	3	R. Elliot & Co. buy 130 pieces of material on account for $58/each, terms 2/10, n/30.
	5	A check for $5,684 is received from the Jeltz Co. in payment of an invoice dated June 26 for $5,800, terms 2/10, n/30.
	9	An additional investment of $5,000 in cash is made in the business by Celine Dion, the proprietor.
	10	Cash sales totaled $10,150, 175 pieces of material at $58/each. (Cost will be automatically figured by the system.)
	13	Sold 450 pieces of material to Beck Co. for $58/each, terms 2/10/, n/30.
	12	A check is received for $7,389 from R. Elliot & Co. in payment of a $7,540 invoice dated July 3, terms 3/10, n/30.
	15	A customer advance of $700 cash is received for future sales.
	20	Cash sales total $45,530 for 785 pieces of material sold at $58/each. (Again, cost will be automatically figured by the system.)
	22	A check for $5,880 is received from Beck Company in payment of $6,000 incoivcie dated July 13, terms 2/10, n/30.
	29	Cash sales total $17,600.
	31	Cash of $200 is received on interest earned for July.

Instructions:

a. Journalize and Post the above transactions.
b. Run the following reports to check your work:
    a. Cash Receipts Journal
    b. Invoice Register
    c. Sales Journal
    d. Income Statement

Cash Sales Invoice (Be sure to change the A/R account number at the bottom to #101, Cash.)

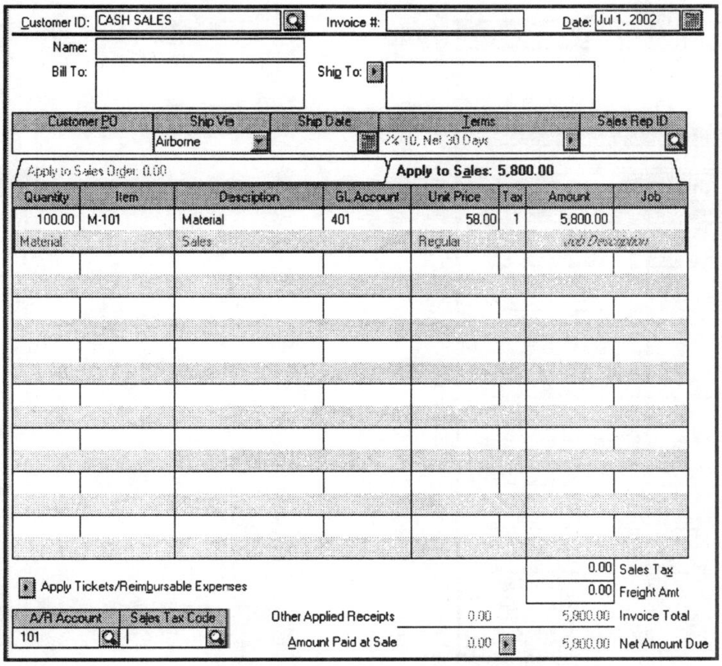
Customer ID: CASH SALES Invoice #: Date: Jul 1, 2002
Name:
Bill To: Ship To:

Customer PO	Ship Via	Ship Date	Terms	Sales Rep ID
	Airborne		2% 10, Net 30 Days	

Apply to Sales Order: 0.00 Apply to Sales: 5,800.00

Quantity	Item	Description	GL Account	Unit Price	Tax	Amount	Job
100.00	M-101	Material	401	58.00	1	5,800.00	
Material		Sales		Regular		Job Description	

Apply Tickets/Reimbursable Expenses
0.00 Sales Tax
0.00 Freight Amt
A/R Account: 101 Sales Tax Code:
Other Applied Receipts 0.00 5,800.00 Invoice Total
Amount Paid at Sale 0.00 5,800.00 Net Amount Due

Check received on account.

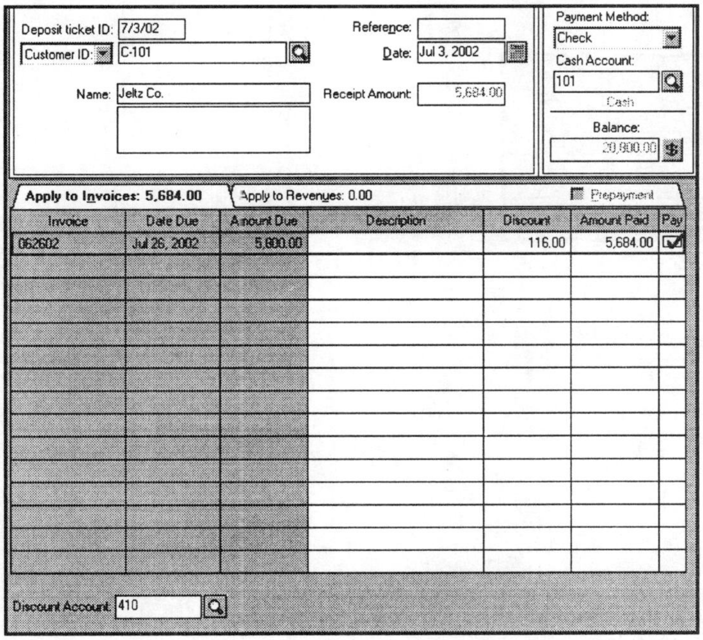
Deposit ticket ID: 7/3/02 Reference:
Customer ID: C-101 Date: Jul 3, 2002
Name: Jeltz Co. Receipt Amount: 5,684.00
Payment Method: Check
Cash Account: 101 Cash
Balance: 20,900.00

Apply to Invoices: 5,684.00 Apply to Revenues: 0.00 Prepayment

Invoice	Date Due	Amount Due	Description	Discount	Amount Paid	Pay
062602	Jul 26, 2002	5,800.00		116.00	5,684.00	✓

Discount Account: 410

R. Elliot Purchase

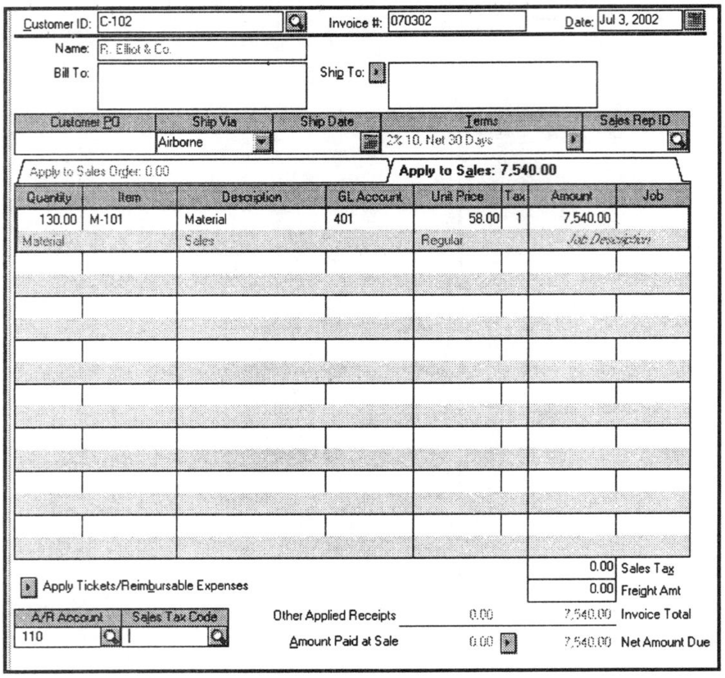

Customer ID: C-102 Invoice #: 070302 Date: Jul 3, 2002

Name: R. Elliot & Co.

Bill To: Ship To:

Customer PO	Ship Via	Ship Date	Terms	Sales Rep ID
	Airborne		2% 10, Net 30 Days	

Apply to Sales Order: 0.00 Apply to Sales: 7,540.00

Quantity	Item	Description	GL Account	Unit Price	Tax	Amount	Job
130.00	M-101	Material	401	58.00	1	7,540.00	
Material		Sales		Regular		Job Description	

Apply Tickets/Reimbursable Expenses

0.00 Sales Tax

0.00 Freight Amt

A/R Account	Sales Tax Code
110	

Other Applied Receipts 0.00 7,540.00 Invoice Total

Amount Paid at Sale 0.00 7,540.00 Net Amount Due

General Journal entry for additional investment.

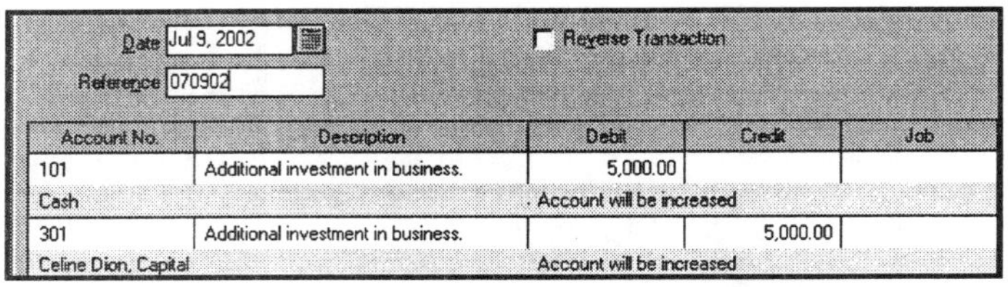

Date Jul 9, 2002 Reverse Transaction

Reference 070902

Account No.	Description	Debit	Credit	Job
101	Additional investment in business.	5,000.00		
Cash	Account will be increased			
301	Additional investment in business.		5,000.00	
Celine Dion, Capital	Account will be increased			

Invoice for Cash Sales.

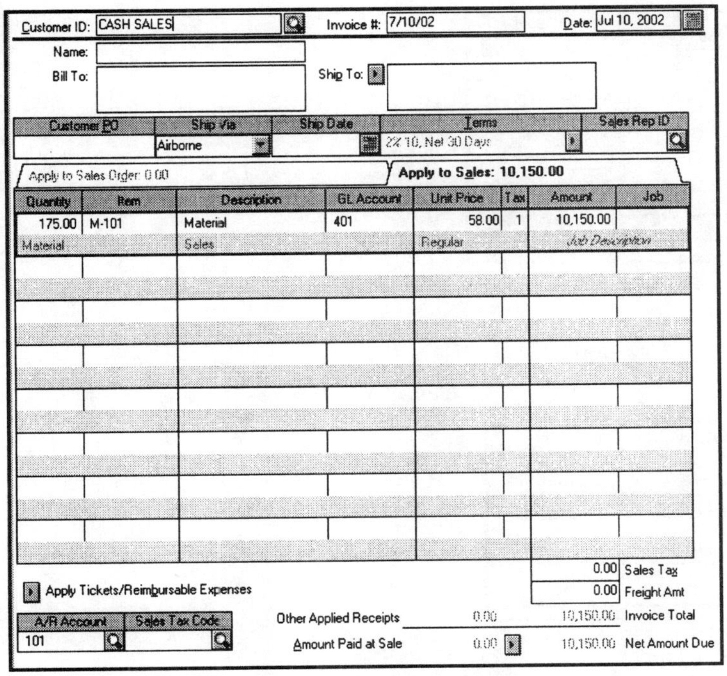

Check received within discount period from R. Elliot & Co.

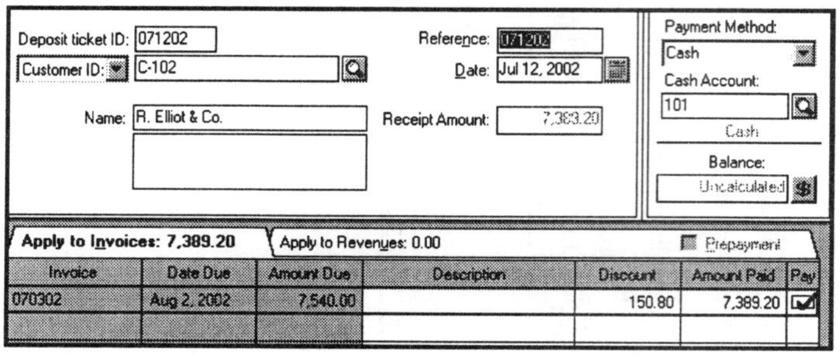

Deposit ticket ID: 071202
Customer ID: C-102
Name: R. Elliot & Co.
Reference: 071202
Date: Jul 12, 2002
Receipt Amount: 7,389.20
Payment Method: Cash
Cash Account: 101
Cash
Balance: Uncalculated
Apply to Invoices: 7,389.20 | Apply to Revenues: 0.00 | Prepayment

Invoice	Date Due	Amount Due	Description	Discount	Amount Paid	Pay
070302	Aug 2, 2002	7,540.00		150.80	7,389.20	☑

General Journal entry to record Unearned Revenue.

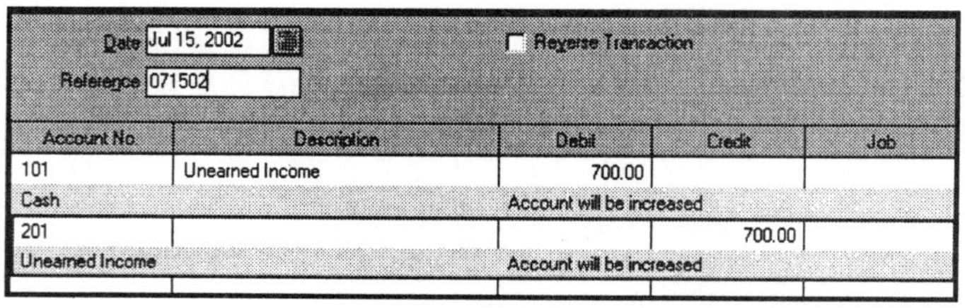

Date: Jul 15, 2002
Reference: 071502
Reverse Transaction

Account No.	Description	Debit	Credit	Job
101	Unearned Income	700.00		
Cash		Account will be increased		
201			700.00	
Unearned Income		Account will be increased		

Recording cash sales.

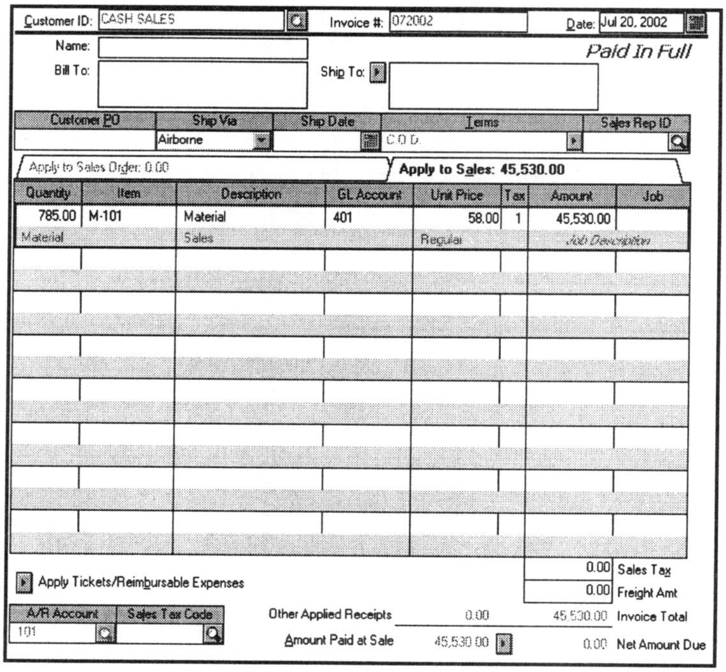

Customer ID: CASH SALES
Invoice #: 072002
Date: Jul 20, 2002
Name:
Bill To:
Ship To:
Paid In Full

Customer PO	Ship Via	Ship Date	Terms	Sales Rep ID
	Airborne		C.O.D.	

Apply to Sales Order: 0.00 | Apply to Sales: 45,530.00

Quantity	Item	Description	GL Account	Unit Price	Tax	Amount	Job
785.00	M-101	Material	401	58.00	1	45,530.00	
Material		Sales		Regular		Job Description	

Apply Tickets/Reimbursable Expenses
A/R Account: 101
Sales Tax Code:
0.00 Sales Tax
0.00 Freight Amt
Other Applied Receipts 0.00
45,530.00 Invoice Total
Amount Paid at Sale 45,530.00
0.00 Net Amount Due

Money received from Beck.

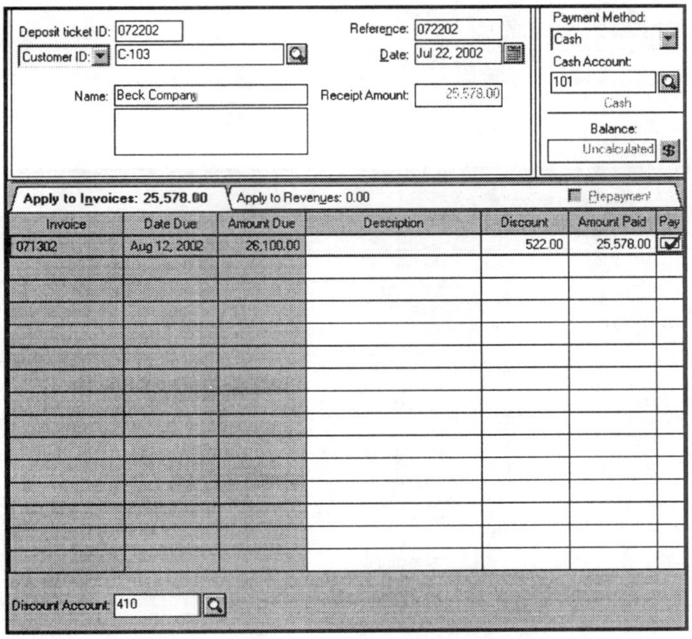

Cash Sales

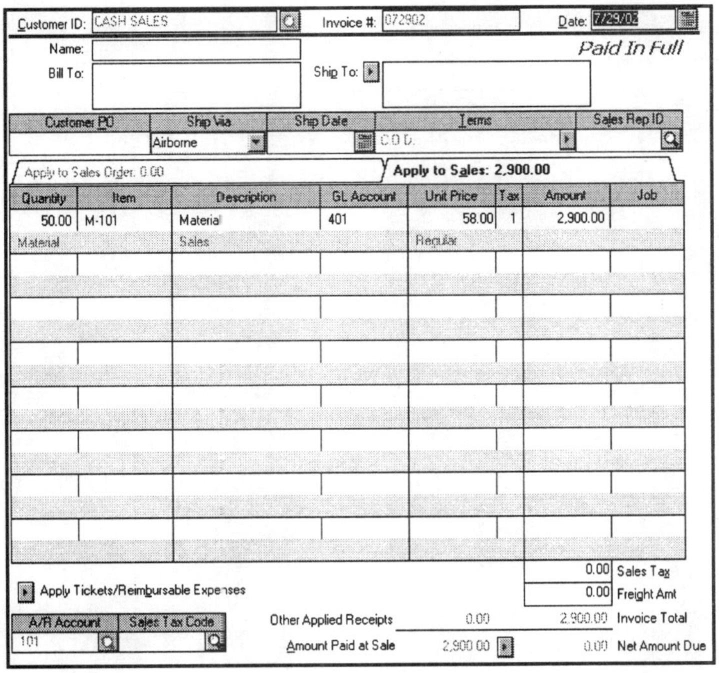

Interest Earned.

Date Jul 31, 2002 ☐ Reverse Transaction
Reference 073102

Account No.	Description	Debit	Credit	Job
101	Interest earned for July	200.00		
Cash	Account will be increased			
402	Interest earned for July		200.00	
Interest Income	Account will be increased			

Cash Receipts Journal

Celine Dion Company
Cash Receipts Journal
For the Period From Jul 1, 2002 to Jul 31, 2002
Filter Criteria includes: Report order is by Check Date. Report is printed in Detail Format.

Date	Account ID	Transaction Ref	Line Description	Debit Amnt	Credit Amnt
7/3/02	410	070302	Discounts Taken	116.00	
	110		Invoice: 062602		5,800.00
	101		Jeltz Co.	5,684.00	
7/3/02	101	070302	Invoice: 070302		5,800.00
	101			5,800.00	
7/10/02	101	071002	Invoice: 07/10/02		10,150.00
	101			10,150.00	
7/20/02	101	072002	Invoice: 072002		45,530.00
	101			45,530.00	
7/22/02	410	072202	Discounts Taken	522.00	
	110		Invoice: 071302		26,100.00
	101		Beck Company	25,578.00	
7/29/02	101	072902	Invoice: 072902		2,900.00
	101			2,900.00	
				96,280.00	96,280.00

Invoice Register

Celine Dion Company
Invoice Register
For the Period From Jul 1, 2002 to Jul 31, 2002
Filter Criteria includes: Report order is by Invoice Number.

Invoice No	Date	Quote No	Name	Amount
07/10/02	7/10/02			10,150.00
070302	7/3/02			5,800.00
070302	7/3/02		R. Elliot & Co.	7,540.00
071302	7/13/02		Beck Company	26,100.00
072002	7/20/02			45,530.00
072902	7/29/02			2,900.00
Total				98,020.00

Sales Journal

Celine Dion Company
Sales Journal
For the Period From Jul 1, 2002 to Jul 31, 2002
Filter Criteria includes: Report order is by Invoice Date. Report is printed in Detail Format.

Date	Account ID	Invoice No	Line Description	Debit Amnt	Credit Amnt
7/3/02	401	070302	Material		5,800.00
	405		Cost of sales	3,480.00	
	115		Cost of sales		3,480.00
	101			5,800.00	
7/3/02	401	070302	Material		7,540.00
	405		Cost of sales	4,524.00	
	115		Cost of sales		4,524.00
	110		R. Elliot & Co.	7,540.00	
7/10/02	401	07/10/02	Material		10,150.00
	405		Cost of sales	6,090.00	
	115		Cost of sales		6,090.00
	101			10,150.00	
7/13/02	401	071302	Material		26,100.00
	405		Cost of sales	15,660.00	
	115		Cost of sales		15,660.00
	110		Beck Company	26,100.00	
7/20/02	401	072002	Material		45,530.00
	405		Cost of sales	27,318.00	
	115		Cost of sales		27,318.00
	101			45,530.00	
7/29/02	401	072902	Material		2,900.00
	405		Cost of sales	1,740.00	
	115		Cost of sales		1,740.00
	101			2,900.00	
		Total		156,832.00	156,832.00

Income Statement

Celine Dion Company
Income Statement
For the Two Months Ending July 31, 2002

		Current Month			Year to Date	
Revenues						
Sales	$	98,020.00	99.80	$	103,820.00	99.81
Interest Income		200.00	0.20		200.00	0.19
Total Revenues		98,220.00	100.00		104,020.00	100.00
Cost of Sales						
Cost of Sales		58,812.00	59.88		62,292.00	59.88
Sales Discounts		638.00	0.65		638.00	0.61
Total Cost of Sales		59,450.00	60.53		62,930.00	60.50
Gross Profit		38,770.00	39.47		41,090.00	39.50
Expenses						
Total Expenses		0.00	0.00		0.00	0.00
Net Income	$	38,770.00	39.47	$	41,090.00	39.50

P7-1a

Lemon Company's chart of accounts includes the following selected accounts already set up on your Student Data Disk.

101	Cash	401	Sales
112	Accounts Receivable	414	Sales Discounts
120	Merchandise Inventory	505	Cost of Goods Sold
301	F. Lemon, Capital		

On April 1, the accounts receivable ledger of Lemon Co. showed the following balances: Horner $1,550, Harris $1,200, Northeast Co. $2,900 and Smith $1,700. These balances need to be inserted as beginning balances in the individual accounts after you create them in Peachtree.

The April transactions involving the receipt of cash were as follows:

April	1	The owner, F. Lemon, invested additional cash in the business, $6,000.
	4	Received check for payment of account from Smith less 2% cash discount.
	5	Received check for $620 in payment of invoice no. 307 from Northeast Co.
	8	Made cash sales of merchandise totaling $7,245. The cost of the merchandise sold was $4,347.
	10	Received check for $800 in payment of invoice no. 309 from Horner.
	11	Received cash refund from a supplier for damaged merchandise $550.
	23	Received check for $1,500 in payment of invoice no. 310 from Northeast Co.
	29	Received check for payment of account from Harris.

Instructions:

a. Journalize and post the above transactions after entering the beginning balances for the customers.

b. Run the following reports to check your work:
   1. Cash Receipts Journal
   2. Invoice Register
   3. Sales Journal
   4. Income Statement

P7-3a

The Chart of Accounts for Hernandez Company includes the following selected accounts that have already been set up on your Student Data Disk:

112	Accounts Receivable	401	Sales
120	Merchandise Inventory	412	Sales Returns and Allowances
126	Supplies	505	Cost of Goods Sold
157	Equipment	610	Advertising Expense
201	Accounts Payable		

In July, the following selected transactions were completed. All purchases and sales were on account. The cost of all merchandise sold was 70% of the sales price.

July	1	Purchased merchandise from Denton Company $7,000
	2	Received freight bill from Johnson Shipping on Denton purchase $400.
	3	Made sales to Lyons Company $1,300 and to Franklin Bros. $1,900.
	5	Purchased merchandise from Grant Company $300.
	8	Received credit on merchandise returned to Grant Company $300.
	13	Purchased store supplies from Brent Supply $720.
	15	Purchased merchandise from Denton Co. $3,600 and from Ruiz Co. $2,900.
	16	Made sales to Martin Co. $3,450 and to Franklin Bros. $1,570.
	18	Received bill fro advertising from Marlin Advertisements $600.
	21	Sales were made to Lyons Co. $310 and to Randee Co. $2,300.
	22	Granted allowance to Lyons Co. for merchandise damaged in shipment $40.
	24	Purchased merchandise from Grant Co. $3,000.
	26	Purchased equipment from Brent Supply $600.
	28	Received freight bill from Johnson Shipping on Grant purchase of July 24th, $380.
	30	Sales were made to Martin Co., $4,900.

Instructions:

a. Journalize and post the above transactions in Peachtree.
b. Run the following reports to check your work:
   1. Cash Receipts Journal
   2. Accounts Payable Journal
   3. Sales Invoice Register
   4. Sales Journal
   5. Income Statement
   6. Cash Flows Statement

P7-5a

Presented below are the handwritten purchases and cash payments journals for Collins Co. for its first month of operation.

Purchases Journal

Date		Account Credited	Ref.	Merchandise Inventory, Dr. Accounts Payable, Cr.
July	4	J. Dixon		6,800
	5	W. Engel		7,500
	11	R. Gamble		3,920
	13	M. Hill		15,300
	20	D. Jacob		8,800

Cash Payments Journal

Date		Account Debited	Other Accounts Dr.	Accounts Payable Dr.	Merchandise Inventory Cr.	Cash Cr.
July	4	Store Supplies	600			600
	10	W. Engel		7,500	75	7,425
	11	Prepaid Rent	6,000			6,000
	15	J. Dixon		6,800		6,800
	19	Collins, Drawing	2,500			2,500
	21	M. Hill		15,300	153	15,147

In addition, the following transactions have not been journalized and posted for July. The cost of all merchandise sold was 65% of the sales price.

July	1	The founder, R. Collins, invests $80,000 in cash in the business.
	6	Sell merchandise on account to Hardy Co. $5,400 terms 1/10, n/30
	7	Make cash sales totaling $4,000
	8	Sell merchandise on account to D. Washburn, $3,600, terms 1/10, n/30
	10	Sell merchandise on account to L. Lemansky $4,900, terms 1/10, n/30
	13	Receive payment in full from D. Washburn
	16	Receive payment in full from L. Lemansky
	20	Receive payment in full from Hardy Co.
	21	Sell merchandise on account to S. Kane $4,000, terms 1/10, n/30
	29	Returned damaged goods to J. Dixon and received cash refund of $450.

Instructions:

a. Open the company R. Collins on your Student Data Disk and create the following accounts:

101	Cash	306	Collins, Drawing
112	Accounts Receivable	401	Sales
120	Merchandise Inventory	414	Sales Discounts
127	Store Supplies	505	Cost of Goods Sold
131	Prepaid Rent	631	Supplies Expense
201	Accounts Payable	729	Rent Expense

The capital accounts has already been created for you.

b. Journalize and post the transactions that have not been journalized.
c. Prepare a trial balance as of July 31, 2002.
d. Determine whether the subsidiary ledgers agree with the control accounts in the general ledger.
e. Make the following adjustments in the General Journal:
    1. A count of supplies indicates that $140 is still on hand.
    2. Recognize rent expense for July, $500.
f. Prepare a General Ledger Trial balance and check your work for errors.
g. Prepare a complete set of Financial Statements including:
    1. Income Statement
    2. Retained Earnings Statement
    3. Balance Sheet
    4. Statement of Cash Flows

Mini Practice Set

A Financial Reporting Problem

The Cheng Co. is converting from a manual bookkeeping system to Peachtree Complete Accounting®. M. Cheng has hired you for the conversion process and to assist him through the first month of the new system.

Below is a list of beginning balances for each of the General Ledger accounts.

Step 1: Open Cheng Co. on your Student Data Disk
Step 2: Create the accounts below and their beginning balances, except for Accounts Receivable and Accounts Payable. Those accounts will get their balances when you set up the subsidiary ledgers.
Step 3: The capital account has been created for you, however you must enter the balance because the current balance is zero.
Step 4: Set up a General Ledger Sales account (Sales or Revenue) and a General Ledger Purchases (Cost of Goods Sold) account.

General Ledger Accounts – Beginning Balances

Account No.	Account Name	Balance
101	Cash	$35,750
112*	Accounts Receivable	$13,000
115	Notes Receivable	$39,000
120	Merchandise Inventory	$18,000
125	Office Supplies	$1,000
130	Prepaid Insurance	$2,000
157	Equipment	$6,450
158	Accumulated Depreciation - Equipment	$1,500
201*	Accounts Payable	$35,000
301	M. Cheng, Capital	$78,700

Cheng would like to use an accounts receivable and an accounts payable subsidiary ledger. Customers, vendors and balances related to both are presented below.

Accounts Payable - Beginning Balances

Vendor ID	V101	V102	V103
Name	S. Jin	R. Manuel	D. Northcutt
Contact	Sin Jin	R. Hand Manuel	Danny Northcutt, III
Account No	#43-1745	#91	#36-AQR
Address	201 5th Street, NW	12 Confederate Ave.	20 Federal Ave.
City	Marietta	Atlanta	Jonesboro
State	GA	GA	GA
Zip	30012	30300	30340
Phone	768.311.0932	404.938.2648	368.451.9120
Beginning Balance	$9,000	$15,000	$11,000

Accounts Receivable – Beginning Balances

Customer ID	C101	C102	C103
Name	R. Danforth	B. Jiminez	S. Levin
Contact	R. Danforth Anchor	Jiminez Krickett	Ira Levin
Account No	101	102	103
Address	2555 Northwinds Dr.	21 Hank Aaron Blvd.	69 Darling Dr.
City	Marietta	Doraville	Chamblee
State	GA	GA	GA
Zip	31104	30351	30381
Phone	770.645.1835	770.357.7835	770.457.1335
Beginning Balance	$1,500	$7,500	$4,000

Below are a series of transactions for Cheng Co. for the month of January 2002. All credit sales terms are 2/10, n/30. The cost of merchandise sold is 60% of the sales price.

Jan	3	Sold merchandise on credit to B. Sanchez, $3,200. Invoice # 510, and to J. Egan, $1,800. Invoice #511.
	5	Purchased merchandise from S. Whitfield, $3,000 and frrm D. Land, $2,000 terms n/30.
	7	Received checks from S Levin, $4,000 and B. Jiminez $2,000. The discount period has elapsed.
	8	Paid freight on merchandise purchased, $180.
	9	Sent checks for payment on account to S. Jin for $9,000 less the 2% cash discount, and on account to D. Northcutt for $11,000 less a 1% cash discount
	9	Issued a credit memo for $300 to J. Egan for merchandise returned.
	10	Summary of daily cash sales total $15,500.
	11	Sold merchandise on credit to R. Danforth $1,300, invoice no. 512, and to S. Levin $900, invoice no. 513.
	12	Paid January's rent to landlord, $1,000.
	13	Received payment in full from B. Sanchez and J. Egan less their cash discounts.
	15	Cheng withdrew $800 cash for his personal use.
	16	Purchased merchandise from D. Northcutt, $16,000, terms 1/10, n/30; S. Jin, $14,200, terms 2/10, n/30 and S. Whitfield, $1,500, terms n/30
	17	Paid $400 cash for office supplies.
	18	Returned $200 of defective merchandise to S. Jin and received credit on account.
	20	Summary of daily cash sales total $17,500.
	21	Issued $15,000 note to R Manual in payment of balance due.
	21	Received payment in full from S. Levin less the cash discount.
	22	Sold merchandise on credit to B. Sanchez, $2,700, invoice no. 514, and to R. Danforth $800, invoice no. 515.
	23	Sent check to D. Northcutt and S. Jin in full payment on account less the cash discounts.
	25	Sold merchandise on account to B. Jiminez $3,500, invoice no. 516 and to J. Egan $6,100, invoice no. 517.
	27	Purchased merchandise from D. Northcutt, $14,500, terms 1/10, n/30; D. Land, $1,200, terms n/30; and S. Whitfield $4,800, terms n/30.
	28	Paid $200 cash for office supplies.
	31	Summary of daily cash sales total $21,300
	31	Paid sales salaries $4,300 and office salaries $2,600

Instructions:

a. Using the proper subsidiary ledgers for sales, purchases and expenses record the January transactions in Peachtree Complete Accounting®.
b. Prepare a working trial balance as of January 31, 2002. The trial balance total should equal $197,000.
c. The following notes will help you make adjusting entries:
    1. Office supplies inventory on January 31st totaled $500.
    2. Insurance coverage expires on October 31, 2002.
    3. Annual depreciation on equipment is $1,500.
    4. Interest of $60 has accrued on the note payable.
d. Prepare an Income Statement, Owner's Equity Statement, Balance Sheet and a Statement of Cash Flows for the month.

CHAPTER 8

Internal Control and Cash

OBJECTIVES

- Define internal control.
- Explain the applications of internal control to principles tc cash receipts.
- Identify the principles of internal control.
- Explain the application of internal control principles tc cash disbursements.
- Describe the operaticn of a petty cash fund.
- Indicate the control features of a bank account.
- Prepare a bank reconciiation.
- Explain the reporting of cash.

INTERNAL CONTROL

Internal control consists of the plan of organization and all the related methods and measures adopted within a business to:

- Safeguard its assts from employee theft, robbery, and unauthorized use.
- Enhance the accuracy and reliability of its accounting records.
- Reduce the risk of errors and irregularities in the accounting process.

PEACHTREE ACCOUNTING REPORTS THAT AID IN THE CONTROL OF CASH

Segregation of duties involving cash is paramount in assuring an accurate cash flow. For example, one employee may be responsible for cash register receipts. That worker in turn gives the receipts and all paperwork to a second worker who double checks the receipts and records them into Peachtree.

Look at the cash receipts journal for High Cotton Farms.

Step 1: Open "High Cotton Farms" on your student data disk.
Step 2: Run a "Cash Receipts" report found under "Reports" on the menu bar, and clicking on Accounts Receivable.
Step 3: Click on "Cash Receipts Journal" to obtain the report shown in Figure 8.1 below.

High Cotton Farms
Cash Receipts Journal
For the Period From Jan 1, 2002 to Jan 31, 2002
Filter Criteria includes: Report order is by Check Date. Report is printed in Detail Format.

Date	Account ID	Transaction Ref	Line Description	Debit Amnt	Credit Amnt
1/10/02	40000	Reg Sales	Cash Sales		586.10
	10200		Cash Sales	586.10	
1/16/02	40000	Reg Sales	Cash Sales		476.58
	10200		Cash Receipts	476.58	
1/30/02	40000	Reg Sales	Cash Receipts		214.10
	10200		Cash Receipts	214.10	
				1,276.78	1,276.78

Figure 8. 1 Cash Receipts Journal (High Cotton Farms)

Notice the date(s) for each transaction along with the Account Number, in our case Sales (#40000) and Cash (#10200). The Transaction Reference refers to Cash Register Sales (Reg Sales). The line description refers either to cash receipts or cash sales. The amount on the debit side increases the asset cash whereas the amount on the credit side increases the revenue account, sales.

Just opposite the cash receipts journal is the cash disbursements journal, which was discussed in the previous chapter. For review, let's revisit the report. Look at the Cash Disbursements Journal for High Cotton Farms.

Step 1: If not already open, open "High Cotton Farms" on your student data disk.
Step 2: Run a "Cash Disbursements" report found under "Reports" on the menu bar, and clicking on Accounts Payable.
Step 3: Click on "Cash Disbursements Journal" to obtain the report shown in Figure 8.2 below.

High Cotton Farms
Cash Disbursements Journal
For the Period From Jan 1, 2002 to Jan 31, 2002
Filter Criteria includes: Report order is by Date. Report is printed in Detail Format.

Date	Check #	Account ID	Line Description	Debit Amou	Credit Amo
1/1/02	147	60100	Advertising Expense	1,259.95	
		10200	Atlanta Journal Constitution		1,259.95
1/7/02	148	61000	Auto Expenses	568.14	
		10200	Bobby's Exxon		568.14
1/8/02	149	80500	Telephone Expense	289.74	
		10200	Bell South		289.74
1/14/02	150	81000	Travel Expense	398.99	
		10200	Delta Airlines		398.99
1/15/02	151	72500	Legal and Accounting	1,200.00	
		10200	Pam Collins		1,200.00
1/15/02	152	67500	Feed and Grain Expense	235.75	
		10200	Cobb Feed 'n Seed		235.75
1/16/02	153	83500	Rent-Office	3,200.00	
		10200	Pope and Land Realty		3,200.00
1/17/02	154	78000	Laundry and Cleaning	72.00	
		10200	Chung Xao Pan		72.00
1/18/02	155	67000	Entertainment Expense	53.89	
		10200	Gold Club		53.89
1/20/02	156	70500	Insurance Expense	750.00	
		10200	J. Smith Lanier		750.00
	Total			8,028.46	8,028.46

Figure 8. 2 Cash Disbursements Journal.

Each check is listed as written for the current period. The appropriate expense account number along with the cash account number follows with the line description. Because these are all paid expense items, the debit amount will be for the expense and the credit amount will be for the decrease in the asset Cash. The Check Register is the next report.

Look at the Check Register Journal for High Cotton Farms.

Step 1: If not already open, open "High Cotton Farms" on your student data disk.
Step 2: Run the "Check Register" report found under "Reports" on the menu bar, and click on Accounts Payable.
Step 3: Click on "Check Register" to obtain the report shown in Figure 8.3.

High Cotton Farms
Check Register
For the Period From Jan 1, 2002 to Jan 31, 2002

Filter Criteria includes: Report order is by Date.

Check #	Date	Payee	Cash Account	Amount
147	1/1/02	Atlanta Journal Constitut	10200	1,259.95
148	1/7/02	Bobby's Exxon	10200	568.14
149	1/8/02	Bell South	10200	289.74
150	1/14/02	Delta Airlines	10200	398.99
151	1/15/02	Pam Collins	10200	1,200.00
152	1/15/02	Cobb Feed 'n Seed	10200	235.75
153	1/16/02	Pope and Land Realty	10200	3,200.00
154	1/17/02	Chung Xao Pan	10200	72.00
155	1/18/02	Gold Club	10200	53.89
156	1/20/02	J. Smith Lanier	10200	750.00
Total				8,028.46

Figure 8. 3 Check Register Report

Each check that has been written during this accounting period is listed along with to whom it was paid, the cash account charged, and the amount of the check. Remember that a company may have several checking accounts. If the total amount is deducted from the cash receipts journal, you should have your cash balance for the company.

This check register will be used later in the chapter when our bank statement arrives. Both will be used to reconcile the bank statement with our books. Note that the current check book balance is $29.82.

ESTABLISHING THE PETTY CASH FUND

Better internal control over cash disbursements is possible when payments are made by check. However, writing a check for small amounts can be impractical and inconvenient. Many businesses handle the situation by setting up a petty cash fund which is a fund used to pay relatively small amounts. It is technically called an imprest system that involves a three-step process:

1. Establishing the fund.
2. Making payments from the fund.
3. Replenishing the fund.

Establishing the Fund

The two essential steps in establishing a petty cash fund are: (1.) appointing a petty cash custodian who will be responsible for the fund and (2.) determining the size of the fund. Normally, the amount would be set to cover anticipated expenses over the monthly accounting period. To establish the account, we will write a check for $15 directly to the account. Writing a check is easy in Peachtree. In fact, we'll be doing a lot of check writing in the accounts payable section.

To write a check to the Petty Cash Fund.

Step 1: On the navigation bar, click on "Purchases."
Step 2: In the middle of the "Navigation Aid", Figure 8.4, click on "Write Checks."

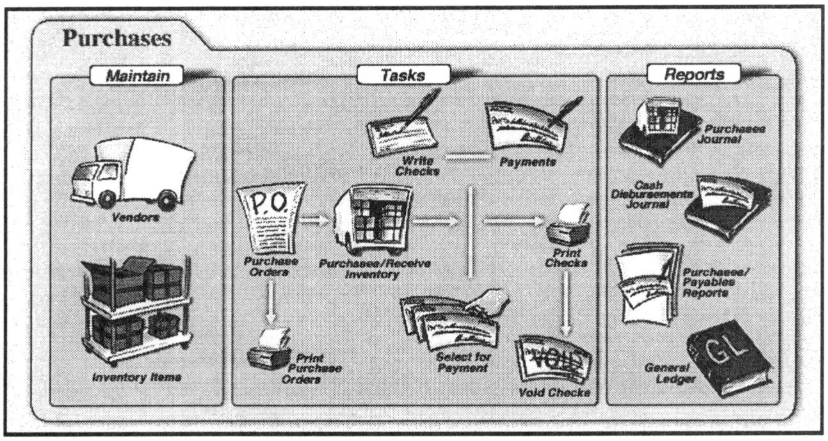

Figure 8. 4 Purchases "Navigation Aid"

Step 3: The Check Writing form, Figure 8.5, will appear.
Step 4: Make the check payable to Petty Cash Fund; the "expense account" will be Account No. 10000, the Petty Cash Fund.

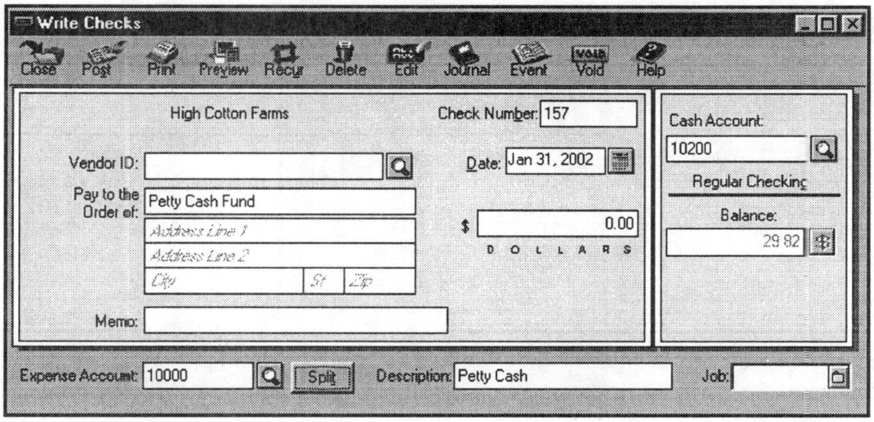

Figure 8. 5 Check Writing Form

Normally when a check is written it would be charged to or debited to an expense, thus increasing the expense item (a debit) and decreasing (a credit) cash, an asset. If we were to increase a cash account, such as Petty Cash, that account would have to be debited also.

Making Payments from the Fund

The custodian of the petty cash fund has the authority to make payments from the fund. Usually, management limits the size of expenditures that may be made. Each payment from the fund must be documented on a prenumbered petty cash receipt or voucher. This would be an internal system that is not available in Peachtree.

Replenishing the Fund

When the moneys in the petty cash fund reaches a minimum level, the fund is replenished. The Petty Cash account (#10000) will not be affected by the reimbursement entry. Instead a General Journal entry is made to record the transaction.

To make the General Journal entry to replenish the Petty Cash Fund:

Step 1: On February 1, 2002, it is determined the fund needs replenishing because it is discovered that the fund contains $2. That $2 plus the $5 spent for postage and the $8 spent for supplies make up the $15 balance shown on the Balance Sheet.

Step 2: Make a General Journal entry debiting the appropriate expense accounts and crediting cash, thus raising the actual cash balance in Petty Cash to $15. (see Figure 8.6) <u>*Do not post your entry at this time*</u>.

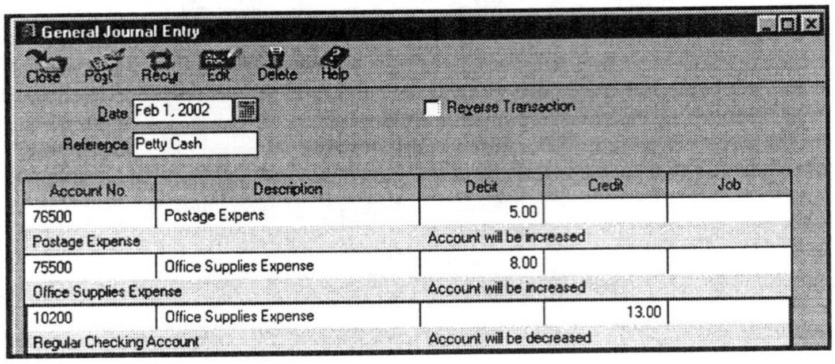

Figure 8. 6 General Journal Entry replenishing the Petty Cash Fund.

RECONCILING THE BANK ACCOUNT

The bank and the depositor always maintain independent records of the checking account. The two balances are seldom the same at any given time. It is then necessary to make the balance in the books agree with the balance according to the bank. This process is called reconciling the bank account and is an easy automated step in Peachtree.

During the current accounting period, High Cotton had 13 banking transactions; 10 checks numbered 147 – 156 were written and three bank deposits were made. According to our books, our bank deposit is $29.82 based on the information in our General Ledger.

Run a General Ledger report and compare yours with Figure 8.7. Look at the Cash Account and each transaction that made the total $29.82.

High Cotton Farms
General Ledger
For the Period From Jan 1, 2002 to Jan 31, 2002
Filter Criteria includes: Report order is by ID. Report is printed with Truncated Transaction Descriptions and in Detail Format.

Account ID Account Description	Date	Reference	Jrnl	Trans Description	Debit Amt	Credit Amt	Balance
10200	1/1/02			Beginning Balance			6,781.50
Regular Checking Accoun	1/1/02	147	CDJ	Atlanta Journal Constitution		1,259.95	
	1/7/02	148	CDJ	Bobby's Exxon		568.14	
	1/8/02	149	CDJ	Bell South		289.74	
	1/10/02	Reg Sales	CRJ	Cash Sales	586.10		
	1/14/02	150	CDJ	Delta Airlines		398.99	
	1/15/02	151	CDJ	Pam Collins		1,200.00	
	1/15/02	152	CDJ	Cobb Feed 'n Seed		235.75	
	1/16/02	153	CDJ	Pope and Land Realty		3,200.00	
	1/16/02	Reg Sales	CRJ	Cash Receipts	476.58		
	1/17/02	154	CDJ	Chung Xao Pan		72.00	
	1/18/02	155	CDJ	Gold Club		53.89	
	1/20/02	156	CDJ	J. Smith Lanier		750.00	
	1/30/02	Reg Sales	CRJ	Cash Receipts	214.10		
				Current Period Change	1,276.78	8,028.46	-6,751.68
	1/31/02			Ending Balance			29.82

Figure 8. 7 Cash Account from the General Ledger

When we received our bank statement, the balance was $807.13. Check #'s 151 for $1,200.00 and 155 for $53.89 had not cleared the bank. Neither had the deposit on January 16th for $476.58.

Let's reconcile our bank account.

Step 1: Click on "Tasks" then toward the bottom of the pull down menu, click on "Account Reconciliation,"

Step 2: Enter the account number being reconciled. It will be the Regular Checking account #10200, the Peachtree account number, in the box provided just under the tool bar.

Step 3: At the bottom of the window, by "Statement Ending Balance" enter the balance as shown on the bank statement $807.13.

Step 4: Looking at the bank statement we know all but two checks #151 and #155 have cleared the bank. The deposit on January 16 for $476.58 did not clear either. Check the boxes on the account reconciliation form by clicking in the box for those items *that have* cleared the bank.

Step 5: Your completed reconciliation should look like that shown in Figure 8.8. Notice the tally at the bottom of the window. Also, bear in mind that not all information will be shown because scroll boxes (list boxes) are utilized.

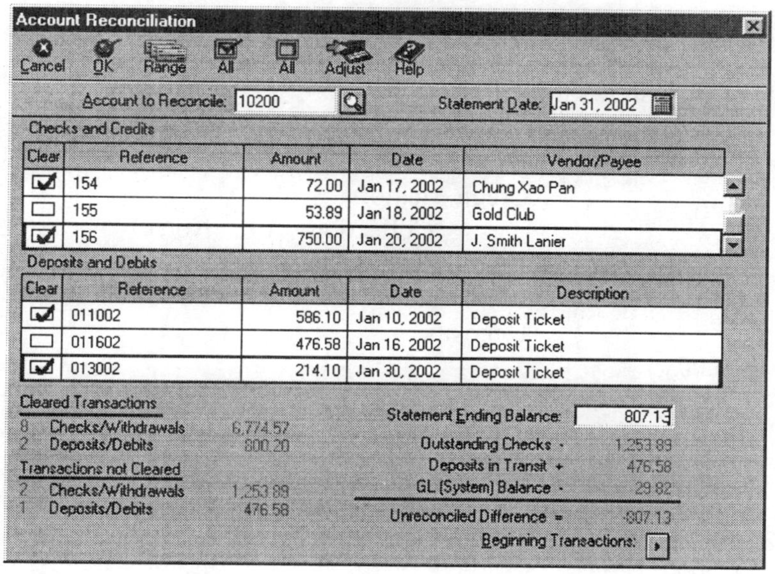

Figure 8. 8 The completed Account Reconciliation window.

The Peachtree system will add up the outstanding checks as shown, $1,253.89 and subtract that amount from the Statement Ending Balance. The deposits in transit, those not yet recorded by the bank will then be added to that running total. The system balance will be subtracted leaving us with the "Unreconciled Difference of -$807.13. If that figure is added to the Statement Ending Balance, the answer should be zero, meaning we're in balance again.

Demonstration Problem

Open Trillo Co. on your Student Data Disk and run an Account Register (Checkbook Register) report. It is shown below.

Trillo Company
Account Register
For the Period From May 1, 2002 to May 31, 2002
101 - Cash

Filter Criteria includes: Report order is by Date

Date	Trans No	Type	Trans Desc	Deposit Amt	Withdrawal Am	Balance
			Beginning Balance			4,520.00
5/3/02	2147	Withdrawal	Chicago Sun /Times		839.00	3,681.00
5/5/02	2148	Withdrawal	Mikie's Texaco		378.00	3,303.00
5/6/02	2149	Withdrawal	Bell Atlantic		193.00	3,110.00
5/7/02	0507	Deposit	Cash Sales	390.00		3,500.00
5/10/02	2150	Withdrawal	American Airlines		265.00	3,235.00
5/12/02	2151	Withdrawal	Chani Xio		600.00	2,635.00
5/14/02	2152	Withdrawal	Michigan Avenue Parks		156.00	2,479.00
5/15/02	2153	Withdrawal	Biship Reality		880.00	1,599.00
5/21/02	0521	Deposit	Cash Sales	317.00		1,916.00
5/23/02	2154	Withdrawal	Pan American Club		53.00	1,863.00
5/24/02	2155	Withdrawal	Silverado Grill		79.00	1,784.00
5/27/02	2156	Withdrawal	John Hancock		500.00	1,284.00
5/29/02	0529	Deposit	Cash Sales	230.00		1,514.00
			Total	937.00	3,943.00	

The bank statement for May 2002 shows the following data:

Balance 5/1:	$4,520.00	Balance 5/30:	$2,376.00
		Credit Memo:	
		Collection of Notes Receivable	$505
Checks:		Deposits:	
2147	839.00	5/7	390.00
2148	378.00	5/29	230.00
2149	193.00		
2150	265.00		
2152	156.00		
2153	880.00		
2154	53.00		
2156	500.00		

Your review of your data reveals the following:

1. The note collected by the bank was a $500, 3-month, 12% note. The bank charged a $10 collection fee. No interest has been accrued.
2. There were two outstanding checks: #2151 and #2155.
3. The deposit dated 5/21 was still in transit at the time of the release of the statement. It was determined it was deposited on 5/30.

Instructions:

a. Use Peachtree Accounting to prepare a bank reconciliation on May 31 for the Trillo Co.
b. Journalize any entries required by the reconciliation.

Solutions:

Adjustments to bank reconciliation.

Trillo Company
Account Register
For the Period From May 1, 2002 to May 31, 2002
101 - Cash

Filter Criteria includes: Report order is by Date.

Date	Trans No	Type	Trans Desc	Deposit Amt	Withdrawal Am	Balance
			Beginning Balance			4,520.00
5/3/02	2147	Withdrawal	Chicago Sun /Times		839.00	3,681.00
5/5/02	2148	Withdrawal	Mikie's Texaco		378.00	3,303.00
5/6/02	2149	Withdrawal	Bell Atlantic		193.00	3,110.00
5/7/02	0507	Deposit	Cash Sales	390.00		3,500.00
5/10/02	2150	Withdrawal	American Airlines		265.00	3,235.00
5/12/02	2151	Withdrawal	Chani Xio		600.00	2,635.00
5/14/02	2152	Withdrawal	Michigan Avenue Parks		156.00	2,479.00
5/15/02	2153	Withdrawal	Biship Reality		880.00	1,599.00
5/21/02	0521	Deposit	Cash Sales	317.00		1,916.00
5/23/02	2154	Withdrawal	Pan American Club		53.00	1,863.00
5/24/02	2155	Withdrawal	Silverado Grill		79.00	1,784.00
5/27/02	2156	Withdrawal	John Hancock		500.00	1,284.00
5/29/02	0529	Deposit	Cash Sales	230.00		1,514.00
			Total	937.00	3,943.00	

Account (#101) Reconciliation Window.

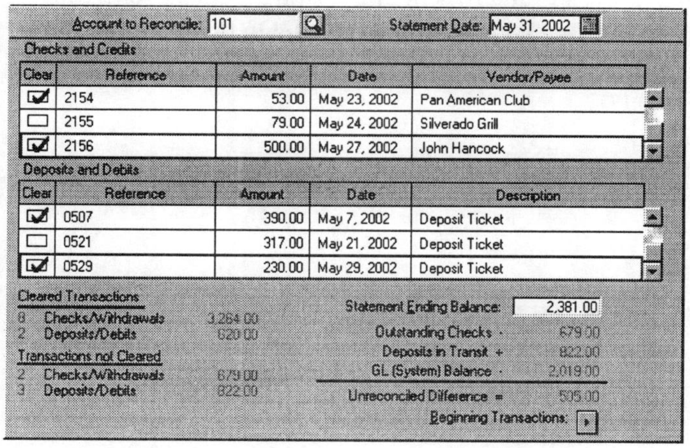

The adjustment to Notes Receivable was made through the adjusting window along with the recognition of the Interest Income.

P8-2a

Maple Park Company maintains a petty cash fund for small expenditures. The following transactions occurred over a 2-month period.

July 1 Established a petty cash fund by writing a check for $200.

15 Replenished the petty cash fund by writing a check for $197.00. On this date, the fund consisted of $3.00 in cash and the following petty cash receipts:

- Freight out, $94.00
- Postage Expense, $42.40
- Entertainment Expense, $46.60
- Miscellaneous Expense, $11.90

31 Replenished the petty cash fund by writing a check for $192.00. On this date, the fund consisted of $8.00 in cash and the following petty cash receipts:

- Freight out, $82.10
- Charitable Contributions, $40.00
- Postage Expense, $27.80
- Miscellaneous expense, $42.10

August 15 Replenished the petty cash fund by writing a check for $187.00. On this date, the fund consisted of $13.00 in cash and the following petty cash receipts:

- Freight out, $74.60
- Entertainment Expense, $43.00
- Postage Expense, $33.00
- Miscellaneous Expense, $37.00

16 Increased the amount of the petty cash fund to $300 by writing a check for $100.

31 Replenished petty cash fund by writing a check for $284.00. On this date, the fund consisted of $16.00 in cash and the following petty cash receipts:

- Postage Expense, $140.00
- Travel Expense, $95.60
- Freight out, $46.40

Instructions:

a. Journalize the petty cash transactions.
b. What internal control features exist in this petty cash fund?

P8-5a

Open Videosoft Co. on your Student Data Disk and run an Account Register (Checkbook Register) report. It is shown below.

Videosoft Co.
Account Register
For the Period From Jul 1, 2002 to Jul 31, 2002
101 - Cash

Filter Criteria includes: Report order is by Date.

Date	Trans No	Type	Trans Desc	Deposit Amt	Withdrawal Am	Balance
			Beginning Balance			1,265.00
7/3/02	468	Withdrawal	Creative Loafing		830.00	435.00
7/7/02	0707	Deposit	Cash Sales	390.00		825.00
7/10/02	469	Withdrawal	Greyhound Bus Express		265.00	560.00
7/12/02	470	Withdrawal	Alyce N. Chains		600.00	-40.00
7/14/02	471	Withdrawal	Peachtree Pavilion Amuseme		156.00	-196.00
			Total	390.00	1,851.00	

The bank statement for July 2002 shows the following data.

Balance 7/1: $1,265.00   Balance 7/31: $395.00

Checks:	Deposits:
$839.00	$390.00
$265.00	
$156.00	

Your review of the data shows there is one outstanding check, #2151.

Instructions:

a. Use Peachtree Accounting to prepare a bank reconciliation on July 31 for Videosoft Co.
b. Journalize any entries required by the reconciliation.

CHAPTER 9

Accounting for Receivables

OBJECTIVES

- Explain how accounts receivable are recognizied in accounts
- Identify the different types of receivables
- Distinguish between the methods and basics used to value accounts receivable.
- Describe the entries to record the disposition of accounts receivable.
- Explain how notes receivable are recognized in the accounts.
- Describe how notes receivable are valued.
- Describe the entries to record the disposition of notes receivable.
- Explain the statement presentation and analysis of receivables.

TYPES OF RECEIVABLES

The term *receivable* refers to amounts due from individuals and other companies. They are claims that are expected to be collected in cash. Receivables are frequently classified as:

1. Accounts
2. Notes
3. Other

Accounts Receivable

Accounts receivable are the amounts owed by customers on their account. They result from the sale of goods and services. These receivables generally are expected to be collected within 30 to 60 days. They are the most significant type of claim held by a company.

Notes Receivable

Notes receivables are claims for which formal instruments of credit are issued as proof of the debt. A note receivable normally requires the debtor to pay interest. Notes and accounts receivable that results from sales transactions are often called trade receivables.

Other Receivables

Other receivables include nontrade receivables such as interest receivable, loans to company officers, advances to employees, and income taxes refundable. These are unusual and are generally classified and reported as separate items on the balance sheet.

Three primary accounting issues are associated with accounts receivable:

- Recognizing the receivable
- Valuing the accounts receivable
- Disposing of accounts receivable.

RECOGNIZING ACCOUNTS RECEIVABLE

Recognizing accounts receivable is relatively straightforward; most of the work was done in Chapter 5. To review, let's work through a sale using a simple company.

Step 1: On your student data disk, open "Jordache Co."
Step 2: Click on the "Sales Navigation Aid" at the bottom of the Peachtree window
Step 3: Click on "Sales/Invoicing" about midway on the navigation aid.
Step 4: You will be presented with the blank sales invoice.
Step 5: Use C101, The name of the customer is the Polo Co. located at 54 W. 52nd Street in New York.
Step 6: Make the "purchase entry" Polo buys 100 pairs of jeans at $10/each. The total due should be $1,000.
Step 7: Make sure the terms read: 2/10, net/30.
Step 8: Check your work with the completed form as shown in Figure 9.1.

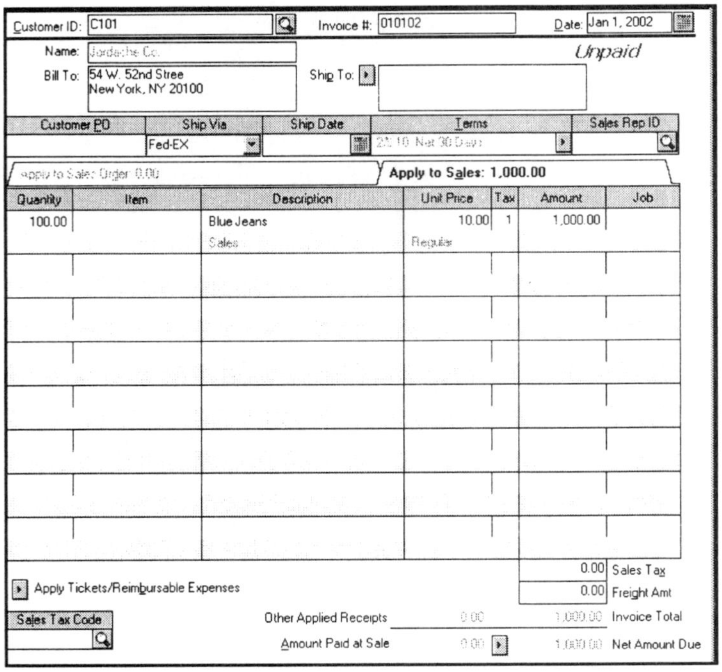

Figure 9. 1 Completed sales invoice.

On January 8, payment from Polo is received for the balance due which should include a $20 discount because they paid within the 10-day time limit.

Step 1: Click on "Purchases" on the navigation bar.
Step 2: Click on "Receipts" to get the window.
Step 3: Click on the "Customer ID" and you are presented with all of the open invoices for that specific customer as shown in Figure 9.2.

<u>**Note:**</u> Because we are within the discount period, the discount (2% of the total invoice) is automatically recognized and posted to the proper account when the account is posted.

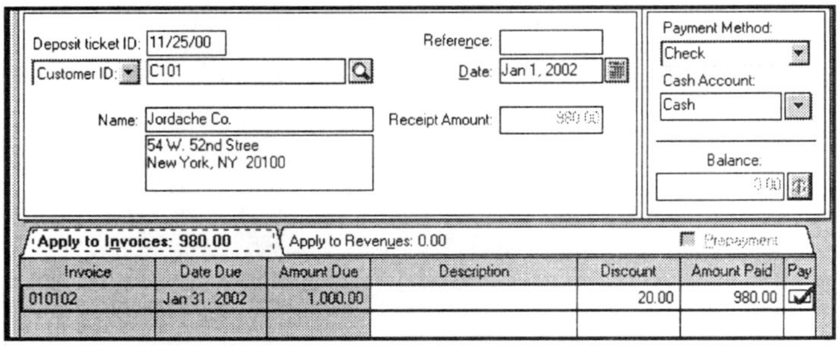

Figure 9. 2 The completed Receipts window.

Write Off of a Customer Bad Debt

In some cases customers will not pay money owed, and the accounts receivable must be written off to bad debt expense. There are two methods for writing off bad debts.

> **Direct Method:** Each invoice that is a bad debt is posted to Bad Debt Expense (an expense account) as the bad debt is recognized.
>
> **Allowance Method:** A percentage of your accounts receivables is written off periodically or at the end of each fiscal year. The amount that is written off depends on the percentage of bad debt you believe your company incurs throughout the year. Normally, you would make a General Journal entry affecting an accounts receivable (used as a contra-asset) account titled "Allowance for Doubtful Accounts" and Bad Debt Expense (an expense account). Then, each invoice is written off to Allowance for Doubtful Accounts as the bad debt is recognized.

To directly write off an invoice(s) whether partially paid or not paid at all in Accounts Receivable as a bad debt, follow the procedure below.

On February 2, 2003, Zaxby's Restaurant purchased $750 in goods and equipment from us. It was determined a few months later the restaurant went out of business and was unable to pay their bill. Thus, it is to be written off as a bad debt

Step 1: Open "Jordache Co." from your student data disk, if it is not already open.
Step 2: From the "Navigation Aid," select "Sales" then "Receipts." Peachtree displays the receipts window.
Step 3: Identify and click on Zaxby's customer number ZAXB01 There is only one invoice, number 7465, for Zaxby to be written off as a bad debt.
Step 4: Peachtree displays the outstanding invoice that is due.
Step 5: Enter a reference number that will help identify the write off (e.g. WO-001).
Step 6: In the Cash Account list, select "Bad Debt Expense" from the pull down menu
Step 7: On the "Apply to Invoices" tab, select the "Pay" check box next to the invoice you wish to write off. The completed form is shown in Figure 9.3.

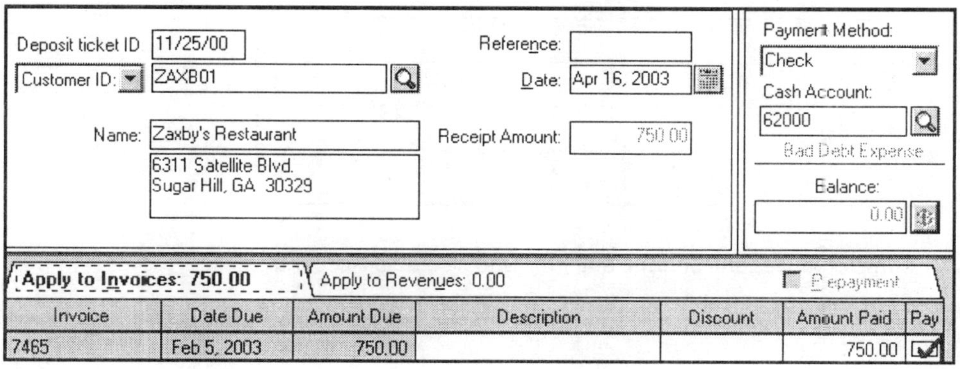

Figure 9. 3 Receipts form used to write off bad debt.

Allowance for Uncollectible Accounts

Under the direct write-off method, bad debts expense is often recorded in a period in which the revenue was recorded. No attempt is made to match bad debts expense to sales revenues in the income statement.

On the other hand, the allowance method of accounting for bad debts involves estimating uncollectible accounts at the end of each period. This method provides better matching on the income statement and ensures that receivables are stated at their cash (net) realizable value, which is the net amount, expected to be received in cash. It excludes amounts that the company estimates it will not collect. Receivables are therefore reduced by estimated uncollectible receivables on the balance sheet through use of this method.

The allowance method is required for financial reporting purposes when bad debts are material in amount. The allowance for doubtful accounts is entered through a General Journal entry similar to the entry in Figure 9.4.

To illustrate the allowance method, assume Hampson Furniture has credit sales of $1,200,000. of that amount, $200,000 remains uncollected at the end of year, December 31st. the credit manager estimates $12,000 of these sales will be uncollectible. The general journal entry is shown in Figure 9.4 below.

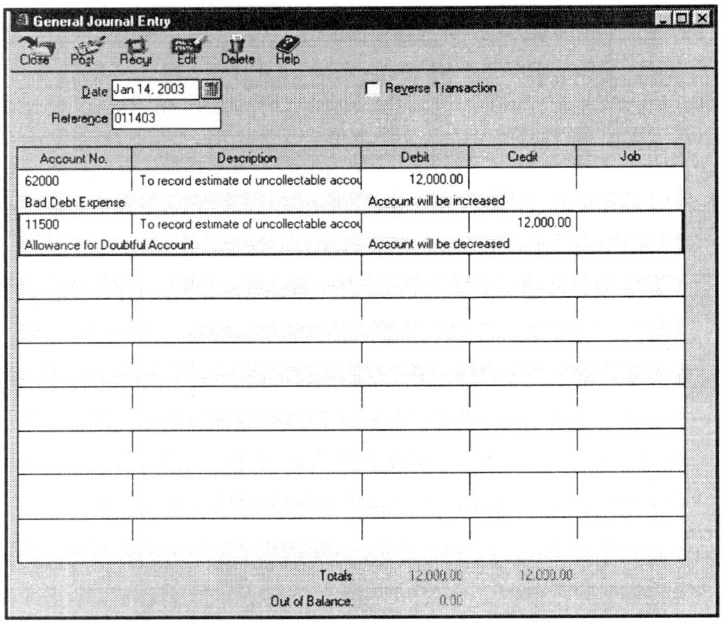

Figure 9. 4 Completed General Journal entry for Uncollectable Accounts

AGED RECEIVABLES REPORT

An aging schedule for accounts receivable is a listing of customer balances that are classified by the length of time they have been unpaid.

To obtain a sample aging report:

Step 1: Open on your student disk, Bellwether Garden Service, Peachtree's tutorial company.

Step 2: Click on reports, then click on accounts receivable

Step 3: Click on aged receivables on the reports list.

A portion of the aged receivables report is shown in Figure 9.5. Compare that with additional information provided in your text. Data may not be the same on your system. However, the basic format of the information should be similar.

Bellwether Garden Supply
Aged Receivables
As of Mar 31, 2003

Filter Criteria includes: Report order is by ID. Report is printed in Detail Format.

Customer ID Customer Contact Telephone 1	Invoice No	0 - 30	31 - 60	61 - 90	Over 90 days	Amount Due
Coleman Realty Chris Coleman 770-555-1005	10306	184.29				184.29
COLEMAN-01 Coleman Realty		184.29		57.20		241.49
CUNNINGHAM-01 Cunningham Construction Betty Cunningham 770-555-1147	10307	180.18				180.18
CUNNINGHAM-01 Cunningham Construction		180.18				180.18
ERTLEY-01 Ertley Bulldog Sports Lee Ertley 770-555-6660	10205 10208	 504.22		252.13		252.13 504.22
ERTLEY-01 Ertley Bulldog Sports		504.22		252.13		756.35

Figure 9. 5 Portion of Aged Receivables Report from Bellwether Garden Supply

CREDIT CARD SALES

Credit card sales are usually considered cash sales by the retailer. Upon receipt of credit card sales slips from the retailer, the bank immediately adds that amount to the seller's bank account. Credit card slips are recorded on the deposit much like the way in which checks are recorded. A fee ranging from 2 to 6 percent of the credit card sales is charged to the customer.

Before you can begin recording credit card transactions in Peachtree Accounting, you must consider the following questions.

When are credit card payments deposited into the company's bank account? Are payments received when the bank receives the credit card transactions (within 24 hours)? Or, is payment received three or more days after submitting the charges?

When does the bank debit from your bank account the credit card processing fee? Is the processing fee deducted from each customer's credit card use? Or, does the credit card company charge one processing fee for the entire month?

Set Up Peachtree Accounting to Accept Credit Card Receipts

Before you can record a credit card receipt from a customer, you must first set up an expense account in the Chart of Accounts in which to charge the credit card processing fees. Again, make sure Jordache Co. is open on your Student Disk.

Step 1: Click on "Maintain" from the main menu bar. Select Chart of Accounts. Peachtree displays the Maintain Chart of Accounts window.
Step 2: Enter a new expense account ID. The account number needs to be associated with the expense area of your chart of accounts.
Step 3: Type a description for your account: Credit Card Processing Fees.
Step 4: Select Expense as the account type, and click the Save button.

If you receive the entire credit card payment in one lump sum, then no other special accounts are required. However, if there is a delay between the time your customer makes the charge and when the credit card company reimburses you, you may want to set up unique accounts receivable accounts to track money owed by the credit card company. Still using Jordache Co.:

Step 1: In the Maintain Chart of Accounts window, enter a new account ID associated with the accounts receivable area of your chart of accounts. Type a description for your account; for example, AMEX Receivable.
Step 2: Select Accounts Receivable as the account type.
Step 3: Click the Save button and close the window.

You also must set up the credit card company that deposits money in your bank account as a *vendor*, not *a customer*. This way you can record and track processing-fee expenses.

Set Up a Credit Card Vendor for Customer Receipts

You must set up a vendor from whom you will receive monthly credit card reimbursements.

Step 1: From the Maintain menu, within the Jordache Co., select Vendors. Peachtree displays the Maintain Vendors window.
Step 2: Enter a vendor ID that represents the credit card (e.g., AMEX).
Step 3: Enter a vendor name that represents the bank or firm of your credit card (e.g., American Express or Wachovia Bank VISA).
Step 4: Enter any additional information, as needed on the General tab. Then, select the Purchase Defaults tab.
Step 5: Select the Processing Fee Expense account as the purchase account default.
Step 6: When finished entering vendor information, select Save, and close the window.

Enter Customer Credit Card Receipts

When recording credit card receipts, always enter customer payments using "Receipts" from the Tasks menu. Apply the customer credit card receipts to open invoices or to revenue (prepayment). You cannot manage credit card receipts effectively when using the Amount Paid field in "Invoicing." You will also be unable to edit the invoice, if needed, later.

To keep the customer's ledger accurate and up-to-date, record the amount paid in Receipts as the "full" amount of the credit card charge, regardless of how the bank handles processing fees.

NOTES RECEIVABLE

Credit may also be granted in exchange for a promissory note, which is a written promise to pay a specified amount of money on demand or at a specific time. Promissory notes may be used when individuals or companies lend or borrow money; when the amount of the transaction and the credit period exceed normal limits or in settlement of accounts receivable.

The entry to recognize a Note Receivable is shown in Figure 9.6. Use the "Receipts" process from the Navigation Bar to make the entry changing the Cash Account to the Notes Receivable Account as shown.

Note that the $11,000 balance shown in the balance window reflects the balance in the Cash account (#14200) not the receivable. The receivable balance is $614.77 as indicated in the Invoice due area.

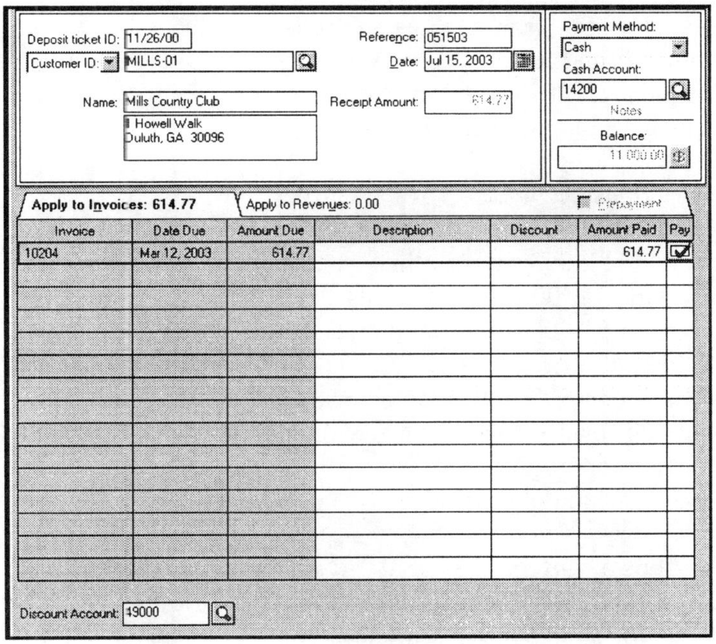

Figure 9. 6 Transferring an amount from Accounts Receivable to Notes Receivable.

Demonstration Problem

On your Student Data Disk, open the Falcetto Company. Set up the following defaults:

a. On the menu bar, click "Maintain", then "Customer Defaults". Change the finance charge to 18% annual interest (1.5% monthly). Charge a finance charge on all unpaid balances over 30 days.
b. Make sure customers are set for a $5,000 credit limit and have available a 2/10, n/30 sales discount available.
c. In Peachtree, under maintain customers; create the following customer's accounts and their beginning balances:

Customer ID:	C-101	C-102	C-103
Name of Company:	Potter Co.	Juno, Inc.	Collins Education
Contact Name:	Henry Potter	Jano Juno	A. Collins
Address:	153 Northside Dr.	351 Morningside Dr.	531 Riverside Dr.
City/State/Zip:	Atlanta, GA 30341	Atlanta, GA 30342	Atlanta, GA 30343
Balance Forward:	$1,800	$1,497	$2,658

In January, the following transactions occurred:

Jan	1	Potter Co. purchased $1,200 worth of goods.
	3	Juno purchased $750 worth of goods.
	9	Collins purchased $600 worth of goods.
	15	Received check for $750 from Potter on account.
	16	Received check for $400 from Juno on account.
	17	Received check for $500 from Collins on account.
	30	a. Computed finance charges on Accounts Receivable. b. Run aging report. c. Changed accounting period.

In February, the following transactions occurred:

Feb	1	Collins purchased $1,000 worth of goods.
	3	Received check for $2,000 from Collins on account.
	5	Potter Co. purchased $500 worth of goods.
	10	Received check for $1,000 from Potter on account.
	15	Juno purchased $200 worth of goods.
	25	Received check for $1,500 from Juno on account.
	28	a. Computed finance charges on Accounts Receivable. b. Run aging report. c. Changed accounting period.

In March, the following transactions occurred:

Mar	1	Received check for $500 from Collins on account.
	5	Received check for $450 from Potter on account.
	15	Received check for $400 from Juno on account.
	31	a. Computed finance charges on Accounts Receivable. b. Run aging report. c. Changed accounting period.

Instructions:

a. Based on the entries you made into the system above, print a set of Billing Statements for Falcetto Co. as of close of business March 31.
b. Run an Income Statement, Retained Earnings Statement, Balance Sheet and Cash Flows statement for the 3rd Accounting Period (Mar 1 – Mar 31).

Solution to Demonstration Problem

Setting Up Finance Charge

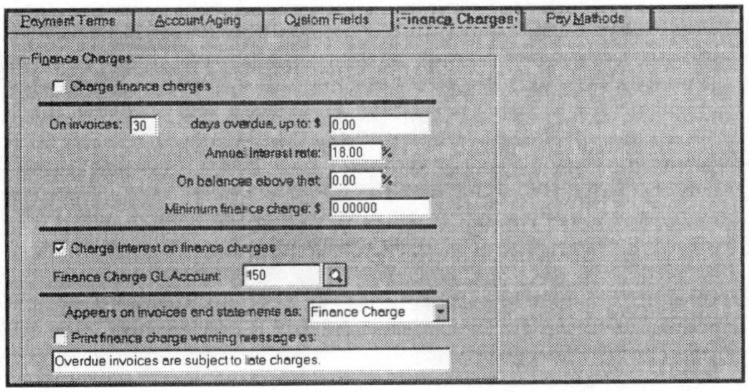

Setting Up Sales Discount and Credit Limit

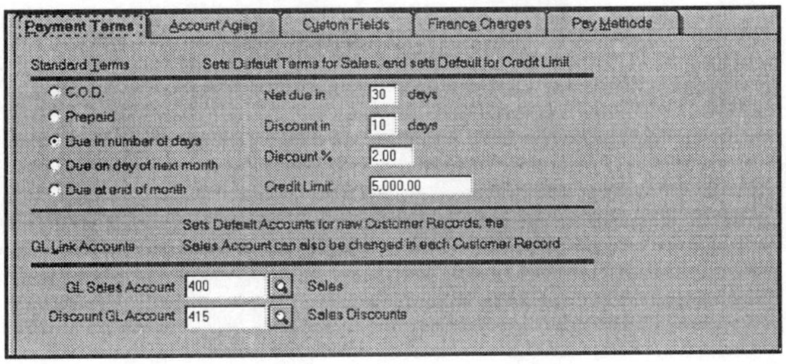

Balance Forward for Current Customers

Invoices for: C-101 The Potter Company — Customer Balances

Invoice Number	Date	Purchase Order Number	Amount	A/R Account
Balance Forward	Jan 1, 2002		1,800.00	130

Invoices for: C-102 Juno, Inc. — Customer Balances

Invoice Number	Date	Purchase Order Number	Amount	A/R Account
Balance Forward	Jan 1, 2002		1,497.00	130
			0.00	

Invoices for: C-103 Collins Education — Customer Balances

Invoice Number	Date	Purchase Order Number	Amount	A/R Account
Balance Forward	Jan 2, 2002		2,658.00	130
			0.00	

Account Balance: 2,658.00
Number of Transactions: 2
Beginning Accounts Receivable Balance: 5,955.00

January Aging (there were no finance charges for the month)

Falcetto Company
Aged Receivables
As of Jan 31, 2002

Filter Criteria includes: Report order is by ID. Report is printed in Detail Format.

Customer ID Customer Contact Telephone 1	Invoice No	0-30	31-60	61-90	Over 90 days	Amount Due
C-101 The Potter Company Henry Potter	Balance For 010102	1,050.00 1,200.00				1,050.00 1,200.00
C-101 The Potter Company		2,250.00				2,250.00
C-102 Juno, Inc Jano Juno	Balance For 010302	1,097.00 750.00				1,097.00 750.00
C-102 Juno, Inc		1,847.00				1,847.00
C-103 Collins Education A. Collins	Balance For 010303	2,658.00 600.00				2,658.00 600.00

February Aging (again, everything falls within 30 days, no finance charges)

Falcetto Company
Aged Receivables
As of Feb 28, 2002

Filter Criteria includes: Report order is by ID. Report is printed in Detail Format.

Customer ID Customer Contact Telephone 1	Invoice No	0-30	31-60	61-90	Over 90 days	Amount Due
C-101	Balance For	50.00				50.00
The Potter Company	010102	1,200.00				1,200.00
Henry Potter	020103	500.00				500.00
C-101 The Potter Company		1,750.00				1,750.00
C-102	Balance For	-403.00				-403.00
Juno, Inc.	010302	750.00				750.00
Jano Juno	020104	200.00				200.00
C-102 Juno, Inc.		547.00				547.00
C-103	Balance For	658.00				658.00
Collins Education	010303	600.00				600.00
A. Collins	020102	1,000.00				1,000.00

March Aging

Falcetto Company
Aged Receivables
As of Mar 31, 2002

Filter Criteria includes: Report order is by ID. Report is printed in Detail Format.

Customer ID Customer Contact Telephone 1	Invoice No	0-30	31-60	61-90	Over 90 days	Amount Due
C-101	Balance For		-400.00			-400.00
The Potter Company	010102		1,200.00			1,200.00
Henry Potter	020103	500.00				500.00
C-101 The Potter Company		500.00	800.00			1,300.00
C-102	Balance For		-403.00			-403.00
Juno, Inc.	010302		350.00			350.00
Jano Juno	020104	200.00				200.00
C-102 Juno, Inc.		200.00	-53.00			147.00
C-103	Balance For		158.00			158.00
Collins Education	010303		600.00			600.00
A. Collins	020102	1,000.00				1,000.00

Income Statement (note that there were no sales during March)

Falcetto Company
Income Statement
For the Three Months Ending March 31, 2002

		Current Month			Year to Date	
Revenues						
Sales	$	0.00	0.00	$	4,250.00	100.00
Total Revenues		0.00	0.00		4,250.00	100.00
Cost of Sales						
Total Cost of Sales		0.00	0.00		0.00	0.00
Gross Profit		0.00	0.00		4,250.00	100.00
Expenses						
Total Expenses		0.00	0.00		0.00	0.00
Net Income	$	0.00	0.00	$	4,250.00	100.00

Retained Earnings Statement

Falcetto Company
Statement of Retained Earnings
For the Three Months Ending March 31, 2002

Beginning Retained Earnings	$	0.00
Adjustments To Date		0.00
Net Income		4,250.00
Subtotal		4,250.00
Ending Retained Earnings	$	4,250.00

Asset portion of Balance Sheet (Explain why there is a "negative balance" in Accounts Receivable.)

Falcetto Company
Balance Sheet
March 31, 2002

ASSETS

Current Assets				
Cash	$	7,000.00		
Accounts Receivable		<2,750.00>		
Total Current Assets				4,250.00
Property and Equipment				
Total Property and Equipment				0.00
Other Assets				
Total Other Assets				0.00
Total Assets			$	4,250.00

P9-5a

Melanie Griffith Company closes its books monthly. On September 30th, selected ledger account balances are:

Notes Receivable	$28,000
Interest Receivable	216

Notes receivable include the following:

Date	Maker	Face	Term	Interest
August 16	Foran, Inc.	$8,000	60 days	12%
August 25	Drexler Co.	$8,000	60 days	12%
September 30	Sego Corp.	$12,000	6 months	9%

Interest is computed using a 360 day year. During October, the following transactions were completed. Peachtree Accounting does not have a method of computing Notes Receivable. You must use the General Journal feature to journalize your entries.

Oct	7	Made sales of $6,900 on Melanie Griffith credit cards.
	12	Made sales of $750 on MasterCard credit cards. The credit card service charge is 4%.
	15	Added $485 to Melanie Griffith customer balance for finance charges on unpaid balances.
	15	Received payment in full from Foran Inc. on the amount due.
	24	Received notice that Drexler note has been dishonored. (Assume that Drexler is expected to pay in the future.)

Instructions:

a. Journalize the October transactions and the October 31st adjusting entry for accrued interest receivable.
b. Enter the balances at October 1st in the receivable accounts. Post the entries to all of the receivable accounts.
c. Show the balance sheet presentation of the receivable accounts as of October 31st.

CHAPTER 10

Plant Assets

OBJECTIVES

- Be able to set up a plant asset account
- Be able to set up an accumulated depreciation account
- Design and execue reoccurring transactions
- Be able to journalize depreciation and depreciation expense

SETTING UP A PLANT ASSET ACCOUNT

Plant assets are tangible resources that are used in the operations of a business and are not intended for sale to customers. In accounting, they are also called property, plant, and equipment; plant and equipment; or fixed assets. These assets are generally long-lived and are expected to provide services to the company for a number of years. With the exception of plant assets decline in service potential over their useful lives.

Plant assets often are split into four classes:

Land – the building site
Land Improvements – driveways, parking lots, fences, underground sprinkler systems, etc.
Buildings – stores, offices, factories, and warehouses
Equipment – checkout counters, cash registers, office furniture, factory machinery, and delivery equipment

In Peachtree, all property, plant, and equipment; plant and equipment; or fixed assets will be classified as Fixed Assets when the account is created as shown in Figure 10.1. On the balance sheet, they are classified as Property and Equipment as shown in Figure 10.2

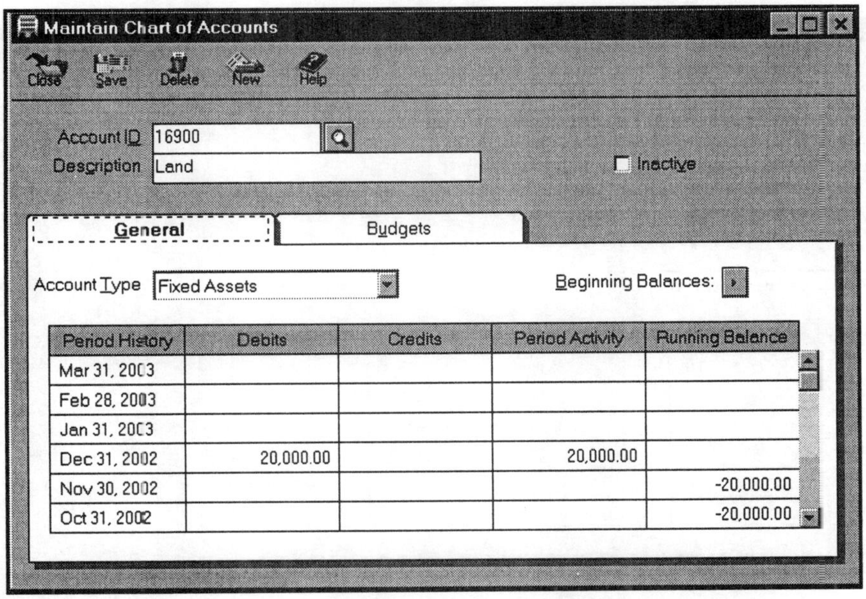

Figure 10. 1 Example of Fixed Asset in Maintain Chart of Accounts

Bellwether Garden Supply
Balance Sheet
March 31, 2003

Property and Equipment		
Furniture and Fixtures	62,769.25	
Equipment	38,738.33	
Vehicles	86,273.40	
Other Depreciable Property	6,200.96	
Buildings	185,500.00	
Building Improvements	26,500.00	
Accum. Depreciation-Furniture	<54,680.57>	
Accum. Depreciation-Equipment	<33,138.11>	
Accum. Depreciation-Vehicles	<51,585.26>	
Accum. Depreciation-Other	<3,788.84>	
Accum. Depreciation-Buildings	<34,483.97>	
Accum. Depreciation-Bldg Imp	<4,926.28>	
Total Property and Equipment		223,378.91

Figure 10. 2 Property and Equipment section (Fixed Assets) of balance sheet.

Accumulated depreciation is a contra asset account to depreciable (fixed) assets. For example, depreciation will be charged against buildings, machinery, and equipment. The depreciable basis (expense) is the difference between an asset's cost and its estimated salvage value. Recording depreciation is a way to indicate that assets have declined in service potential. Accumulated depreciation represents total depreciation taken to date on the assets.

An example from "Maintain Chart of Accounts" is shown in Figure 10.3.

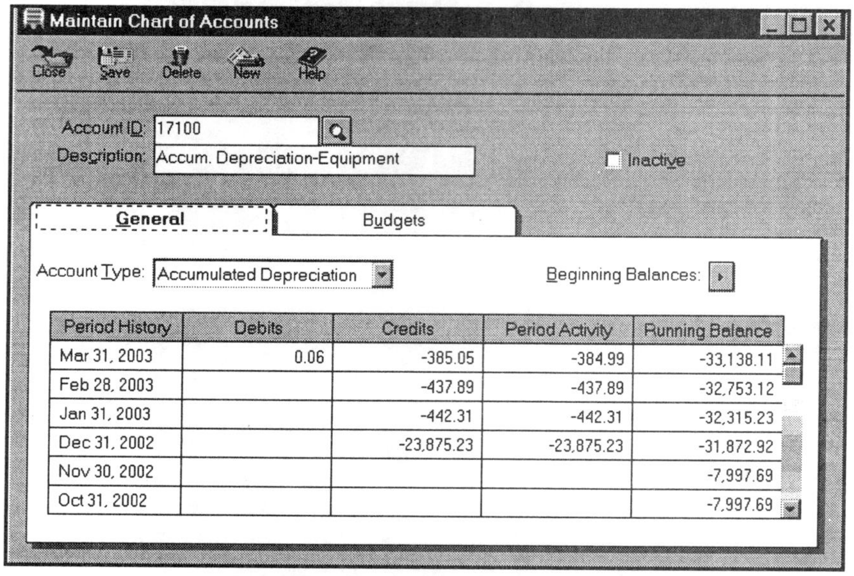

Figure 10. 3 Example of Accumulated Depreciation in Maintain Chart of Accounts

Peachtree does not provide any special way of entering transactions for the purchase of Fixed Assets or entering transactions for Accumulated Depreciation besides a General Journal entry, which was covered previously. Depreciable calculations must be done in advance and entered as a General Journal entry.

There is one exception, however, Straight Line Depreciation can be *automatically* handled for you through a reoccurring General Journal entry.

Creating the Fixed Asset Account(s)

Two accounts will be created in this exercise. The first account to be created is for the purchase of a piece of property (Land) for $150,000. The second account to be created is for the purchase of the building that sits on the land for $250,000.

Create the Fixed asset accounts for the purchase of Land and Building and their appropriate Accumulated Depreciation and Depreciation Expense Accounts.

Step 1: Open "Beyer Video" on your student data disk. Be sure to use your most updated file.
Step 2: The Account No. for Land will be 110 and the account type will be Fixed Assets.
Step 3: The Account No. for Building will be 115 and the account type will be Fixed Assets.
Step 4: The Account No. for Accum Deprec – Building will be 115.1 and the account type will be Accumulated Depreciation
Step 5: The Account No. for Depreciation Expense – Building will be 510 and the account type will be Expenses. The four completed accounts are shown in Figure 10.4.

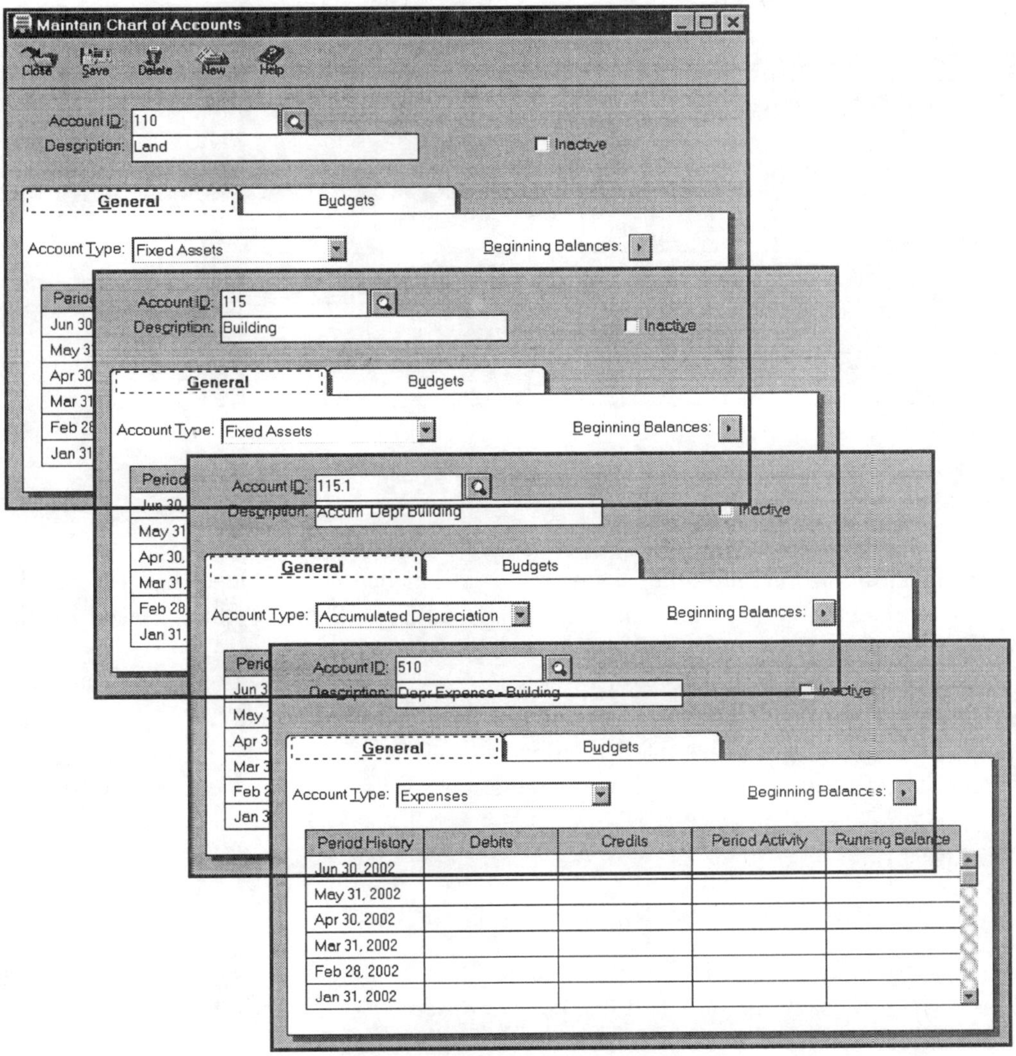

Figure 10. 4 Accounts for Fixed Assets.

Making the Entry

Step 1: Make sure Beyer Video is open to the most up to date file. You will be making a compound General Journal entry on June 18, 2002.

Step 2: Since the asset Land is being increased by $150,000, that account is to be debited.

Step 3: In the same way, the Building account would be debited by $250,000.

Step 4: In order to pay for the new purchases, Notes Payable, a liability account, will be credited for $400,000. The compound General Journal entry is shown in Figure 10.5.

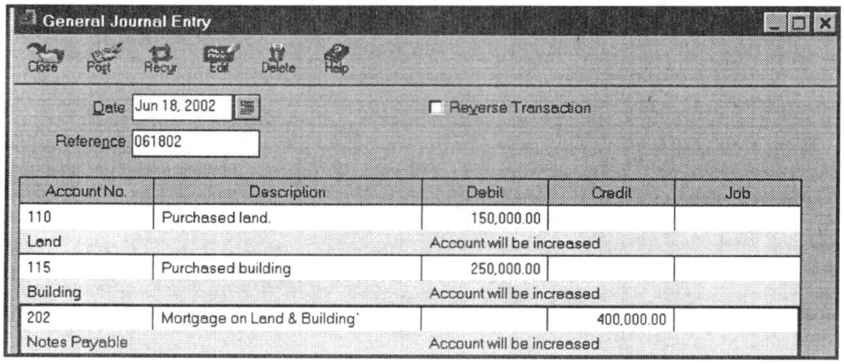

Figure 10. 5 General Journal entry to show purchase of land & building.

Using the straight line method of depreciation, it has been determined that the useful life of the building will be 20 years and that the salvage value will be \$15,000. Based on those figures, the monthly depreciation for the building will be \$979.17

Cost of the Building – Salvage Value = Depreciable Value	250,000 – 15,000 = 235,000
Depreciable Value / 20 years = Yearly Depreciation	235,000 / 20 = 11,750
Yearly Depreciation / 12 months = Monthly Depreciation	11,750 / 12 = 979.17

Recognizing Monthly Depreciation for the Building

You learned how to make this basic entry in Chapter 3, Adjusting Entries. However, since this will be a recurring transaction, one that happens the same way, every time, Peachtree can automate that step for you.

Recurring Transactions:

Step 1: Make the general journal entry as you normally would to expense depreciation.
Step 2: Debit the Depreciation Expense – Building account no. 510 for \$979.17
Step 3: Credit the Accumulated Depreciation – Building Account No. 115.1 for \$979.17. The entry is shown in Figure 10.6

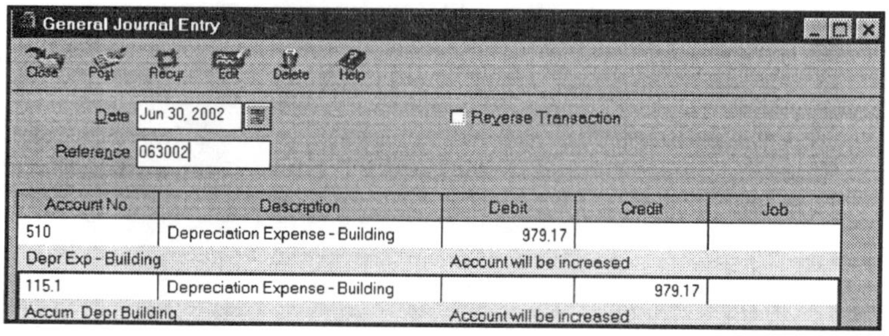

Figure 10. 6 Entry for monthly depreciation of the building.

Step 4: Instead of posting the transaction as you did previously, click on "Recur" on the toolbar as shown in Figure 10.7 below

Figure 10. 7 Menu Bar for General Journal entry.

Step 5: You will be presented with the pull down menu as shown in Figure 10.8. Click "Monthly" and enter "24" as the number of accounting periods this transaction will occur; 24 is entered instead of 240 because Peachtree only recognizes 24 accounting periods at a time.

Step 6: Click "OK" and on the 30 of every month for the next two years, Peachtree will automatically make this entry for you.

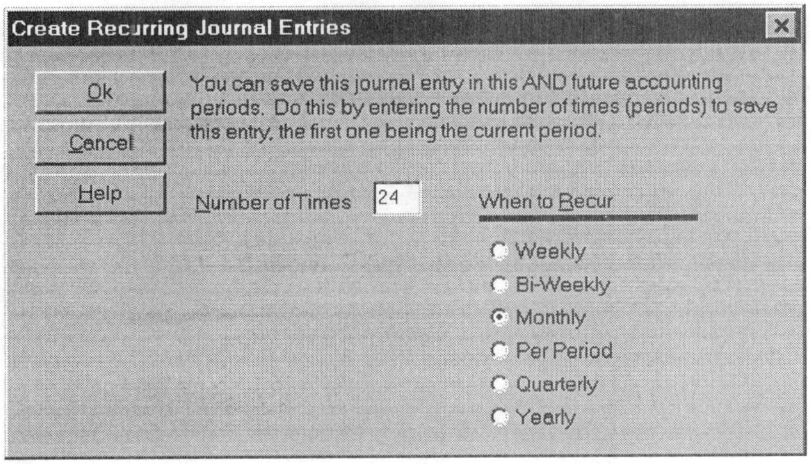

Figure 10. 8 Create Recurring Journal Entries window.

Run a copy of the Balance Sheet for Beyer Video. Look specifically at the assets section of the report, Figure 10.9. Notice the addition of the two accounts for building and land. Also, notice the Accumulated Depreciation account for the building.

If you scroll down a bit farther, you will immediately see how your entries affected the Notes Payable account in the liabilities section, Figure 10.10.

Beyer Video
Balance Sheet
June 30, 2002

ASSETS

Current Assets				
Accounts Receivable	$	3,281.50		
Merchandise Inventory		29,063.00		
Total Current Assets				32,344.50
Property and Equipment				
Land		150,000.00		
Building		250,000.00		
Accum Depr Building		<979.17>		
Total Property and Equipment				399,020.83
Other Assets				
Total Other Assets				0.00
Total Assets			$	431,365.33

Figure 10. 9 Beyer Video's Asset Section of the Balance Sheet.

Beyer Video
Balance Sheet
June 30, 2002

LIABILITIES AND CAPITAL

Current Liabilities				
Accounts Payable	$	31,475.00		
Notes Payable		400,000.00		
Total Current Liabilities				431,475.00
Long-Term Liabilities				
Total Long-Term Liabilities				0.00
Total Liabilities				431,475.00
Capital				
Net Income		<109.67>		
Total Capital				<109.67>
Total Liabilities & Capital			$	431,365.33

Figure 10. 10 Beyer Video's Liabilities & Capital section of the balance sheet.

CHAPTER 11

Payroll and Liabilities

OBJECTIVES

- Discuss the objectives of internal control for payroll.
- Describe and record employer payroll taxes
- Compute and record the payroll for a pay period
- Understand other liabilities of the company.

OVERVIEW

The payroll system is totally automated in Peachtree Complete Accounting® following a setup process for the company and each of your employees. Once you have set up the defaults and records you only have to select each employee using the payroll tasks. Peachtree Accounting automatically computes the paycheck. Checks can be printed in batches or on an individual basis.

The payroll process in Peachtree is divided into four distinct levels:

- **Employee Defaults:**
  - This is the area in which you set up your company's defaults for your employees including General Ledger accounts, pay levels, customized fields and payroll fields.
- **Employee Information**:
  - This is the area where you set up employee information such as name, address, social security number, tax filing status, and individual pay levels.
- **Payroll Journal Entries:**
  - This is the area where you actually process payroll checks.
- **Payroll Reports**
  - This is the area that analyzes the data you enter including period and quarterly earnings, 941 and W-2 forms.

PAYROLL NAVIGATION AID

The Payroll Navigation Aid found at the bottom of the main Peachtree window can be used to complete most of the required payroll tasks. It is shown in Figure 11.1.

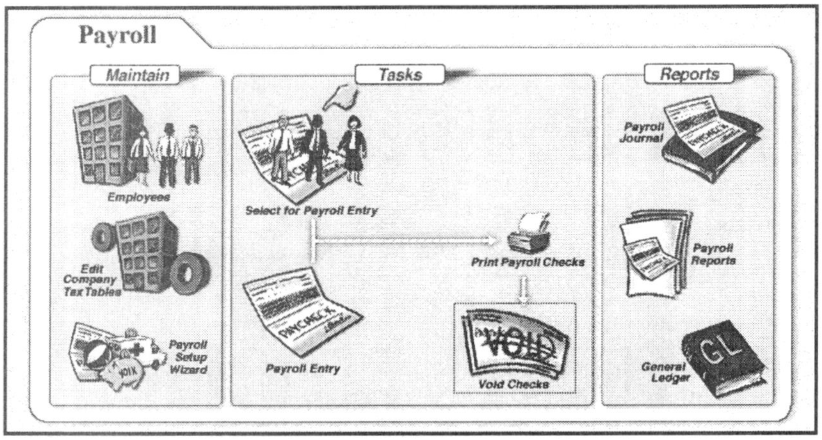

Figure 11. 1 Payroll navigation aid.

Step 1: Open the data files for "Beyer Video"; making sure that you are using the latest version of the data.
Step 2: On the main menu bar, click "Maintain" to get the pull down menu.
Step 3: On the pull down menu, click "Default Information" and then "Payroll Setup Wizard." You will be presented with the screen as illustrated in Figure 11.2. Or click on "Payroll Setup Wizard" on the Navigation Bar.

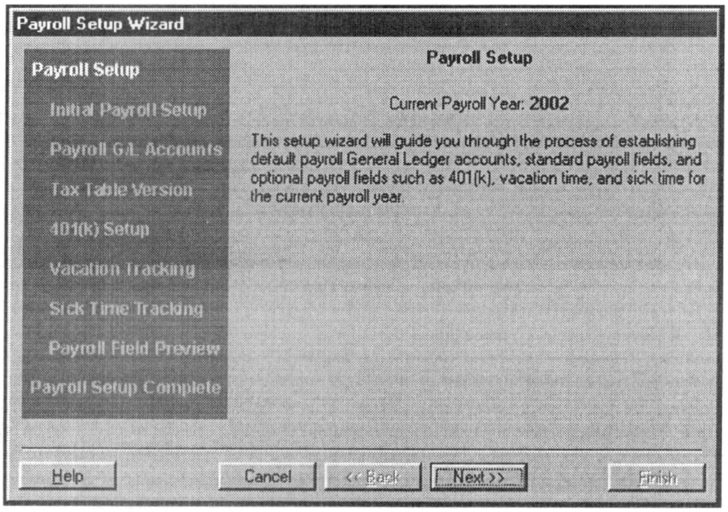

Figure 11. 2 Initial payroll wizard setup screen.

Payroll Defaults

Step 1: Click "Next" at the bottom of the screen to get the initial payroll setup screen as shown in Figure 11.3.

Step 2: Select from the drop-down list the state abbreviation for the primary state in which your employees work. Use "GA" for Georgia. Leave locality blank for now. This would be used if the city where "Beyer Video" was located levied a local withholding tax.

Step 3: Enter the unemployment percentage that the state requires your company to pay. Enter 2.7% (e.g., enter 2-point-7 for 2.7%). This is used to create the calculation for SUI or State Unemployment Insurance. Your company's accountant will provide this number to you.

Step 4: By default, the Tips and Meals fields (predominantly for restaurants) are memo fields. Their amounts are logged for reporting and tax calculations. Check your entries with Figure 11.3.

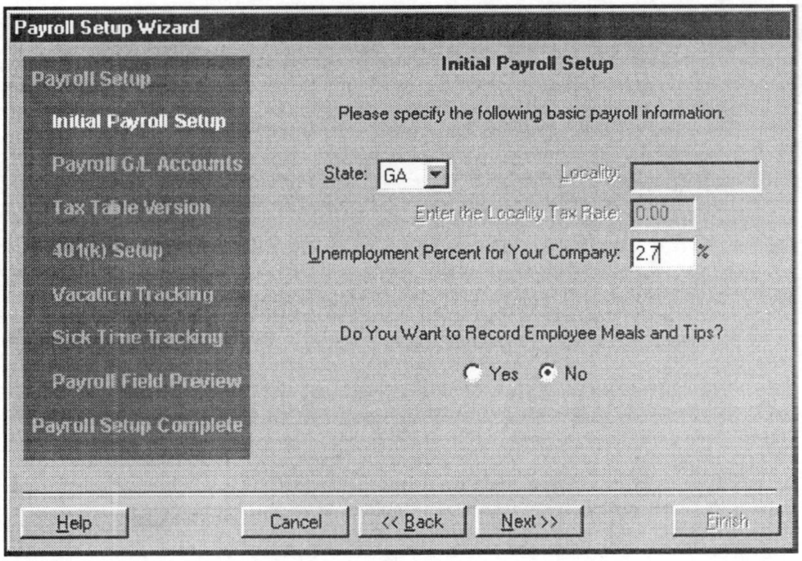

Figure 11. 3 Initial Payroll Setup (cont.)

Default Payroll General Ledger Accounts

We now need to set up the General Ledger accounts associated with our standard payroll fields. The "Wages Expense" account, "Payroll Tax Payable" account, and "Payroll Tax Expense" accounts must be established.

These are new accounts that must be created.

Step 1: Create the accounts for the General Ledger using Account No. 510 for Wages Expense (an Expense type), using Account No. 205 for Payroll Tax Payable (an Other Current Liability type), and using Account No. 520 for Payroll Tax Expense (an Expense type).

Step 2: Enter the account numbers in the spaces designated and compare your entries with those in Figure 11.4.

Step 3: Click on "Next" on the bottom of the screen to continue.

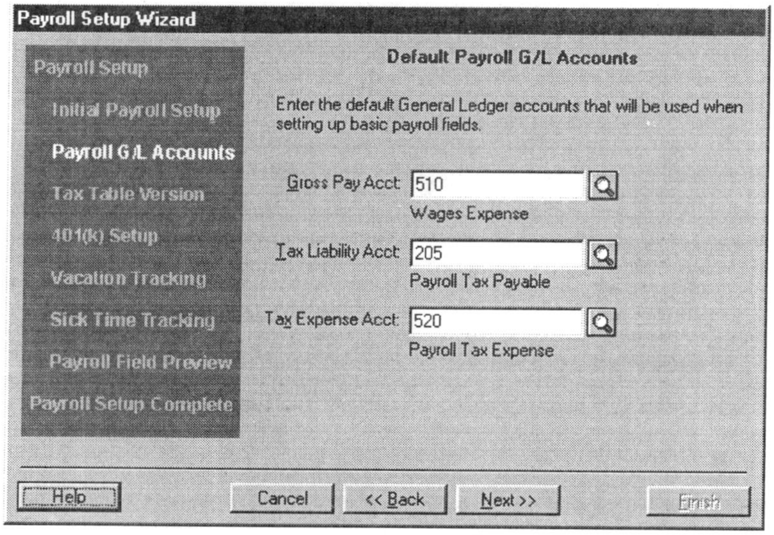

Figure 11. 4 General Ledger Accounts for Payroll

Tax Table Information

Peachtree Accounting provides tax tables through a subscription service. These "standard" tables, known as "Global Tax Tables" are used to calculate Federal, state, and local payroll taxes. A tax table was included on the Peachtree CD provided with this book.

Many professional bookkeepers subscribe to the Peachtree Tax Service to receive annual global tax table updates. Because Peachtree software keeps track of all the latest changes, it can save you time by providing this information.

Keep the default information provided on the screen as shown in Figure 11.5.

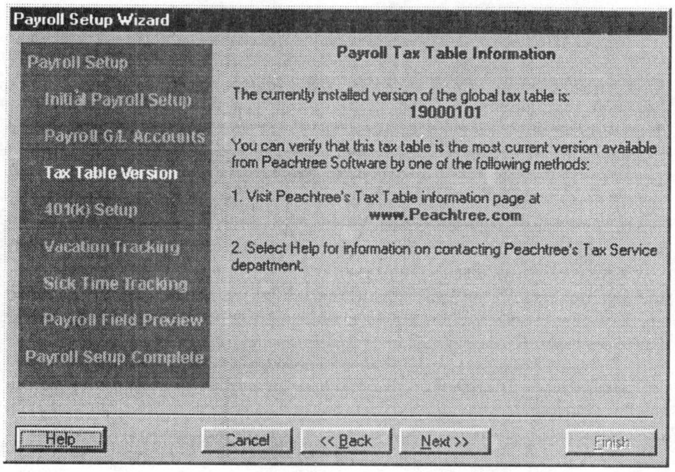

Figure 11. 5 Default Tax Table Information.

401(k) Setup Information

The next step concerns 401(k) pretax deductions. A company's 401(k) plan allows a specified percentage of an employee's gross wage to be taken out prior to taxes and placed into a savings type plan set up by the company. The contributions and the savings plan proceeds are tax deferred by the U.S. government.

There is not a 401(k) plan at Beyer Video, so click the "Next" button to continue.

Vacation and Sick Time Tracking

Peachtree Accounting can track vacation and sick time in your company. Vacation and sick time for employees can be set up two ways:

- Employees earn all their hours at one time, or
- Employees earn a specified number of hours each payroll period, which accrues throughout the year.

When employees go on vacation or are out sick, the used hours are recorded on their paychecks and are subtracted from their total hours allowed or earned. The remaining hours are continually tracked throughout the payroll year.

Step 1: No entries are required on this screen or the next, click "Next" two times to continue to the Payroll Fields Preview Screen shown below in Figure 11.6.

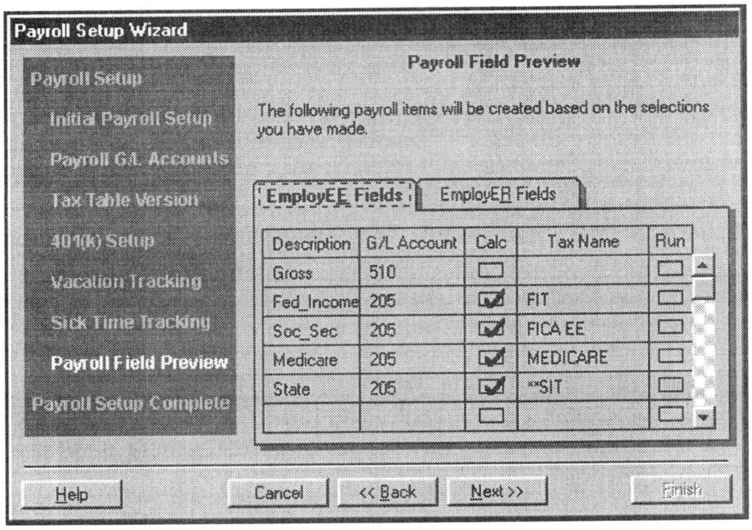

Figure 11. 6 Payroll Field Preview screen.

Each of the accounts, as you set them up, appears on this window together with their matching General Ledger account number. The specific tax is shown on the right side with its matching account on the left side of the form.

Step 2: If there are no errors, click "Next" to get the screen shown on the next page, Figure 11.7.

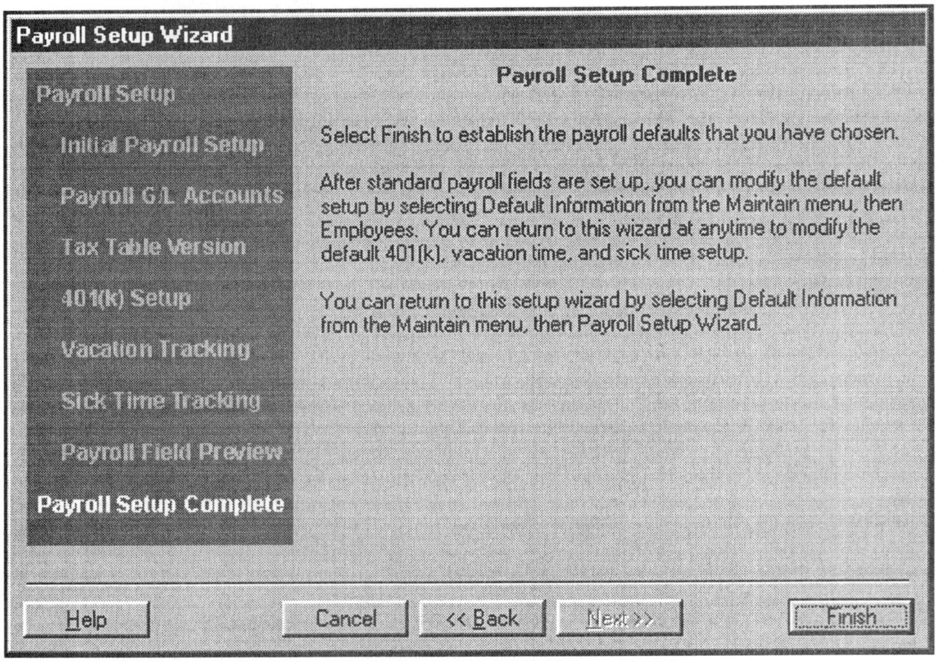

Figure 11. 7 Final screen in Payroll Setup Wizard.

Step 3: Click "Finish" to complete Payroll Setup.

EMPLOYEE DEFAULT ENTRIES

Modifying the payroll setup to match your company's specific needs is the next task. The date found on the Employee Defaults window displays standard employee information that will be considered during payroll entry.

Step 1: On the "Main Menu" bar, select "Maintain," and then select Default information, then "Employees" to get the screen in Figure 11.8.

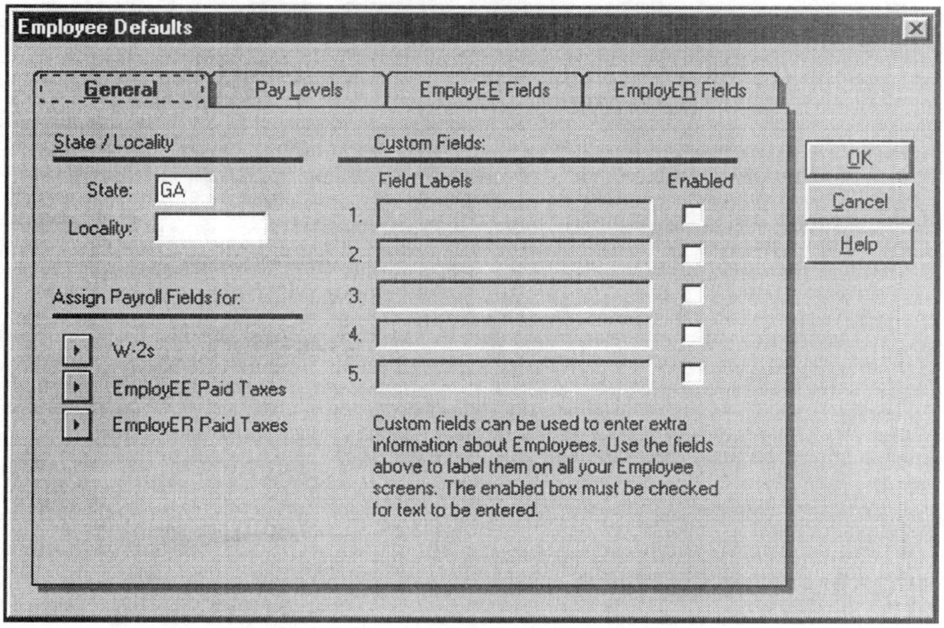

Figure 11. 8 Employee Defaults Screen

Constant information that serves as the basis for payroll processing is entered in Employee Defaults. Notice the last two tabs: EmployEE fields affecting your workers and EmployER fields for your company defaults.

Step 2: Select the "General" tab on the Employee Defaults window.
Step 3: Enter your state and/or locality codes. These codes are already preset for you if the Payroll Setup Wizard was completed previously.
Step 4: The custom fields allow you to enter you own field labels to keep track of specific information. For example, you could enter "Birthday" as a field label and maintain employees' birthday records. The information entered plays no part in the actual calculation of your payroll – it is for record keeping only.

Step 5: Part of the payroll process includes setting up fields for W-2 Forms and paid taxes by the EmployEE and the EmployER. These fields are used to calculate and post employee deductions and allowances and employer taxes. Use the defaults already set up as shown in Figure 11.9. The information used in the forms are also used for corresponding amounts on other forms

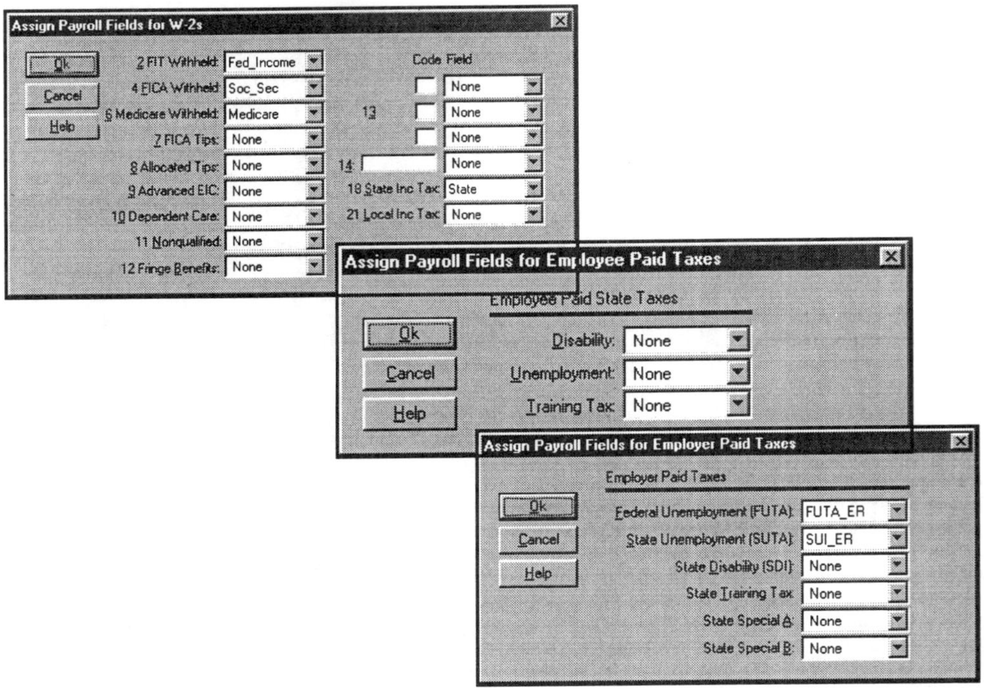

Figure 11. 9 The three assign payroll fields windows

PAY LEVEL INFORMATION ENTRIES

The second tab of the Employee Defaults window is for levels of employee pay. You may enter both hourly and salary levels in this window. A maximum of 20 different pay levels and names can be entered.

Make or keep the entries as they appear in Figure 11.10. Each of the payroll entries will be entered in the "generic" Payroll Expense Account (Account No. 510), which you set up earlier.

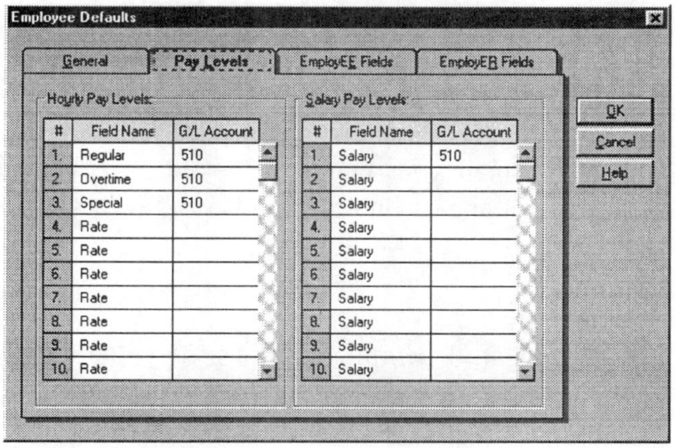

Figure 11. 10 Pay Level Information

EMPLOYEE FIELDS INFORMATION ENTRIES

The payroll fields listed in Figure 11.11 serve three basic functions:

- Payroll deductions and allowances that combine with the gross to compute the net pay.
- Memo amounts, such as Vacation and Sick hours, Tips and Meals are also tracked for reporting and tax calculations but not posted to the General Ledger.
- Tax Amounts, tracked for computing the employee's W-2 amounts.

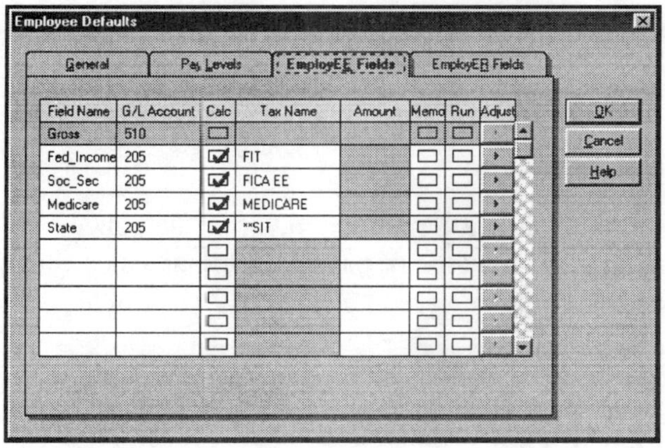

Figure 11. 11 Employee Entry defaults.

These fields are used to hold amounts that should be accumulated and updated when your payroll gets posted. These fields can be changed if necessary, but for our example leave the defaults as they appear in Figure 11.11. These are fields you set up earlier.

EMPLOYER INFORMATION FIELDS ENTRIES

Employer fields are the expenses for payroll which your company would be responsible for during payroll entry. These specific fields will not appear on an employee's paycheck. Two new accounts must be created for this form.

Step 1: Make sure "Beyer Video" is open.
Step 2: Create Account No. 210 titled State Unemployment Tax Payable and Account No. 211 State Unemployment Tax Expense.
Step 3: Enter State Unemployment Tax Payable, Account No. 210 to the blank on the EmployER Information Fields window. It is illustrated in Figure 11.12.

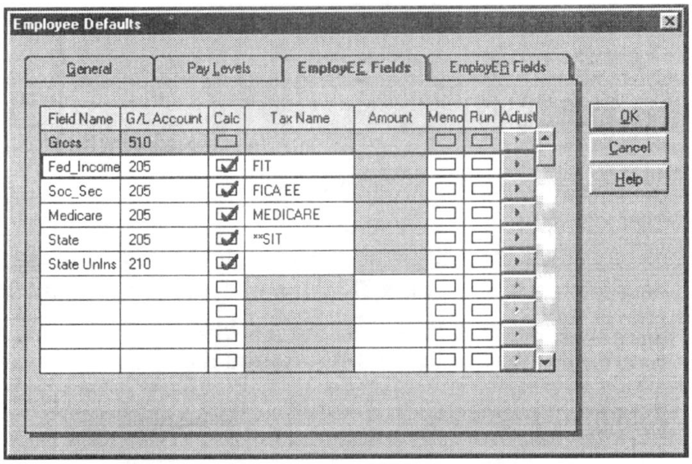

Figure 11. 12 Employee Defaults with new field.

Before employees and transactions are entered in the next section, note that once you start entering payroll transactions, you may not change the name of payroll field names or change the order in which payroll field names are listed.

EMPLOYEE MAINTENANCE INFORMATION ENTRIES

The information in the "Maintain Employees" window is displayed below as a completed form in Figure 11.13 and includes five working tabs on the form plus the header at the top of the form.

Step 1: Under "Maintain" on the main menu bar, click on "Employees/Sales Representatives." You will be presented with the blank form where you will enter Employee Information.
Step 2: Using the General Tab, enter the employee's ID, name and address information. The first employee's ID is #34, the employee's name is Valarie King, the address is 2555 Northwinds Parkway, Apt. 3, in Atlanta, GA 30341.

Step 3: Enter the employee's social security number 256-70-1116; skip Type, but enter 770.555.4900 as the phone number.

Step 4: Enter the hire date: April 15, 1977 and the last pay raise date: April 15, 2000. The employee still works for Beyer Video so leave the "Terminated" field blank.

Step 5: Complete the witholding information including the filing status for federal, state and local tax authorities. Use the Employee's W-4 form for this information. Any allowances and additional withholding amounts are entered here as well. Valarie is single with one federal and state exemption. The completed form is shown in Figure 11.13.

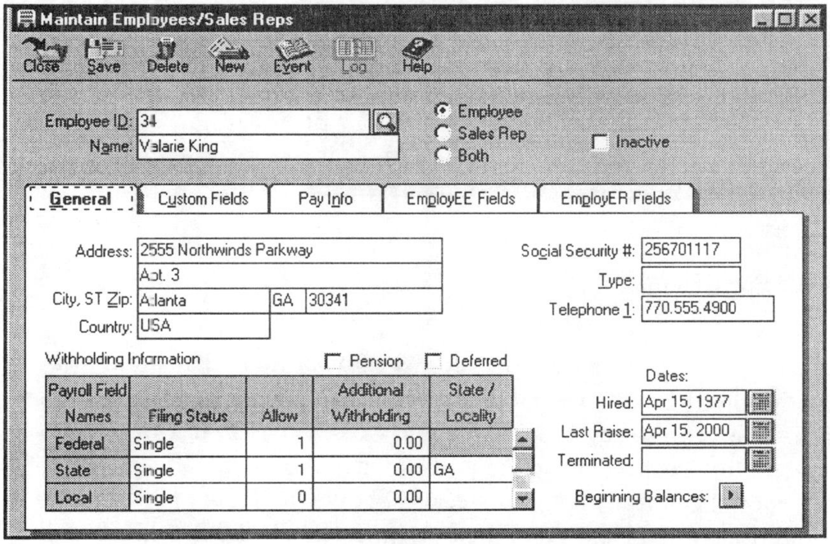

Figure 11. 13 Maintain Employees entry form.

If you had previous Payroll information you could, at this point, click on the "Beginning Balances" tab to fill in all of the payroll information to date. Click on the arrow to see what is available; however, do not enter any information. Beyer Video, our sample company, is new and has no previous employee history.

Three of the remaining tabs are set and do not require any changes. At this time, there are no custom fields to worry about. EmployEE fields and EmployER fields were set up earlier and require no further attention. However, we still must enter the Pay Information for Valarie so that she is paid correctly this pay period.

Step 1: Click on the "Pay Info" tab. The completed form is shown in Figure 11.14.

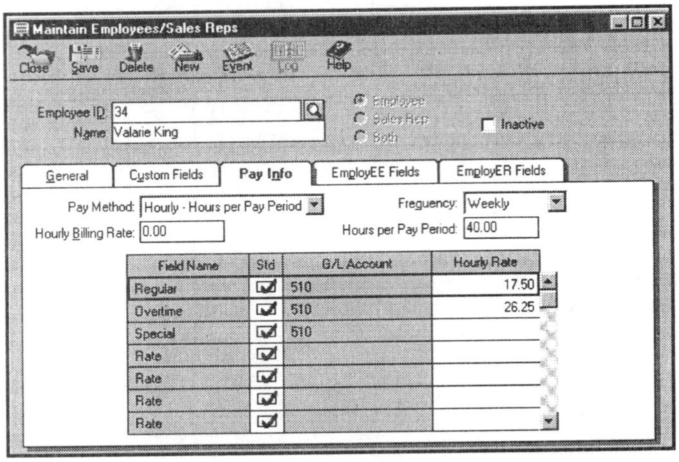

Figure 11. 14 Completed Payroll form.

Step 2: Complete the entry. Valarie works for \$17.50 per hour. The hourly pay rate is set in the "Pay Method" box. Other methods include per piece, salary, and so on.

Step 3: Because the employees are paid on a weekly basis at Beyer Video, set the Frequency box to "weekly" using the pull-down menu.

Step 4: Valarie works a normal 40-hour week as shown in "Hours per Pay Period.

Step 5: And, the wage rate (17.50) and the overtime rate (17.50/2 + 17.50) are entered in the "Hourly Rate" blanks.

Step 6: Compare your work with Figure 13.13 and correct any errors.

Step 7: Click "Save" on the toolbar when completed.

You may use the "Payroll Navigation Aid" at the bottom of the Peachtree main window, (Figure 11.15) whenever you wish to update employee or payroll information.

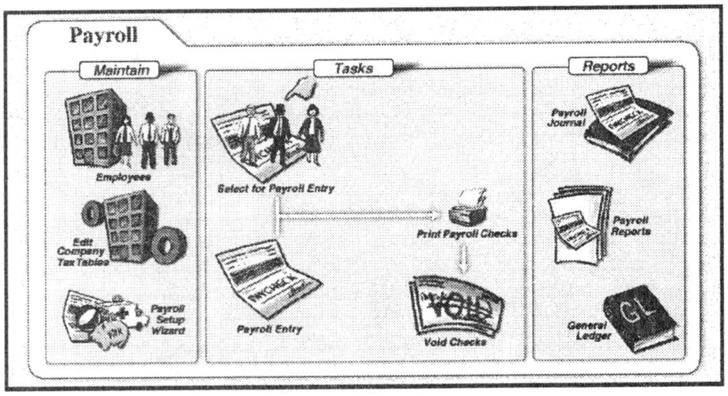

Figure 11. 15 Payroll Navigation Aid

Step 1: Click on the Payroll Navigation Aid.
Step 2: Click on , in the left section labeled "Maintain," "Employees"
Step 3: Enter the following three employees from Table 11.1 below.

Table 11. 1 Employee Listing for Beyer Video Payroll

ID	21	5	20
Name:	Mike Crofton	John Caine	Karen Cattz
Address	340 14th St., NE	15 W. Peachtree St.	21 5th Street., NW
City/ST/Zip	Atlanta, GA 30344	Atlanta, GA 30321	Marietta, GA 30321
SSN	256-90-5881	255-10-4467	010-14-7375
Phone	770.555.1943	770.555.7950.	404.555.9959
Date Hired	4/12/00	7/1/97	7/4/98
Last Raise	4/12/01		7/4/99
Filing Status	Married – 2 allowances	Married – 1 allowance	Single – 3 allowances
Pay Method	Salary	Hourly	Hourly
Frequency	Weekly	Weekly	Weekly
Hour/pay period	40	40	40
Regular Pay Rate	$575.00	$35.00	$25.00
Overtime Pay	None	Time and a half	Double time.

Double check your work by running a "Payroll List" from the Reports menu on the main menu bar. Your report should look similar to the one shown in Figure 11.16.

Beyer Video
Employee List

Filter Criteria includes: Report order is by ID.

Employee ID Employee	Address line 1 Address line 2 City ST ZIP	SS No	Fed Filing Stat	Pay Type
20 Karen Cattz	21 5th Street., NW Marietta, GA 30321 USA	010-14-7375	Single	Hourly
21 Mike Crofton	340 14th St., NE Atlenta,, GA 30344 USA	256-90-5881	Married	Salaried
34 Valarie King	2555 Northwinds Parkway Apt. 3 Atlanta, GA 30341 USA	256701117	Single	Hourly
5 John Caine	15 W. Peachtree St. Atlanta,, GA 30321 USA	255104461	Married	Hourly

Figure 11. 16 Employe List.

PAYROLL TAXES AND TAX TABLES

Tax tables in Peachtree are used with employee and employer payroll field. Changing and editing payroll tax tables is beyond the scope of this workbook. It is unlikely you would want to change these anyway. Even though there are additional costs involved you may depend on a tax service provided by Peachtree Software. (This feature is not available in your edition of Peachtree.) In calculating payroll in the next section we will use the tax tables and percentages as of January 2001. These percentages are always subject to change based on current federal, state and local ordinances.

CREATING THE PAYROLL AND ISSUING PAYCHECKS

Once your payroll is set up in Peachtree, there is little work left to do. When it is time to pay your employees:

- Enter or select the employee ID of the person(s) you wish to pay.
- Specify the pay period.
- Enter any special amounts.
- Verify the information
- Save, Post, and Print the paychecks

All entries made in Payroll are posted to the General Ledger and the Employee File. Once a valid employee ID has been entered, the rest of information is filled in automatically. You entered enough information in the Maintain Employees record previously to determine what a "normal" paycheck would be. If those data are correct (verification process), save the paycheck and proceed to next employee.

Here's how it is done:

Step 1: Click on the "Payroll Navigation Aid" and select "Select for Payroll Entry." If necessary, refer to Figure 11.16.

Step 2: You will be presented with the "Select Employees – Filter Selection" dialog window as shown in Figure 11.17.

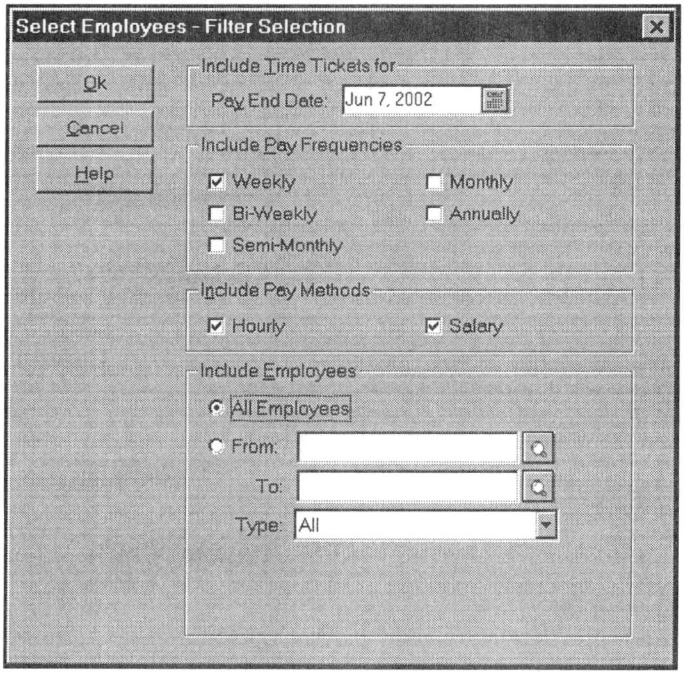

Figure 11. 17 Select Employees - Filter Selection window.

Step 3: The pay end date is June 7, 2002. Include all weekly pay frequencies. Checks will be issued on June 10, 2002.

Step 4: We have two types of pay, hourly or salary. Select both to include this pay period.

Step 5: Finally, include all employees to be paid.

Step 6: Check your work with Figure 11.16, correct any errors and Click "OK" to continue.

Step 7: The "Select Employees to Pay" window appears. Make sure the employees you wish to pay have check marks next to them. Your deductions should have been figured for you.

Step 8: Double check your payroll; if satisfied, print the paychecks.

Demonstration Problem

Indiana Jones Company had the following selected transactions. Assume the Peachtree Complete Payroll system was not used and all entries are General Journal entries. Open the Indiana Jones Company on your Student Data Disk.

Feb 1 Signs a $50,000, 6-month, 9%- interest bearing note payable to Citibank and receives $50,000 in cash.

10 Cash register sales total $43,200, which includes an 8% sales tax.

28 The payroll for the month consists of Sales Salaries $32,000 and Office Salaries $18,000. All wages are subject to 8% FICA taxes. A total of $8,900 federal income taxes are withheld. The salaries are paid on March 1.

Feb 28 The following adjustment data are developed:

1. Interest expense of $375 has been incurred on the note.
2. Employer payroll taxes include 8% FICA taxes, a 5.4% state unemployment tax and a 0.8% federal unemployment tax.
3. Some sales were made under warranty. Of the units sold under warranty, 350 are expected to become defective. Repair costs are estimated to be $40 per unit.

Instructions:

a. Journalize the February transactions.
b. Journalize the adjusting entries at February 28th.

Solution to Demonstration Problem

Journal Entry for Note Payable. (Since the note is due in 6 months, you may recognize the note as a current liability.)

Date: Feb 1, 2002   Reverse Transaction
Reference: Demo Prob 1

Account No.	Description	Debit	Credit	Job
101 Cash	Issued 6 month note to CitiBank	50,000.00 Account will be increased		
225 Notes Payable	Issued 6 month note to CitiBank	Account will be increased	50,000.00	

Journal Entry to recognize Cash Sales and Sales Tax due (payable).

Date: Feb 10, 2002   Reverse Transaction
Reference: Demo Prob 2

Account No.	Description	Debit	Credit	Job
101 Cash	Sales & Sales Tax Collected & Payabl	43,200.00 Account will be increased		
400 Sales	Sales & Sales Tax Collected/Payable	Account will be increased	40,000.00	
230 Sales Tax Payable	Sales & Sales Tax Collected/Payable	Account will be increased	3,200.00	

To Journalize February salaries and taxes due.

Date: Feb 28, 2002 ☐ Reverse Transaction
Reference: Demo Prob 3

Account No.	Description	Debit	Credit	Job
610		32,000.00		
Sales Salaries Expense		Account will be increased		
615		18,000.00		
Office Salaries Expense		Account will be increased		
250			4,000.00	
FICA Tax Payable		Account will be increased		
255			8,900.00	
Federal Income Tax Payable		Account will be increased		
260			37,100.00	
Salaries Payable		Account will be increased		

Part "B"

To record accrued interest for February.

Date: Feb 28, 2002 ☐ Reverse Transaction
Reference: Demo Prob 4

Account No.	Description	Debit	Credit	Job
510	Accrued Interest for February	375.00		
Interest Expense		Account will be increased		
226	Accrued Interest for February		375.00	
Interest Payable		Account will be increased		

To record employer's payroll taxes on February payroll.

Date: Feb 28, 2002 ☐ Reverse Transaction
Reference: Demo Prob 5

Account No.	Description	Debit	Credit	Job
620	Feb employer's payroll taxes.	7,100.00		
Payroll Tax Expense		Account will be increased		
250			4,000.00	
FICA Tax Payable		Account will be increased		
256			400.00	
Fed Unemployement Tax Payable		Account will be increased		
257			2,700.00	
GA Unemployement Tax Payable		Account will be increased		

To record Warranty Expense.

Date: Feb 28, 2002 ☐ Reverse Transaction
Reference: Demo Prob 5

Account No.	Description	Debit	Credit	Job
515	Est warranty liability	14,000.00		
Warranty Expense		Account will be increased		
227	Ext warranty liability		14,000.00	
Estimated Warranty Liability		Account will be increased		

P11-1a

On January 1, 2002, the ledger of Twyla Co., found on your Student Data Disk, contains the following liability accounts:

Accounts Payable	$52,000
Sales Taxes Payable	7,000
Unearned Service Revenue	16,000

During January, the following selected transactions occurred:

Jan	5	Sold merchandise for cash totaling $16,632, which includes 8% sales taxes.
	12	Provided services for customers who had made advance payments of $10,000
	14	Paid state revenue department for sales taxes collected in December 2001 ($7,700)
	20	Sold 500 units of a new product on credit at $50 per unit, plus 8% sales tax. This new product is subject to a 1-year warranty.
	21	Borrowed $18,000 from UCLA Bank on a 3-month, 10%, $18,000 note.
	25	Sold merchandise for cash totaling $11,340, which includes 8% sales taxes.

Instructions:

a. Open the file and journalize the January transactions.
b. Journalize the adjusting entries at January 31st for:
    1. The outstanding notes payable, and
    2. Estimated warranty liability, assuming warranty costs are expected to equal 7% of sales of the new product.
c. Prepare the current liabilities section of the balance sheet at January 31, 2002. assume no change in accounts payable.

P11-4a

The following payroll liability accounts are included in the ledger of Nam Viet Company on January 12, 2002.

FICA Tax Payable	$ 760.00
Federal Income Taxes Payable	1,004.60
State Income Taxes Payable	108.95
Federal Unemployment Taxes Payable	288.95
State Unemployment Taxes Payable	1,954.40
Union Dues Payable	870.00
U.S. Savings Bonds Payable	360.00

In January, the following transactions occurred:

Jan 10 Sent check for $870 to union treasure for union dues.

12 Deposited check for $1,764.60 in Federal Reserve bank for FICA taxes and federal income taxes withheld.

15 Purchased U.S. Savings Bonds for employees by writing check for $360

17 Paid state income taxes withheld from employees

31 Completed monthly payroll register, which shows office salaries $14,600, store wages $28,400, FICA taxes withheld $3,440, Federal income taxes payable $1,684, state income taxes payable $360, union dues payable $400, United Fund Contributions payable $1,888 and net pay $35,228.

31 Prepared payroll checks for the net pay and distributed checks to employees.

At January 31st, the company also makes the following accrued adjustments pertaining to employee compensation.

1. Employer payroll taxes: FICA taxes 8%, federal unemployment taxes 0.8%, and state unemployment taxes 5.4%
2. Vacation pay: 6% of gross earnings.

CHAPTER 12

Accounting Principles

OBJECTIVES

- Explain the meaning of generally accepted accounting principles.
- Identify the key items of the conceptual framework.
- Discuss the elements of financial statements.
- Discuss the qualitative characteristics of accounting information.
- Describe the basic objectives of financial reporting.
- Describe the operating guidelines of financial reporting.

THE CONCEPTUAL FRAMEWORK OF ACCOUNTING

What you have learned up to this point is the automated process of entering and extracting data from Peachtree Complete Accounting®. The goal of all of your data entry leads to the preparation of financial reports about a company - the company's financial statements.

In regards to Financial Accounting, the accounting profession has established a set of standards and rules that are recognized as a general guide for financial reporting. This recognized set of standards is called generally accepted accounting principles (GAAP). "Generally accepted" means that these principles must have "substantial authoritative support." That support usually comes from two standard setting bodies: the Financial Accounting Standards Board (FASB) and the Securities and Exchange Commission (SEC).

In fact, the FASB has even developed a conceptual framework that serves as the basis for resolving accounting and reporting problems. "... a constitution, a coherent system of interrelated objectives and fundamentals," is how the Board view its conceptual framework.

The FASB's conceptual framework consists of the following four items:

1. Objectives of financial reporting.
2. Qualitative characteristics of accounting information.
3. Elements of financial statements.
4. Operating guidelines (assumptions, principles and constraints).

Objectives of Financial Reporting

Who uses financial statements? Why? What information do they need? How knowledgeable about business and accounting are financial statement users? How should financial information be reported so that it is best understood?

In answering these questions, the FASB decided that the objectives of financial reporting are to provide data that:

1. Is useful to those making investment and credit decisions.
2. Is helpful in assessing future cash flows.
3. Identifies the economic resources (assets), the claims to those resources (liabilities) and the changes in those resources and claims.

Qualitative Characteristics of Accounting Information

To be useful, information should possess the following qualitative characteristics:

Relevance

Accounting information has relevance if it makes a difference in a decision. Relevant information has either predictive or feedback value or both. Predictive value helps users forecast future events. Feedback value confirms or corrects prior expectations.

Reliability

Reliability of information means that the information is free or error and bias. Accounting information must be verifiable and a faithful representation of what it purports to be. Accounting information also must be neutral. It cannot be selected, prepared, or presented to favor one set of interested users over another.

Comparability

Accounting information about an enterprise is most useful when it can be compared with accounting information about other enterprises. Comparability results when different companies use the same accounting principles.

Consistency

Consistency means that a company uses the same accounting principles and methods from year to year. When financial information has bee reported on a consistent basis, the financial statements permit meaningful analysis of trends within a company. A company can change to a new method of accounting, but management must justify that the new method results in more meaningful financial information.

Elements of Financial Statements

An important part of the accounting conceptual framework is a set of definitions that describe the basic terms used in accounting. The FASB refers to this set of definitions as the elements of financial statements. They include such terms as assets, liabilities, equity, revenues, and expenses.

Because these elements are so important, it is crucial that they be precisely defined and universally applied. A good set of definitions should provide answers to many questions. Because you have already learned most of these definitions in previous chapters, they will not be repeated here.

Operating Guidelines

The objectives of financial reporting, the qualitative characteristics of accounting information, and the elements of financial statements are very broad. Because practicing accountants must solve practical problems, more detailed guidelines are needed. We classify these guidelines as assumptions, principles, and constraints. These guidelines are well established and accepted in accounting.

Assumptions

Assumptions provide a foundation for the accounting process.

Principles

Principles are the specific rules that indicate how economic events should be reported in the accounting process.

Constraints

Constraints on the accounting process allow for a relaxation of the principles under certain circumstances.

CHAPTER 13

Partnerships

OBJECTIVES

- Be able to set up a partnership accounting method
- Be able to Determining partnership retained earnings
- Identify and determine beginning capital in a newly formed partnership
- Prepare the entries for partnership withdrawals.

PARTNERSHIP FORM OF ORGANIZATION

There are basic rules for partnerships set forth by The Uniform Partnership Act. These rules outline the formation and operation of partnerships and are recognized in most states. This act defines a partnership as an association of two or more persons to carry on as co-owners of a business for profit. Partnerships are common in retail establishments and in small manufacturing companies.

Accountants, lawyers, and doctors find it desirable to form partnerships with other professionals in their field.

Partnerships are easy to form in Peachtree Accounting.

SETTING UP A PARTNERSHIP IN PEACHTREE

Step 1: On the Peachtree main menu, follow the directions in "Setting Up a New Company." Everything is self explanatory. Create a new company called "Paul England & Partners." Make sure to highlight "Partnership" in the "Business Type" box as shown in Figure 13.1.

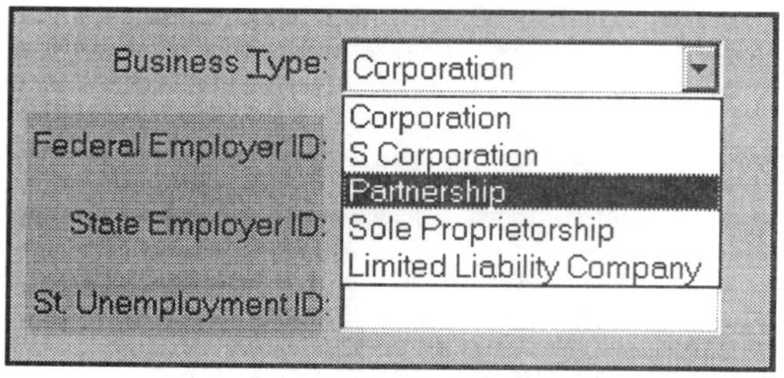

Figure 13. 1 Business Type section of New Company Information.

Step 2: Set up the "Chart of Accounts" for Paul England as shown in Figure 13.2. Note specifically how the equity accounts are set up. Each partner has an account for his contributions (which doesn't close) plus the Equity, and a Retained Earnings account.[1]

Paul England & Partners
Chart of Accounts
As of Jan 31, 2002
Filter Criteria includes: Report order is by ID. Report is printed with Accounts having Zero Amounts and in Detail Format.

Account ID	Account Description	Activ	Account Type
101	Cash	Yes	Cash
105	Accounts Receivable	Yes	Accounts Receivable
201	Accounts Payable	Yes	Accounts Payable
301	Retained Earnings	Yes	Equity-Retained Earnings
310	Paul England, Capital	Yes	Equity-doesn't close
315	Charles Door, Capital	Yes	Equity-doesn't close
320	Gene Song,Capital	Yes	Equity-doesn't close
400	Sales	Yes	Income

Figure 13. 2 Chart of Accounts for Paul England & Partners

Step 3: Each of the partners contributes various amounts of cash to the company. They could have contributed equipment, fixed assets, or anything else of value. Make a General Journal entry to record the Cash for each partner as listed below.

Paul England	$75,000
Charles Door	$50,000
Gene Song	$25,000

Step 4: Check your G/J entry with the one shown in Figure 13.3 and post the entry.

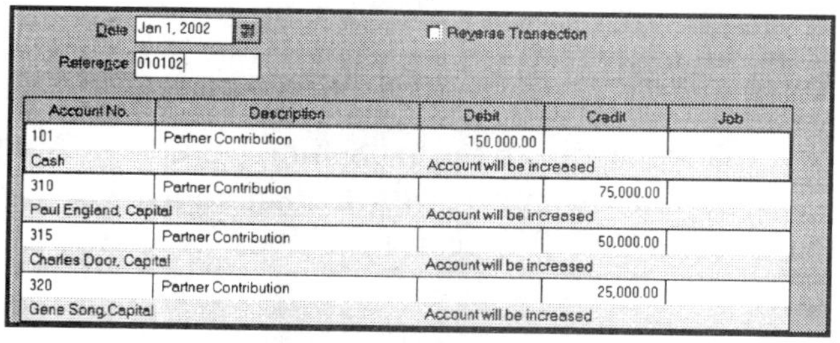

Figure 13. 3 General Journal entry for Partner's contribution.

---

[1] Peachtree Complete Accounting requires a Retained Earnings Account in its set up procedure. Retained Earnings will be covered under corporate accounting.

Step 5: The partners earn $34,000 in sales. Create and post the invoice for the Sale to NBC Entertainment. The completed invoice appears in Figure 13.4.

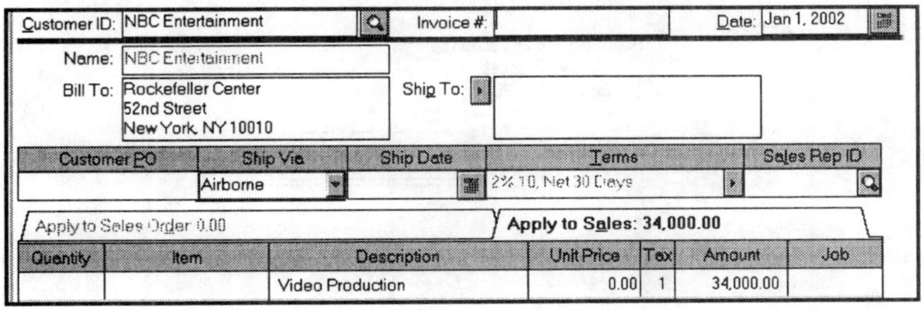

Figure 13. 4 Sales invoice for NBC - recorded as an Account Receivable.

Step 6: Run a copy of the "Balance Sheet" from the "General Ledger" reports section to see how your entries affected the overall financial picture of the company. The complete balance sheet is shown in Figure 13.5.

Step 7: Mr. Door would like to withdraw $10,000 from the business. Create the "Drawing Account" for Mr. Door and create a General Journal entry to record the transaction on January 15th. The entry is shown in as Figure 13.5.

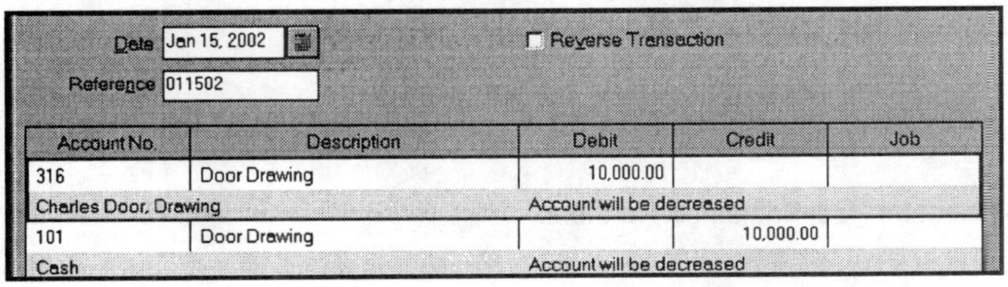

Figure 13. 5 General Journal transaction for Door's withdrawal of funds.

Paul England & Partners
Balance Sheet
January 31, 2002

Total Assets		$ 184,000.00
LIABILITIES AND CAPITAL		
Current Liabilities		
Total Current Liabilities		0.00
Long-Term Liabilities		
Total Long-Term Liabilities		0.00
Total Liabilities		0.00
Capital		
Paul England, Capital	$ 75,000.00	
Charles Door, Capital	50,000.00	
Gene Song,Capital	25,000.00	
Net Income	34,000.00	
Total Capital		184,000.00
Total Liabilities & Capital		$ 184,000.00

Figure 13. 6 Balance Sheet for Paul England & Partners.

Demonstration Problem

On January 1,2002, the capital balances in Hollingsworth Company are Lois Holly $26,000, and Jim Worth $24,000. In 2002, the partnership reports net income of $30,000. The income ratio provides for salary allowances of $12,000 for Holly and $10,000 to Worth and the remainder equally. Neither partner had any drawings in 2002.

Assume that the following independent transactions occur on January 1, 2003.

1. Donna Reichenbacher purchases one-half of Holly's capital interest for $25,000.
2. Marsha Mears is admitted with a 25% capital interest by a cash investment of $40,000.
3. Stan Wells is admitted with a #5% capital interest by a cash investment of $40,000.

Instructions:

a. Using any popular spreadsheet application, prepare a schedule showing the distribution of net income among the partners for 2002.
b. Open the Hollingsworth Company on your Student Data Disk and run a Balance Sheet report to give a reference point as to the current position of each of the partners.
c. Journalize, in Peachtree, the division of the 2002 net income to the current partners.
d. Create the new partner accounts, change accounting periods and journalize the admittance of the new partners that occurred on January 1, 2003.
e. Run a balance sheet report to give another reference point as to the position of each of the old and new partners in Hollingsworth Company.

Solution to Demonstration Problem

a.

Net Income		$30,000	
	Division of Net Income		
	Lois Holly	Jim Worth	Total
Salary Allowance	$12,000	$10,000	$22,000
Remaining Income	$4,000	$4,000	$8,000
Total Division of Net Income	$16,000	$14,000	$30,000

b.

Hollingsworth Company
Balance Sheet
January 31, 2002

ASSETS

Current Assets		
Cash	$ 50,000.00	
Accounts Receivable	30,000.00	
Total Current Assets		80,000.00
Property and Equipment		
Total Property and Equipment		0.00
Other Assets		
Total Other Assets		0.00
Total Assets		$ 80,000.00

LIABILITIES AND CAPITAL

Current Liabilities		
Total Current Liabilities		0.00
Long-Term Liabilities		
Total Long-Term Liabilities		0.00
Total Liabilities		0.00
Capital		
Lois Holly, Capital	$ 26,000.00	
Jim Worth, Capital	24,000.00	
Net Income	30,000.00	
Total Capital		80,000.00
Total Liabilities & Capital		$ 80,000.00

c. Journalize the close of income to partner's account. (NOTE: This entry is a little misleading. Normally, the retained earnings account would be debited and not sales directly. There were no expenses in this exercise, therefore, sales was debited and not retained earnings.)

Date Dec 31, 2002 ☐ Reverse Transaction
Reference Close Income

Account No.	Description	Debit	Credit	Job
400 Sales	Close Income to Partner's Capital	30,000.00		
	Account will be decreased			
350 Lois Holly, Capital	Close Income to Partner's Capital		16,000.00	
	Account will be increased			
360 Jim Worth, Capital	Close Income to Partner's Capital		14,000.00	
	Account will be increased			

d.

1. Recording the purchase of half of Holly's stake in the partnership. The agreement was figured on Holly's initial investment in the partnership.

Date: Jan 1, 2003 ☐ Reverse Transaction
Reference: Reichenbacher

Account No.	Description	Debit	Credit	Job
350	Purchase of 1/2 Holly's interest.	21,000.00		
Lois Holly, Capital		Account will be decreased		
370	Purchase of 1/2 Holly's interest.		21,000.00	
Donna Reichenbacher, Capital		Account will be increased		

2. Recording the admission of Mears into the partnership.

Date: Jan 1, 2003 ☐ Reverse Transaction
Reference: Mears

Account No.	Description	Debit	Credit	Job
101	Admission of Mears to partnership.	40,000.00		
Cash		Account will be increased		
350	Admission of Mears to partnership		5,000.00	
Lois Holly, Capital		Account will be increased		
360	Admission of Mears to partnership.		5,000.00	
Jim Worth, Capital		Account will be increased		
380	Admission of Mears to partnership.		30,000.00	
Marsha Mears, Capital		Account will be increased		
	Admission of Mears to partnership.			

3. Recording the admission of Wells into the partnership.

Date: Jan 1, 2003 ☐ Reverse Transaction
Reference: Wells

Account No.	Description	Debit	Credit	Job
101	Admission of Wells to partnership	40,000.00		
Cash		Account will be increased		
350	Admission of Wells to partnership	1,000.00		
Lois Holly, Capital		Account will be decreased		
360	Admission of Wells to partnership	1,000.00		
Jim Worth, Capital		Account will be decreased		
390	Admission of Wells to partnership		42,000.00	
Stan Wells, Capital		Account will be increased		

e. New Balance Sheet.

Hollingsworth Company
Balance Sheet
January 31, 2003

ASSETS

Current Assets				
Cash	$	130,000.00		
Accounts Receivable		30,000.00		
Total Current Assets				160,000.00
Property and Equipment				
Total Property and Equipment				0.00
Other Assets				
Total Other Assets				0.00
Total Assets			$	160,000.00

LIABILITIES AND CAPITAL

Current Liabilities				
Total Current Liabilities				0.00
Long-Term Liabilities				
Total Long-Term Liabilities				0.00
Total Liabilities				0.00
Capital				
Lois Holly, Capital	$	25,000.00		
Jim Worth, Capital		42,000.00		
Donna Reichenbacher, Capital		21,000.00		
Marsha Mears, Capital		30,000.00		
Stan Wells, Capital		42,000.00		
Net Income		0.00		
Total Capital				160,000.00
Total Liabilities & Capital			$	160,000.00

P13-1a

The post closing trial balances of two proprietorships on January 1, 2002 are presented below. They may also be found, separately, on your Student Data Disk.

	Mel Company Dr.	Mel Company Cr.	Gibson Company Dr.	Gibson Company Cr.
Cash	14,000		13,000	
Accounts Receivable	17,500		26,000	
Allowance for Doubtful Accounts		3,000		4,400
Merchandise Inventory	26,500		18,400	
Equipment	45,000		28,000	
Accumulated Depreciation – Equipment		24,000		12,000
Notes Payable		20,000		15,000
Accounts Payable		20,000		31,000
Mel, Capital		36,000		
Gibson, Capital				23,000
	103,000	103,000	85,400	85,400

Mel and Gibson decide to form a partnership, the Mel Gibson Co., with the following agreed upon valuations for noncash assets.

	Mel Company	Gibson Company
Accounts Receivable	17,500	26,000
Allowance for Doubtful Accounts	4,500	4,000
Merchandise Inventory	30,000	20,000
Equipment	25,000	18,000

All cash will be transferred to the partnership and the partnership will assume all the liabilities of the two proprietorships. Further, it is agreed that Mel will invest an additional $3,000 in cash and Gibson will invest an additional $18,000 in cash.

Instructions:

a. Open the Mel Gibson Company file on your Student Data Disk.
b. Prepare separate journal entries to record the transfer of each proprietorship's assets and liabilities to the partnership.
c. Journalize the additional cash investment by each partner.
d. Prepare a balance sheet for the partnership on January 1, 2002.

P13-5a

The partners in Wilkowski Company decide to liquidate the firm. The balance is shown below and is also available on your Student Data Disk.

Wilkowski Company
Balance Sheet
May 31, 2002

Assets		Liabilities and Owners' Equity	
Cash	27,500	Notes Payable	13,500
Accounts Receivable	25,000	Accounts Payable	27,000
Allowance for Doubtful Accounts	(1,000)	Wages Payable	3,800
Merchandise Inventory	34,500	S. Wilkowski, Capital	36,000
Equipment	21,000	J. Harkins, Capital	20,000
Accumulated Depreciation	(5,500)	Mick Jagger, Capital	1,200
	$101,500		$101,500

The partners share income and loss ratio is 5:3:2. During the process of liquidation, the following transactions were completed in the following sequence.

1. A total of $53,000 was received from converting noncash assets into cash.
2. Liabilities were paid off in full.
3. Mick Jagger paid his capital deficiency.
4. Cash was paid to the partners with credit balances.

Instructions:

a. Open the Wilkowski Company file on your Student Data Disk.
b. Prepare the entries to record the transactions.
c. Create General Journal entries and post to the cash and individual capital accounts.

CHAPTER 14

The Corporate Form of Organization: Stocks, Dividends, and Retrained Earnings

OBJECTIVES

- Describe the corporate form of a business organization
- Describe the effect of sales on a corporate balance sheet
- Create a new corporation in Peachtree Accounting
- Determine the entries for Treasury Stock

THE CORPORATE FORM OF ORGANIZATION

A corporation is defined as "... an artificial being, invisible, intangible and existing only in contemplation of law." The definition as stated in 1819 by then Chief Justice John Marshall has laid the foundation for the prevailing legal interpretation that a corporation is an entity separate and distinct from its owners.

The initial step in forming a corporation is to file an application with the secretary of state in the state in which incorporation is desired. The application will contain:

- The corporate name
- The purpose of the proposed corporation
- The amounts, kinds, and number of shares of capital stock to be authorized
- The names of the incorporators
- The shares of stock to which each has subscribed

When chartered, the corporation may begin selling ownership rights in the form of shares of stock when a corporation has only one class of stock; which is identified as common stock. Each share of common stock gives the stockholder certain ownership rights. The authorization of capital stock does not result in a formal accounting entry and has no immediate effect on either corporate assets or stockholders' equity.

In a corporation, as compared to a sole proprietorship, owners' equity is now identified as "Stockholders' Equity," "Shareholders' Equity," or "Corporate Capital." Two sections of capital are now presented on the balance sheet, paid in capital (contributed) and retained earnings (earned capital from income). The distinction between paid-in capital and retained earnings is important from both a legal and accounting point of view. Legally, dividends can be declared out of retained earnings. Many states forbid paying dividends out of paid-in capital. From an analysis standpoint, continued existence and growth of a corporation is based on earnings. Paid-in capital is the total amount of cash and other assets paid in to the corporation by stockholders in exchange for capital stock.

RETAINED EARNINGS

We have been talking about Retained Earnings in several chapters, now. The definition of retained earnings: the net income that is retained in a corporation. Peachtree records net income as in Retained Earnings, as earnings occur automatically.

THE NEW CORPORATION

Setting up the new corporation.

Step 1: Create a new corporation called "Hydro Slide." Make sure "Corporation" is checked as the business type.

Step 2: Hydro Slide issues 1,000 shares of $1 par value common stock at par for cash. Make the General Journal entry as shown in Figure 14.1

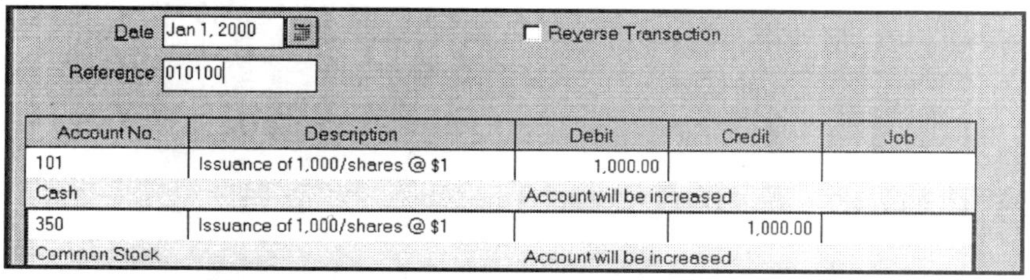

Figure 14.1 General Journal entry for initial stock sale.

TREASURY STOCK

Treasury stock is an asset account that represents a corporations own stock that has been issued, fully paid for by a stockholder, and reacquired by the corporation.

Step 1: Hydro Slide purchases back from shareholders, on January 15, 250 shares of the thousand it issued in the previous activity, for $1. Create the asset account no. 105 for Treasury Stock, which would be classified as "Other Current Assets."

Step 2: Enter the debit amount, $250 for Treasury Stock and credit cash for the same amount. The transaction is shown in Figure 14.2.

Date	Jan 15, 2000		Reverse Transaction	
Reference	011501			
Account No.	**Description**	**Debit**	**Credit**	**Job**
105	Purchase of Treasury Stock	250.00		
Treasury Stock		Account will be increased		
101	Purchase of Treasury Stock		250.00	
Cash		Account will be decreased		

Figure 14 2 Journal entry to record purchase of Treasury Stock

Recording of Sales & Examining the Results:

Step 1: Hydro Slide records sales of $2,850. Use the "Sales" navigation icon to record sales on account to Rapid River Amusement. Enter January 31, 2000 as the date of the invoice.

Step 2: Create a General Journal entry, on January 31, 2000, recording $1,250 in General Expenses (Account No. 500). Cash was paid.

Step 3: Set the date to January 31, 2000 and run a copy of the Income Statement (Figure 14.3), Retained Earnings Statement (Figure 14.4), Balance Sheet (Figure 14.5), and a Cash Flow Statement (Figure 14.6) to see how everything you have entered so far affects Hydro Slide's books.

Hydro Slide
Income Statement
For the One Month Ending January 31, 2000

		Current Month			Year to Date	
Revenues						
General Sales	$	2,850.00	100.00	$	2,350.00	100.00
Total Revenues		2,850 00	100.00		2,350.00	100.00
Cost of Sales						
Total Cost of Sales		0.00	0.00		0.00	0.00
Gross Profit		2,850.00	100.00		2,850.00	100.00
Expenses						
General Expenses		1,250 00	43.86		1,250.00	43.86
Total Expenses		1,250.00	43.86		1,250.00	43.86
Net Income	$	1,600 00	56 14	$	1,600.00	56.14

Figure 14.3 Income Statement

Hydro Slide
Statement of Retained Earnings
For the One Month Ending January 31, 2000

Beginning Retained Earnings	$	0.00
Adjustments To Date		0.00
Net Income		1,600.00
Subtotal		1,600.00
Ending Retained Earnings	$	1,600.00

Figure 14.4 Retained Earnings Statement

Hydro Slide
Balance Sheet
January 31, 2000

ASSETS

Current Assets				
Cash	$	<500.00>		
Treasury Stock		250.00		
Accounts Receivable		2,850.00		
Total Current Assets				2,600.00
Property and Equipment				
Total Property and Equipment				0.00
Other Assets				
Total Other Assets				0.00
Total Assets			$	2,600.00

LIABILITIES AND CAPITAL

Current Liabilities				
Total Current Liabilities				0.00
Long-Term Liabilities				
Total Long-Term Liabilities				0.00
Total Liabilities				0.00
Capital				
Common Stock	$	1,000.00		
Net Income		1,600.00		
Total Capital				2,600.00
Total Liabilities & Capital			$	2,600.00

Figure 14.5 Balance Sheet.

Hydro Slide
Statement of Cash Flow
For the one Month Ended January 31, 2000

		Current Month		Year to Date
Cash Flows from operating activities				
Net Income	$	1,600.00	$	1,600.00
Adjustments to reconcile net income to net cash provided by operating activities				
Treasury Stock		<250.00>		<250.00>
Accounts Receivable		<2,850.00>		<2,850.00>
Total Adjustments		<3,100.00>		<3,100.00>
Net Cash provided by Operations		<1,500.00>		<1,500.00>
Cash Flows from investing activities				
Used For				
Net cash used in investing		0.00		0.00
Cash Flows from financing activities				
Proceeds From				
Common Stock		1,000.00		1,000.00
Used For				
Common Stock		0.00		0.00
Net cash used in financing		1,000.00		1,000.00
Net increase <decrease> in cash	$	<500.00>	$	<500.00>
Summary				
Cash Balance at End of Period	$	<500.00>	$	<500.00>
Cash Balance at Beg of Period		0.00		0.00
Net Increase <Decrease> in Cash	$	<500.00>	$	<500.00>

Figure 14.6 Statement of Cash Flows.

Demonstration Problem

The Rolman Corporation is authorized to issue 1,000,000 shares of $5 par value common stock. In its first year, the company has the following stock transactions:

Jan 10	Issued 400,000 shares of stock at $8 per share.
July 1	Issued 100,000 shares of stock for land. The land had an asking price of $900,000. The stock is currently selling on a national exchange at $8.25 per share.
Sept 1	Purchased 10,000 shares of common stock for the treasury (Treasury Stock) at $9 per share.
Dec 1	Sold 4,000 shares of the treasury stock at $10 per share.

Instructions:

a. Open the Rolman Company file on your Student Data Disk. The equity account, Common Stock and the Cash account have already been created for you.
b. Journalize the transactions.
c. Create two more accounts, Accounts Receivable and Sales (income). The normal beginning balance for both is $200,000.
d. Run a balance sheet to double check your work as of December 31, 2002.

Solution to the Demonstration Problem

b. Record of stock issue

Date: Jan 10, 2002 — ☐ Reverse Transaction
Reference: 1

Account No.	Description	Debit	Credit	Job
101 Cash	Isuance of 400,000 share @ $8	3,200,000.00		
		Account will be increased		
300 Common Stock	Isuance of 400,000 share @ $8		2,000,000.00	
		Account will be increased		
310 Paid In Capital /Excess of Par	Isuance of 400,000 share @ $8		1,200,000.00	
		Account will be increased		

Shares of stock for land

Date: Jul 1, 2002 — ☐ Reverse Transaction
Reference: 2

Account No.	Description	Debit	Credit	Job
150 Land	100,000 shares @ 8.25 for land	825,000.00		
		Account will be increased		
300 Common Stock	100,000 shares @ 8.25 for land		500,000.00	
		Account will be increased		
310 Paid In Capital /Excess of Par	100,000 shares @ 8.25 for land		325,000.00	
		Account will be increased		

Purchase of Treasury Stock

Date: Sep 1, 2002 ☐ Reverse Transaction

Reference: 3

Account No.	Description	Debit	Credit	Job
125	Purchase Treasury Stock at Cost	90,000.00		
Treasury Stock		Account will be increased		
101	Purchase Treasury Stock at Cost		90,000.00	
Cash		Account will be decreased		

Sold Treasury Stock

Date: Dec 1, 2002 ☐ Reverse Transaction

Reference: 4

Account No.	Description	Debit	Credit	Job
101	Sold Treasury Stock @ $10	40,000.00		
Cash		Account will be increased		
125	Sold Treasury Stock @ $10		36,000.00	
Treasury Stock		Account will be decreased		
315	Sold Treasury Stock @ $10		4,000.00	
Paid In Capital /Treasury Stck		Account will be increased		
	Sold Treasury Stock @ $10			

Liabilities and Capital portion of Balance Sheet as of December 31, 2002

Rolman Corporation
Balance Sheet
December 31, 2002

LIABILITIES AND CAPITAL

Current Liabilities			
Total Current Liabilities			0.00
Long-Term Liabilities			
Total Long-Term Liabilities			0.00
Total Liabilities			0.00
Capital			
Common Stock	$ 2,500,000.00		
Paid In Capital /Excess of Par	1,525,000.00		
Paid In Capital /Treasury Stck	4,000.00		
Retained Earnings	200,000.00		
Total Capital			4,229,000.00
Total Liabilities & Capital		$	4,229,000.00

P14-1a

Tiger Corporation was organized on January 1, 2002. It is authorized to issue 10,000 shares of 8%, $100 par value preferred stock, and 500,000 shares of no-par common stock with a stated value of $2 per share. The following stock transactions were completed during the first year.

Jan 10	Issued 80,000 shares of common stock for cash at $3 per share
Mar 1	Issued 5,000 shares of preferred stock for cash at $105 per share
Apr 1	Issued 24,000 shares of Common stock for land. The asking price of the land was $90,000. The fair market value of the was $80,000
May 1	Issued 80,000 shares of common stock for cash at $4 per share.
Aug 1	Issued 10,000 shares of common stock to attorneys in payment of their bill of $50,000 for services rendered in helping the company organize.
Sept 1	Issued 10,000 shares of common stock for cash at $5 per share
Nov 1	Issued 1,000 shares of preferred stock for cash at $109 per share

Instructions:

a. Open the Tiger Corporation file on your Student Data Disk and journalize the transactions.
b. Run a balance sheet to double check the accuracy of your work.

P14-4a

Roberto Moreno Corporation is authorized to issue 10,000 shares of $100 par value, 10% convertible preferred stock and 125,000 shares of $5 par value common stock. On January 1, 2002, the ledger contained the following stockholders' equity balances:

Preferred Stock (5,000 shares)	$500,000
Paid In Capital in Excess of Par Value – Preferred	75,000
Common Stock (70,000 shares)	350,000
Paid In Capital in Excess of Par Value – Common	700,000
Retained Earnings	300,000

During 2002, the following transactions occurred:

Feb 1	Issued 1,000 shares of preferred stock for land having a fair market value of $125,000.
Mar 1	Issued 1,000 shares of preferred stock for cash at $125 per share
July 1	Holders of 2,000 of preferred stock purchased at $110 per share converted the shared into common stock. Each share of preferred was convertible into 8 shares of common stock. Market values were preferred stock $122 and common stock $17.
Sept 1	Issued 400 shares of preferred stock for a patent. The asking price of the patent was $60,000. Market values were preferred stock $125 and patent indeterminable.
Dec 1	Holders of 1,000 shares of preferred stock purchased at $130 per share converted the shares into common stock. Each share of preferred was convertible into 8 shares of common stock. Market values were preferred stock $134 and common stock $16.
Dec 31	Net income for the year was $260,000. No dividends were declared.

Instructions:

a. Journalize the transactions.
b. Enter the beginning balances in the accounts.
c. Run a balance sheet report as of December 31.

CHAPTER 15

Corporations: Dividends, Retained Earnings and Income Reporting

OBJECTIVES

- Describe the form and content of a corporate income statement.
- . Prepare the entries for cash dividends.
- Identify the items that are reported in a retained earnings statement.
- Prepare and analyze a comprehensive stockholders'equity section of the balance sheet

DIVIDENDS

A dividend is usually a cash distribution by a corporation to its stockholders on a proportional basis based on earned profits. Dividends are usually expressed as a percentage of the par or stated value of the stock or as a dollar amount per share. In the financial press, dividends are generally reported quarterly as a dollar amount per share. There are several forms of dividends; however, they are outside the scope of this workbook. We will concentrate only on Cash Dividends.

For a corporation to pay a cash dividend it must have:

- Retained Earnings
- Adequate Cash
- A Declaration of Dividends

PEACHTREE ENTRIES FOR CASH DIVIDENDS

Three dates are important in connection with dividends: the declaration date, the record date, and the payment date. There is normally about a month between the dates. Accounting entries are required for the declaration date and the payment date.

On the declaration date, the board of directors formally announces or declares (authorizes) the cash dividend. The announcement is made to the shareholders. And, at that point, the obligation is binding and cannot be rescinded. The corporation has now entered into a liability for the declared dividends.

Hydro Slide would like to pay a small dividend to its shareholders and on February 1, declares a cash dividend of $1.00 per outstanding share.

Step 1: Open "Hydro Slide" on your student data disk. Change the accounting period to February 1, 2000.

Step 2: Create a new account: Dividends Payable, Account No. 230. The account type is "Other Current Liabilities" and an Equity – Gets Closed, Account No. 305 titled Dividends

Step 3: Create a General Journal entry debiting the Dividends account for $1,000 and crediting Dividends Payable for the same amount. The completed entry is shown in Figure 15.1.

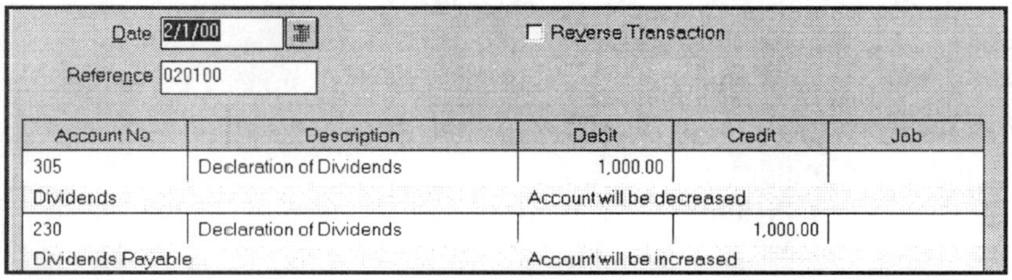

Figure 15. 1 General Journal entry to declare dividends.

Dividends Payable is a current liability that will be paid within the next few months.

The next step is the Record Date, which identifies the stockholders who will receive the dividend. The stockholder must be of register by the Record Date. No entry is required for Record Date.

On the Payment Date, assuming it is April 1, dividend checks are mailed to the stockholders and the payment of the dividend is recorded. Make the following General Journal entry as shown in Figure 15.2.

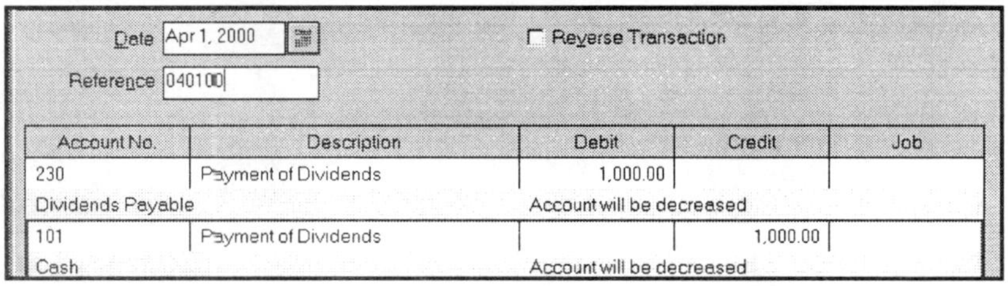

Figure 15. 2 General Journal entry to pay dividends.

Run a Retained Earnings Statement, Figure 15.3, to see how your entries affected the Retained Earnings of the company. Be sure to set the Accounting Period ahead to April.

Hydro Slide
Statement of Retained Earnings
For the Four Months Ending April 30, 2000

Beginning Retained Earnings	$	0.00
Adjustments To Date		0.00
Net Income		1,600.00
Subtotal		1,600.00
Dividends		<1,000.00>
Ending Retained Earnings	$	600.00

Figure 15. 3 Retained Earnings Statement.

The previous statement (Figure 15.3) represents the net income that is retained in the business. The balance in retained earnings is part of the stockholders' claim on the total assets of the corporation. It does not represent a claim on any specific asset, nor can the amount of retained earnings be associated with the balance of any asset account (i.e., Cash).

CORPORATE INCOME STATEMENTS IN PEACHTREE

In Peachtree Accounting, income statements for corporations are the same as the statements for proprietorships, including the way income tax and income tax expense is handled. Income Tax Expense is listed as a normal expense item.

You may redesign forms in Peachtree Accounting, which is outside the scope of this workbook.

Problem Sets

P15-1a

On January 1, 2002, Hayslett Corporation had the following stockholders' equity accounts:

Common Stock ($20 par value, 65,000 shares and outstanding	$1,300,000
Paid In Capital in Excess of Par Value	200,000
Retained Earnings	600,000

During the year, the following transactions occurred:

Feb 1	Declared a $1 cash dividend per share to stockholders of record on February 15, payable March 1.
Mar 1	Paid the dividend declared in February
Apr 1	Announced a 4-for-1 stock split. Prior to the split, the market price per share was $36.
July 1	Declared a 5% stock dividend to stockholders of record on July 15, distributable July 31. On July 1, the market price of the stock was $13 per share.
July 31	Issued the shares for the stock dividend.
Dec 1	Declared a $.50 per share dividend to stockholders of record on December 15, payable January 5, 2000.
31	Determined that net income for the year was $350,000

Instructions:

a. Open the Hayslett Corporation file on your Student Data Disk.
b. Journalize the transactions.
c. Run a balance sheet to check for errors.

P15-2a

The stockholders' equity accounts of Greene Company at January 1, 2002 are as follows:

Preferred Stock, 9%, $50 par	$600,000
Common Stock, $2 par	500,000
Paid-In Capital in Excess of Par Value - Preferred Stock	200,000
Paid-In Capital in Excess of Par Value - Common Stock	300,000
Retained Earnings	800,000

There were no dividends in arrears on preferred stock. During 2002, the company had the following transactions and events.

July	1	Declared a $.50 cash dividend on common stock.
Aug	1	Discovered $45,000 understatement of 2001 depreciation. Ignore income taxes.
Sept	1	Paid the cash dividend declared on July 1
Dec	1	Declared 10% stock dividend on common stock when the market value of the stock was $18 per share.
Dec	15	Declared a 9% cash dividend on preferred stock payable January 15, 2003.
	31	Determined that net income for the year was $385,000.
	31	Recognized a $200,000 restriction of retained earnings for plant expansion.

Instructions:

a. Enter the beginning balances in the accounts.
b. Journalize the transactions and events.
c. Run a retained earnings statement for the year.
d. Run a balance sheet report paying particular interest to the stockholders' equity section.

CHAPTER 16

Bonds and Long-Term Liabilities

OBJECTIVES

- Prepare entries for issuance of bonds and interest expense
- Describe and prepare entries for a bond sinking fund.
- Prepare the entries when bonds are redeemed
- Describe the accounting for long-term notes payable

BOND BASICS

Bonds are a form of interest bearing notes payable. Like common stock, bonds are sold in small denominations (usually $1,000). A corporation may also use long-term financing other than bonds, such as notes payable. To obtain large amounts of long-term capital, corporate management usually must decide whether to issue common stock (equity financing) or issue bonds.

The major disadvantage resulting from the use of bond financing is that interest must be paid on a periodic basis and the principal (face value) of the bonds must be paid at maturity. A company with fluctuating earnings and a relatively weak cash position will have difficulty making interest payments when earnings are slow. (Your text discusses the several types of bond issues.)

In authorizing a bond issue, the corporation's board of directors stipulates the number of bonds to be authorized, the total face value, and the contractual interest rate.

The face value is the amount of principal the issuer must pay at the maturity date. The contractual interest rate is the rate used to determine the amount of cash interest the borrower (the company) pays to the investor. This is often referred to as the stated rate. Although the contractual rate is stated as an annual rate, it is paid semiannually.

ISSUING BONDS AT FACE VALUE

Bonds may be issued at face value, below face value (a discount) or above face value (a premium). Discounts and Premiums will not be dealt with in this workbook; only face value issues will be discussed.

To illustrate the account for bonds assume that on June 1, Hydro Slide issues 1,000, 10-year, 9%, $1,000 bonds at 100 (100% of face value).

Step 1: Open the "Hydro Slide" file on your student disk. Change the accounting period to July 1.

Step 2: Create the liability account Bonds Payable, Account No. 220, a long-term liability account.

Step 3: Because Cash is being received on the sale of the bonds, the General Journal entry will reflect a Debit to cash,. Account No. 101 for $1,000,000 and a credit to the liability account, Bonds Payable. The million-dollar liability will remain on the books until the 10-year maturity date is reached or when the bonds are paid out earlier.

Step 4: Make the journal entry and check your work with that shown in Figure 16.1.

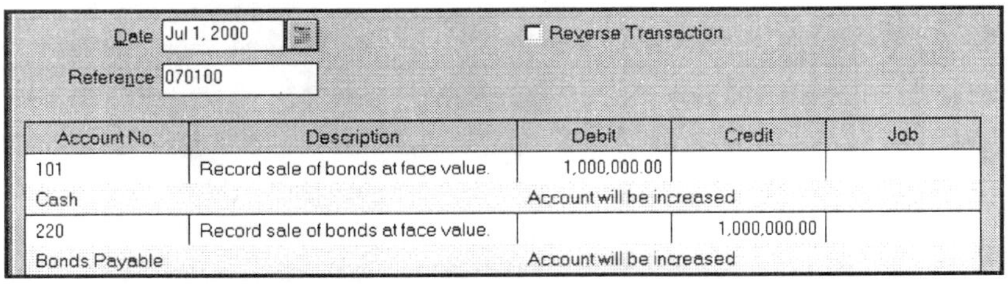
Date Jul 1, 2000

Reverse Transaction

Reference 070100

Account No	Description	Debit	Credit	Job
101 Cash	Record sale of bonds at face value.	1,000,000.00		
		Account will be increased		
220 Bonds Payable	Record sale of bonds at face value.		1,000,000.00	
		Account will be increased		

Figure 16. 1 General Journal entry for sale of bonds.

Over the term (life) of the bonds, entries are required for bond interest. Interest on bonds payable is computed in the same manner as interest on notes payable. Assuming that interest is payable semiannually on January 1 and July 1, our first interest payment will be due on January 1, 2001 for $45,000 ($1,000,000 * 9% * 6/12). Make the entry as described below.

Step 1: Create the new account Interest Payable, Account No. 215 as a Current Liability and Interest Expense, Account No. 520, an Expense.

Step 2: On December 31, recognize the accrued liability, Bond Interest Payable for $45,000 as a credit and debit the expense Bond Interest Expense for the same amount.

Step 3: DO NOT MAKE THIS ENTRY – The next step would be to clear out the liability by debiting the liability and crediting cash, when the interest payment is actually made. However, do not make this entry at this time.

BOND SINKING FUND

Many bond issues require the borrower to make periodic cash contributions to a sinking fund over the life of the bonds. A sinking fund simply is moneys that are set aside to eventually be used to redeem the bonds at maturity. It is like a savings account that is used to repay the bondholders. In fact, the sinking fund can be, and usually is invested in some sort of high quality income, with the hope that the deposits plus the earnings from the invested sinking fund will equal the face value of the bonds at maturity.

Returning to the previous activity, Hydro Slide issued 1,000, 10-year, 9%, $1,000 bonds at 100 (100% of face value). The terms of the bond indenture indicate that Hydro Slide must make annual deposits with a sinking fund trustee, starting at the end of the first year. The amount of the annual cash contribution is contracted at $83,000.

The entry would be a debit to the asset Bond Sinking Fund and a credit (decrease) to the asset account cash.

Step 1: Create the new account Bond Sinking Fund, Account No.102. It is a Current Asset Account because the cash in the account is not used for general operating purposes.

Step 2: On December 31, 2000, make the General Journal entry debiting the Bond Sinking Fund Account for $83,000 and crediting the Cash account for the same amount. Make sure your entry is the same as Figure 16.2. Make any corrections before posting the entry.

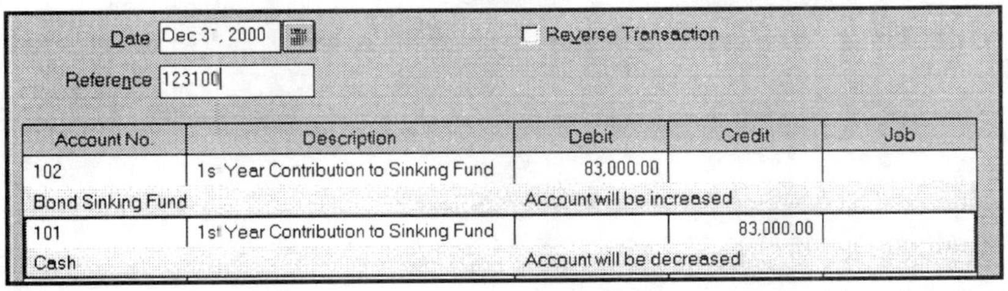

Date Dec 31, 2000 Reverse Transaction

Reference 123100

Account No.	Description	Debit	Credit	Job
102	1st Year Contribution to Sinking Fund	83,000.00		
Bond Sinking Fund		Account will be increased		
101	1st Year Contribution to Sinking Fund		83,000.00	
Cash		Account will be decreased		

Figure 16. 2 G/J entry for Bond Sinking Fund

At the end of the second year, Hydro Slide records the actual earnings from the investment of the sinking fund of $16,500 together with the required $83,000 contribution to the fund. A revenue account must be created: Bond Sinking Fund Revenue, it would be Account No. 410 and would be classified as income. The entry is shown in Figure 16.3. **DO NOT MAKE THIS ENTRY.**

Date Dec 31, 2001 ☐ Reverse Transaction

Reference 123101

Account No.	Description	Debit	Credit	Job
102	2nd Year Contribution to Sinking Fund	99,500.00		
Bond Sinking Fund		Account will be increased		
101	2nd Year Contribution to Sinking Fund		83,000.00	
Cash		Account will be decreased		
410	2nd Year Investment return from Sinking		16,500.00	
<Undefined Account>		Account will be increased		

Figure 16. 3 2nd Year G/L entry for sinking fund contribution and investment return.

Two assumptions now need to be made. First, let's assume that at the maturity date of the bonds, 10 years from now, the sinking fund assets will be used to redeem the bonds. Second, let's assume the investment of the sinking fund will continue to return a steady $16,500 over the 10 year period.

At the maturity of the bonds the entry would be similar to the one shown in Figure 16.4. **AGAIN, DO NOT MAKE THIS ENTRY.**

Date Dec 31, 2010 ☐ Reverse Transaction

Reference 123110

Account No.	Description	Debit	Credit	Job
220	Redeem Bonds at Maturity	1,000,000.00		
Bonds Payable		Account will be decreased		
102	Redeem Bonds at Maturity		995,000.00	
Bond Sinking Fund		Account will be decreased		
101	Redeem Bonds at Maturity		5,000.00	
Cash		Account will be decreased		

Figure 16. 4 Entry to redeem bonds in 10 years.

In the previous case, Hydro Slide had to make up for the deficiency by paying an additional $5,000 in cash. If the sinking fund happened to have excess cash, it would be returned to Hydro.

LONG-TERM NOTES PAYABLE

The use of Notes Payable in long-term debt financing is also common. Long-term notes are similar to short-term interest bearing notes except that the terms will exceed a year. The accounting procedures are similar to account for bonds, creating accounts for the actual Note Payable and its corresponding interest payable and interest expense.

CHAPTER 17

Investments

OBJECTIVES

- Discuss why corporations invest in debt securities.
- Explain the accounting for stock investments
- Indicate how debt and stock investments are valued and reported on the financial statements.
- . Describe the use of consolidated financial statements.
- Explain the accounting for debt investments
- Distinguish between short term and long term investments.

WHY CORPORATIONS INVEST

There are three reasons why corporations purchase investments in either debt or securities:

1. A corporation may have excess cash that it does not need for the immediate purchase of operating assets or for general operations.
2. Some companies purchase investments to generate investment income. For example, although banks make most of their earnings by lending money, they also generate earnings by investing in debt and equity securities.
3. Strategic reasons is the third basis for investing. A company may purchase a noncontrolling interest in another firm in a related industry in which it wishes to establish a presence.

ACCOUNTING FOR DEBT INVESTMENTS

Three types of entries are required for debt investing such as government or corporate bonds:

1. The acquisition
2. The interest revenue
3. The sale

At acquisition, the cost principle applies. The cost will include all expenditures necessary to acquire these investments. For example, the price paid and commissions would be included in the cost. Kuhl Corporation acquires 50 Doan, Inc. 12%, 10-year, $1,000 bonds on January 1, 2002, for $54,000, including brokerage fees of $1,000.

Step 1: Open the file "Kuhl Corporation" on your student data disk.

Step 2: To record the initial investment: debit Debt Investments, Account no. 115 for $54,000 and credit Cash for the same amount as shown in Figure 17.1.

Date Jan 1, 2002 ☐ Reverse Transaction

Reference 010102

Account No.	Description	Debit	Credit	Job
115 Debt Investment	Purchase of 50 Doan, Inc. bonds	54,000.00		
	Account will be increased			
101 Cash	Purchase of 50 Doan, Inc. bonds		54,000.00	
	Account will be decreased			

Figure 17. 1 Acquisition of Bonds

The bonds pay interest of $3,000 ($50,000 * 12% * ½) semiannually on July 1 and January 1. Record the entry in Figure 17.2 for Kuhl Corporation.

Date Jul 1, 2002 ☐ Reverse Transaction

Reference 070102

Account No.	Description	Debit	Credit	Job
101 Cash	Receipt of Interest on Doan bonds	3,000.00		
	Account will be increased			
401 Interest Revenue	Receipt of Interest on Doan bonds		3,000.00	
	Account will be decreased			

Figure 17. 2 Receipt of interest on bonds.

If Kuhl's fiscal year ends on December 31, an accrual of the interest of $3,000 earned since July 1 must be recorded. It is an adjusting entry as shown in Figure 17.3. Make the adjusting entry.

Date: Dec 31, 2002 ☐ Reverse Transaction
Reference: 123102

Account No.	Description	Debit	Credit	Job
110	Accred interest on Doan Inc. bonds	3,000.00		
Interest Receivable	Account will be increased			
401	Accred interest on Doan Inc. bonds		3,000.00	
Interest Revenue	Account will be decreased			

Figure 17. 3 Adjusting entry for accrued interest on bonds.

Interest receivable is reported as a current asset in the balance sheet and interest revenue is reported under revenues on the income statement generated by Peachtree. The balance sheet as of December 31, 2002 is shown in Figure 17.4.

Kuhl Corporation
Balance Sheet
December 31, 2002

ASSETS

Current Assets				
Cash	$	24,000.00		
Interest Receivable		3,000.00		
Debt Investment		54,000.00		
Total Current Assets				81,000.00
Property and Equipment				
Total Property and Equipment				0.00
Other Assets				
Total Other Assets				0.00
Total Assets			$	81,000.00

LIABILITIES AND CAPITAL

Current Liabilities				
Total Current Liabilities				0.00
Long-Term Liabilities				
Total Long-Term Liabilities				0.00
Total Liabilities				0.00
Capital				
Stockholders Equity	$	75,000.00		
Net Income		6,000.00		
Total Capital				81,000.00
Total Liabilities & Capital			$	81,000.00

Figure 17. 4 Balance Sheet as of 12/31/02

When interest is received on January 1, 2003, the entry is:

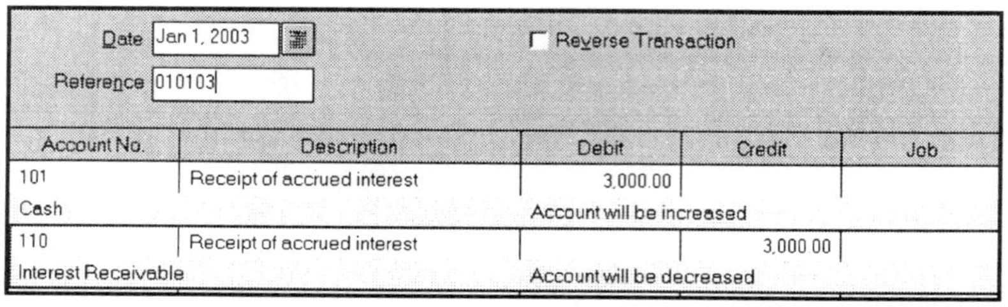
Date Jan 1, 2003 ☐ Reverse Transaction
Reference 010103

Account No.	Description	Debit	Credit	Job
101 Cash	Receipt of accrued interest	3,000.00		
		Account will be increased		
110 Interest Receivable	Receipt of accrued interest		3,000.00	
		Account will be decreased		

Figure 17. 5 Receipt of accrued interest.

When the bonds are sold, it is necessary to credit the investment account for the cost of the bonds and recognize any gain or loss on the sale.

For example, Kuhl Corporation receives net proceeds of $58,000 on the sale of the Doan bonds, which they sell on January 1, 2003. The sell is made soon after the receipt of due. Since the securities cost $54,000, a gain of $4,000 will be realized. The interest earned does not come into play here; it has already been received, recorded, and probably spent.

The entry appears as Figure 17.6.

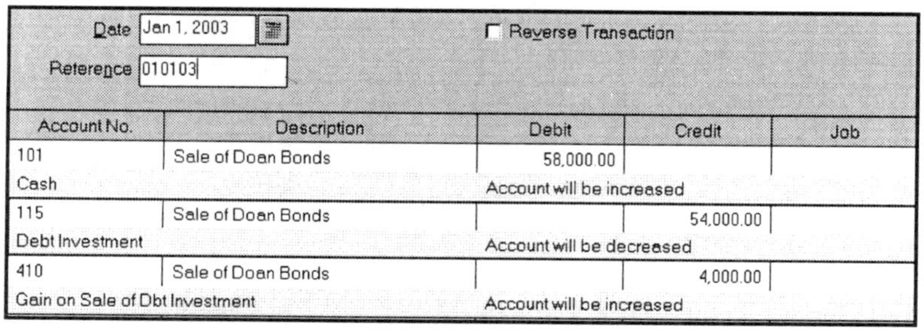
Date Jan 1, 2003 ☐ Reverse Transaction
Reference 010103

Account No.	Description	Debit	Credit	Job
101 Cash	Sale of Doan Bonds	58,000.00		
		Account will be increased		
115 Debt Investment	Sale of Doan Bonds		54,000.00	
		Account will be decreased		
410 Gain on Sale of Dbt Investment	Sale of Doan Bonds		4,000.00	
		Account will be increased		

Figure 17. 6 Sale of Doan Bonds

The gain on the sale of debt investments is reported under "Income" in the income statement.

The accounting for other types of short-term and long-term debt investments is similar. The major exception is when bonds are purchased at a premium or discount.

Run an income statement, Figure 17.7 as of January 1, 2003 for Kuhl Corporation to see the effect of the preceding transactions.

Kuhl Corporation
Income Statement
For the One Month Ending January 31, 2003

		Current Month			Year to Date	
Revenues						
Interest Revenue	$	6,000.00	60.00	$	0.00	0.00
Gain on Sale of Dbt Investment		4,000.00	40.00		4,000.00	100.00
Total Revenues		10,000.00	100.00		4,000.00	100.00
Cost of Sales						
Total Cost of Sales		0.00	0.00		0.00	0.00
Gross Profit		10,000.00	100.00		4,000.00	100.00
Expenses						
Total Expenses		0.00	0.00		0.00	0.00
Net Income	$	10,000.00	100.00	$	4,000.00	100.00

Figure 17. 7 Income Statement for Kuhl Corporation.

Demonstration Problem

In its first year of operations, DeMarco Company had the following selected transactions in stock investments that are considered trading securities. Open the DeMarco file on your Student Data Disk. The accounts have been created for you. The cash account, accounts receivable, stockholders' equity – common, and retained earnings all have current balances.

June 1	Purchased for cash 600 shares of Sanburg common stock at $24 per share, plus $300 brokerage fees.
July 1	Purchased for cash 800 shares of Cey common stock at $33 per share, plus $600 brokerage fees.
Sept 1	Received a $1 per share cash dividend from Cey Corporation.
Nov 1	Sold 200 shares of Sanburg common stock for cash at $27 per share, less $150 brokerage fees.
Dec 15	Received a $.50 per share cash dividend on Sanburg common stock.

On December 31, the fair values per share were:

Sandburg	$25
Cey	$30

Instructions:

a. Run a balance sheet report as of May 31, 2002 to understand the current position of the corporation.
b. Journalize the transactions.
c. Recognize and journalize any unrealized gain or loss.
d. Run an income statement to see and understand the effect the transactions had on the company.
e. Run a balance sheet to understand the new position of the company at close of business December 31.

Solution to Demonstration Problem

Purchase of Sanburg stock

Date: Jun 1, 2002 ☐ Reverse Transaction
Reference: 1

Account No.	Description	Debit	Credit	Job
125 Stock Investments	Purchased Sanburg stock	14,700.00 Account will be increased		
101 Cash	Purchased Sanburg stock	Account will be decreased	14,700.00	

Purchase of Cey Stock

Date: Jul 1, 2002 ☐ Reverse Transaction

Reference: 2

Account No.	Description	Debit	Credit	Job
125 Stock Investments	Purchase of Cey Stock	27,000.00		
	Account will be increased			
101 Cash	Purchase of Cey Stock		27,000.00	
	Account will be decreased			

Receipt of cash dividend.

Date: Sep 1, 2002 ☐ Reverse Transaction

Reference: 3

Account No.	Description	Debit	Credit	Job
101 Cash	Receipt of cash dividend	800.00		
	Account will be increased			
430 Dividend Revenue	Receipt of cash dividend		800.00	
	Account will be increased			

Sold shares of Sanburg stock

Date: Sep 1, 2002 ☐ Reverse Transaction

Reference: 4

Account No.	Description	Debit	Credit	Job
101 Cash	Sold Sandburg stock (200 sh)	5,250.00		
	Account will be increased			
125 Stock Investments	Sold Sandburg stock (200 sh)		4,900.00	
	Account will be decreased			
425 Gain on Sale of Stock Inv	Sold Sandburg stock (200 sh)		350.00	
	Account will be increased			

Receipt of dividends on remaining Sanburg stock

Date: Dec 15, 2002 ☐ Reverse Transaction

Reference: 5

Account No.	Description	Debit	Credit	Job
101 Cash	Receipt of dividends on Sanburg	200.00		
	Account will be increased			
430 Dividend Revenue	Receipt of dividends on Sanburg		200.00	
	Account will be increased			

Recognized loss yearly security trades.

Investment	Cost	Fair Value	Unrealized Gain/Loss
Sanburg Common Stock	9,800	10,000	200
Cey Common Stock	27,000	24,000	(3,000)
Totals	36,800	34,000	(2,800)

Journal Entry

Date Dec 31, 2002 ☐ Reverse Transaction

Reference 7

Account No.	Description	Debit	Credit	Job
435	Record yearly loss on investments	2,800.00		
Unrealized Loss - Income		Account will be decreased		
550	Record yearly loss on investments		2,800.00	
Market Adjustment - Trading		Account will be decreased		

Income Statement

DeMarco Company
Income Statement
For the Twelve Months Ending December 31, 2002

		Current Month			Year to Date	
Revenues						
Gain on Sale of Stock Inv	$	0.00	0.00	$	350.00	24.14
Dividend Revenue		200.00	7.69		1,000.00	68.97
Unrealized Loss - Income		<2,800.00>	<107.69>		<2,800.00>	<193.10>
Total Revenues		<2,600.00>	<100.00>		<1,450.00>	<100.00>
Cost of Sales						
Total Cost of Sales		0.00	0.00		0.00	0.00
Gross Profit		<2,600.00>	<100.00>		<1,450.00>	<100.00>
Expenses						
Market Adjustment - Trading		<2,800.00>	<107.69>		<2,800.00>	<193.10>
Total Expenses		<2,800.00>	<107.69>		<2,800.00>	<193.10>
Net Income	$	200.00	7.69	$	1,350.00	93.10

Balance Sheet

DeMarco Company
Balance Sheet
December 31, 2002

ASSETS

Current Assets				
Cash	$	39,550.00		
Accounts Receivable		5,000.00		
Stock Investments		36,800.00		
Total Current Assets				81,350.00
Property and Equipment				
Total Property and Equipment				0.00
Other Assets				
Total Other Assets				0.00
Total Assets			$	81,350.00

LIABILITIES AND CAPITAL

Current Liabilities				
Total Current Liabilities				0.00
Long-Term Liabilities				
Total Long-Term Liabilities				0.00
Total Liabilities				0.00
Capital				
Common Stock	$	75,000.00		
Retained Earnings		5,000.00		
Net Income		1,350.00		
Total Capital				81,350.00
Total Liabilities & Capital			$	81,350.00

P17-2a

In January 2002, the management of Harris Company concludes that it has sufficient cash to permit some short-term investments in debt and stock securities. During the year, the flowing transactions occurred:

Feb 1	Purchased 400 shares of Alpha common stock for $21,800, plus brokerage fees of $600
Mar 1	Purchased 800 shares of Omega common stock for $20,000, plus brokerage fees of $400
Apr 1	Purchased 40 $1,000, 12% Pop bonds for $40,000, plus $1,000 brokerage fees
July 1	Received a cash dividend of $.60 per share on the Alpha common stock.
Aug 1	Sold 200 shares of Alpha common stock at $58 per share less brokerage fees of $200
Sept 1	Received a $1 per share cash dividend on the Omega common stock.
Oct 1	Received the semiannual interest on the Pop bonds.
Oct 1	Sold the Pop bonds for $41,000 less $1,000 brokerage fees.

On December 31st, the fair value of the Alpha common stock was $55. The fair value of the Omega common stock was $23 per share.

Instructions:

a. Run a balance sheet for Harris Company, after opening the file on your Student Data Disk, as of January 1st. Note: There are no other accounts in this company besides the ones used in this exercise.
b. Create the appropriate accounts before journalizing the transactions above.
c. Run an income statement as of December 31st to double check your work for any errors and to study the current position of the company.
d. Run a balance sheet as of December 31st to compare it to the one you ran for January 1st.

CHAPTER 18

The Statement of Cash Flow

OBJECTIVES

- Indicate the primary purpose of the statement of cash flow
- Analyze a cash flow statement.
- Generate a statement of cash flow using Peachtree Accounting.

THE PURPOSE OF A CASH FLOW STATEMENT

The three basic financial statements presented thus far provide very little information concerning a company's cash flow. An analyst would like to know more in studying the company, more about the cash receipts and cash payments of the firm. For example, balance sheets generated by Peachtree show the increases (or decreases) in property, plant, and equipment during the year, but, they do not show how the additions were paid for or financed.

The income statement shows net income, but it does not show the amount of cash that was generated by operating activities. And, the retained earnings statement shows cash dividend declared but not the cash dividends that were paid during the year.

The primary purpose of the statement of cash flow is to provide information about cash receipts and cash payments during a fiscal period. A secondary objective is to provide information about operating, investing, and financing activities. Reporting the causes of changes in cash helps investors, creditors, and other interested parties understand what is happening to a company's most liquid resource – cash.

The Cash Flow statement for Kuhl Corporation as of December 31, 2002, the one we worked with in the previous chapter is shown in Figure 18.1. Compare that statement with changes made during the next accounting period as shown in the Cash Flow statement for the same corporation as of December 31, 2003 (Figure 18.2). Be sure to change accounting periods for the most up-to-date report.

Kuhl Corporation
Statement of Cash Flow
For the twelve Months Ended December 31, 2002

		Current Month		Year to Date
Cash Flows from operating activities				
Net Income	$	6,000 00	$	6,000.00
Adjustments to reconcile net income to net cash provided by operating activities				
Interest Receivable		<3,000 00>		<3,000.00>
Debt Investment		<54,000 00>		<54,000.00>
Total Adjustments		<57,000.00>		<57,000.00>
Net Cash provided by Operations		<51,000 00>		<51,000.00>
Cash Flows from investing activities				
Used For				
Net cash used in investing		0.00		0.00
Cash Flows from financing activities				
Proceeds From				
Beginning Balance Equity		0.00		0.00
Stockholders Equity		0.00		0.00
Used For				
Beginning Balance Equity		0 00		0.00
Stockholders Equity		0.00		0.00
Net cash used in financing		0.00		0.00
Net increase <decrease> in cash	$	<51,000 00>	$	<51,000.00>
Summary				
Cash Balance at End of Period	$	24,000 00	$	24,000.00
Cash Balance at Beg of Period		<24,000 00>		<75,000.00>
Net Increase <Decrease> in Cash	$	0.00	$	<51,000.00>

Figure 18. 1 Cash Flows statement for the year 2002 for Kuhl Corporation.

The $6,000 net income figure represents the two $3,000 interest payments received on the bonds purchased at the beginning of their fiscal year (January 1, 2002). The negative $3,000 represents the accrued interest payment recognized "this year" but not actually received until "next year." The negative $54,000 represents the moneys paid for the bonds.

The company began the accounting period with a $75,000 cash balance as shown in the summary.

Look at the Cash Flow statement for the next year. It is shown in Figure 18.2.

Kuhl Corporation
Statement of Cash Flow
For the twelve Months Ended December 31, 2003

		Current Month		Year to Date
Cash Flows from operating activities				
Net Income	$	4,000.00	$	4,000.00
Adjustments to reconcile net income to net cash provided by operating activities				
Interest Receivable		3,000 00		3,000.00
Debt Investment		54,000 00		54,000 00
Total Adjustments		57,000.00		57,000.00
Net Cash provided by Operations		61,000 00		61,000.00
Cash Flows from investing activities				
Used For				
Net cash used in investing		0 00		0 00
Cash Flows from financing activities				
Proceeds From				
Beginning Balance Equity		0.00		0.00
Stockholders Equity		0.00		0.00
Used For				
Beginning Balance Equity		0.00		0 00
Stockholders Equity		0.00		0.00
Net cash used in financing		0 00		0 00
Net increase <decrease> in cash	$	61,000.00	$	61,000.00
Summary				
Cash Balance at End of Period	$	85,000.00	$	85,000 00
Cash Balance at Beg of Period		<85,000 00>		<24,000 00>
Net Increase <Decrease> in Cash	$	0.00	$	61,000 00

Figure 18. 2 Cash Flows Statement for 2003.

The net income represents the profit on the sale of bonds. The interest receivable has now been converted to cash. The initial investment of $54,000 has been recouped along with the profit on the sale.

Call up the Cash Flows Statement for Hydro Slide. It is shown in Figure 18.3.

Hydro Slide
Statement of Cash Flow
For the twelve Months Ended December 31, 2000

		Current Month		Year to Date
Cash Flows from operating activities				
Net Income	$	1,600.00	$	1,600.00
Adjustments to reconcile net income to net cash provided by operating activities				
Bond Sinking Fund		0.00		0.00
Treasury Stock		<250.00>		<250.00>
Accounts Receivable		<2,850.00>		<2,850.00>
Dividends Payable		0.00		0.00
Total Adjustments		<3,100.00>		<3,100.00>
Net Cash provided by Operations		<1,500.00>		<1,500.00>
Cash Flows from investing activities				
Used For				
Net cash used in investing		0.00		0.00
Cash Flows from financing activities				
Proceeds From				
Bonds Payable		1,000,000.00		1,000,000.00
Dividends		0.00		0.00
Common Stock		1,000.00		1,000.00
Used For				
Bonds Payable		0.00		0.00
Dividends		<1,000.00>		<1,000.00>
Common Stock		0.00		0.00
Net cash used in financing		1,000,000.00		1,000,000.00
Net increase <decrease> in cash	$	998,500.00	$	998,500.00
Summary				
Cash Balance at End of Period	$	998,500.00	$	998,500.00
Cash Balance at Beg of Period		<998,500.00>		0.00
Net Increase <Decrease> in Cash	$	0.00	$	998,500.00

Figure 18. 3 Cash Flow statement for Hydro Slide.

Starting in the middle of the statement with Cash Flow from Financing Activities note the $1 million bond issue and the $1,000 paid out in stock dividends. At the top of the statement, notice the moneys used to purchase Treasury Stock. Contributions to the Sinking Fund would appear on "next year's" Cash Flow statement.

NOTES

NOTES

NOTES

NOTES

NOTES

NOTES

NOTES

NOTES

PEACHTREE COMPLETE ACCOUNTING--EDUCATIONAL VERSION

Thank you for trying Peachtree Complete Accounting! This is a fully functional version of Peachtree Accounting. It includes a limited-use license intended for educational purposes only and does not require user registration.

To purchase Peachtree Accounting software for your business, visit a local software reseller or contact Peachtree Software, Inc. For information on additional products and services that Peachtree Software provides, call 1-800-336-1420 (within the US), +1-770-724-4000 (outside the US), or visit our Web site at www.peachtree.com.

PEACHTREE SOFTWARE LICENSE AGREEMENT FOR EDUCATIONAL USE
The following states the license agreement that governs your use of this product. You acknowledge and accept this agreement by proceeding with the installation of this computer software from disks or CD-ROM.

LICENSE
PLEASE READ CAREFULLY THIS LICENSE AGREEMENT BEFORE CLICKING YES BELOW. PROCEEDING WITH THE INSTALLATION OF THIS COMPUTER SOFTWARE INDICATES YOUR ACCEPTANCE OF THE TERMS OF THIS LICENSE. IF YOU DO NOT AGREE WITH THESE TERMS, YOU SHOULD CANCEL THE INSTALLATION PROCESS AND RETURN THE PACKAGE AND ITS CONTENTS.

Peachtree Software, Inc. ("Peachtree"), provides the computer software program(s) and documentation (printed manuals, guides, bulletins, and/or online Help) contained in the package as well as any modifications, updates, revisions, or enhancements received by you from Peachtree or its dealers (the "Program"). Peachtree licenses its use under the terms below:

a. You are granted a nontransferable license to use the Program under the terms stated in this Agreement for educational use only. Title and ownership of the Program and of the copyright in the Program remain with Peachtree.

b. You may not make copies, translations, or modifications of or to the Program, except you may copy the Program into a machine-readable or printed form for backup purposes in support of your use of the Program. You must reproduce the copyright notice on any copy of the Program or portion of the Program merged into another program. All copies of the Program and any portion of the Program merged into or used in conjunction with another program are and will continue to be the property of Peachtree and subject to the terms and conditions of this Agreement.

c. You may not assign, sell, distribute, lease, rent, sublicense, or transfer the Program or this license or disclose the Program to any other person. You may not Web-enable the Program or sell, distribute, lease, rent, sublicense, or otherwise offer access to or use of, the Program via the Internet or via any other network available to or accessible by third parties. You may not reverse-engineer, disassemble, or decompile the Program or otherwise attempt to discover the source code or structural framework of the Program.

d. This license terminates if you fail to comply with any provision in this Agreement. You agree upon termination to destroy the Program, together with all copies, modifications, and merged portions in any form, including any copy in your computer memory or on a hard disk.

LIMITED WARRANTY
Peachtree warrants that the Program substantially conforms to the specifications contained in Peachtree's packaging and promotional materials for a period of sixty (60) days from delivery as evidenced by your receipt, provided that the Program is used on the computer operating system for which it was designed. Peachtree further warrants that the media on which the Program is furnished will be free from defects in material or workmanship for a period of sixty (60) days from delivery. All warranties stated in this

Agreement apply only when the Program is used within the United States of America and its territories. Peachtree's sole obligation and liability for breach of the foregoing warranties shall be to replace or correct the Program so that it substantially conforms to the specifications or to replace the defective media, as the case may be.
Any modification of the Program by anyone other than Peachtree voids the foregoing warranty. NO OTHER WARRANTIES ARE EXPRESSED AND NONE SHALL BE IMPLIED. PEACHTREE DOES NOT WARRANT THAT THIS SOFTWARE IS FREE OF BUGS, VIRUSES, IMPERFECTIONS, ERRORS, OR OMISSIONS. PEACHTREE SPECIFICALLY DISCLAIMS AND EXCLUDES ANY IMPLIED WARRANTIES OF MERCHANTABILITY AND FITNESS FOR A PARTICULAR PURPOSE. SOME STATES DO NOT ALLOW THE EXCLUSION OF IMPLIED WARRANTIES, SO THE FOREGOING MAY NOT APPLY TO YOU.

Support

Peachtree Software, Inc. does not provide technical support for education versions of the Program. For assistance, you must refer to your institution or instructor. To receive technical support from Peachtree Software, you must purchase a single-workstation or multiple-workstation license of the Program.

Tax Updates

Peachtree Software, Inc. does not provide tax updates for education versions of the Program. Changes in state, federal, or local tax laws may render this software, or previous versions, obsolete. To continue to operate successfully, you must purchase a single-workstation or multiple-workstation license of the Program. Also, it may be necessary for you to purchase an update. In addition to these fees, Peachtree may require you to purchase an upgrade to a current version of the Program as tax laws change. Peachtree does not update versions of the Program that are not shipping at the time of a change in tax laws.

Links to External Sites

Peachtree provides links in Peachtree Today to other Web sites on the Internet that are owned and operated by third party vendors and other third parties not under the control of Peachtree. These links are provided for your convenience only and are not intended as a warranty of any type regarding the other Web sites or the information or services offered on such Web sites. Under no circumstances shall Peachtree, or its subsidiaries or affiliates, be responsible or liable in any way for the availability of, services or products offered, or the content located on or through any such external Web site.

RECOMMENDED ENVIRONMENT

This Program has been designed to work optimally in the environment documented within the system requirements. Any defects, inconsistencies, or issues arising out of operating outside the parameters set forth therein may require the licensee to pay additional maintenance/upgrade costs to Peachtree to support and/or rectify.

LIMITATION OF LIABILITY

IN NO EVENT SHALL PEACHTREE'S LIABILITY TO YOU FOR DAMAGES HEREUNDER FOR ANY CAUSE WHATSOEVER EXCEED THE AMOUNT PAID BY YOU FOR USE OF THE PROGRAM. IN NO EVENT WILL PEACHTREE BE LIABLE FOR ANY LOST PROFITS OR OTHER INCIDENTAL OR CONSEQUENTIAL DAMAGES ARISING OUT OF THE USE OR INABILITY TO USE THE PROGRAM EVEN IF PEACHTREE HAS BEEN ADVISED OF THE POSSIBILITY OF SUCH DAMAGES.

U.S. Government Restricted Rights

The Program is provided to the Government with RESTRICTED RIGHTS. Use, duplication, or disclosure by the Government is subject to restrictions set forth in subdivision (c) (1) of The Rights in Technical Data and Computer Software clause at 252.227-7013. Contractor/Manufacturer is Peachtree Software, Inc., 1505 Pavilion Place, Norcross, GA 30093.

This Agreement is governed by the laws of the state of Georgia. In the event that any provision of this Agreement is found invalid or unenforceable pursuant to judicial decree, the remainder of this Agreement shall be valid and enforceable according to its terms. ONE-WRITE PLUS, PEACHTREE, and PEACHTREE SOFTWARE are registered trademarks of Peachtree Software, Inc.